IN THE FOOTSTEPS
OF MARCO POLO

About the author

Stanley Johnson, former MEP and Vice-Chairman of the European Parliament's Environment Committee, has worked for the World Bank, the United Nations and the European Commission in Brussels. He won the Newdigate prize for Poetry in 1962, the Greenpeace Prize and the RSPCA's Richard Martin award in 1984, and the RSPB Medal and the WWF Leader of the Living Planet Award in 2015.

Between 2019 and 2023, he served as the International Ambassador for the Conservative Environment Network (CEN). He is currently President of the Gorilla Organisation, Chairman of GEDU-Global Education Advisory Board, and Adviser to the World Coastal Forum.

He has appeared in numerous reality television shows, including I'm a Celebrity, Get Me Out of Here and Celebrity Mastermind where his specialist topic was the works of Sophocles.

He is the author of 12 non-fiction works on environmental and demographic topics, two volumes of memoir and 11 novels, one of which – *The Commissioner* – was made into a film starring John Hurt.

'*In the Footsteps of Marco Polo*' is his 26th book.

IN THE FOOTSTEPS OF MARCO POLO

Stanley Johnson

Published in 2026 by
Unicorn, an imprint of Unicorn Publishing Group
Charleston Studio
Meadow Business Centre
Lewes BN8 5RW
www.unicornpublishing.org

Text copyright © 2026 Stanley Johnson

All rights reserved. No part of the contents of this book may be reproduced, stored in or introduced into a retrieval system, or transmitted, in any form or by any means (electronic, mechanical, photocopying, recording or otherwise), without the prior written permission of the copyright holder and the above publisher of this book.

Every effort has been made to trace copyright holders and to obtain their permission for the use of copyrighted material. The publisher apologises for any errors or omissions and would be grateful to be notified of any corrections that should be incorporated in future reprints or editions of this book.

ISBN 978 1 917458 65 8
10 9 8 7 6 5 4 3 2 1

Published in the United States of America by
Histria Books
7181 N. Hualapai Way, Ste. 130-86
Las Vegas, NV 89166 U.S.A
HistriaBooks.com

Histria Perspectives is an imprint of Histria Books. Titles published under the imprints of Histria Books are distributed in the United States and Canada by Simon & Schuster and worldwide through Unified Book Distribution. We appreciate your support of copyright by purchasing an authorized edition of this book and for respecting intellectual property laws by not reproducing, scanning, or otherwise distributing any part of it by any means without permission. You are supporting authors and enabling Histria Books to continue publishing books for everyone.

ISBN 978-1-59211-774-1 (softbound)

Design by newtonworks.uk
Printed in the Czech Republic

CONTENTS

Acknowledgements — viii

PART ONE
TRACKING MARCO POLO, JUNE 1961 – MAY 2023

1 Oxford, England 1960–61 — 2
2 Three Men on a Motorcycle — 11
3 'Mango Juice, Sahib?' — 21
4 The Grand Trunk Road, Calcutta, Bombay and Home — 31
5 Newdigate Poetry Prize Debt to Marco Polo — 38
6 To China – at Last! 1975 — 43
7 Looking Ahead — 51
8 Returning to China, December 1986 — 59
9 Visits to the Chinese Embassy, January–February 2020 — 63
10 OneTribeTV Comes on Board — 67
11 Enter Dr Rana — 71
12 False Start — 74
13 Dr Telensky Commissions a Bust — 79

PART TWO
TRACKING MARCO POLO IN CHINA, MAY–JUNE 2023

14	Leaving England – High Pamirs	86
15	Buzkashi	94
16	Tashkurgan	100
17	Panlong Ancient Highway	104
18	A Short Walk in the Cryosphere	107
19	Kashgar I	112
20	Kashgar II	119
21	Muqam Music	124
22	Hotan Jade and Carpets	128
23	The Heruo Desert Railway	133
24	Miran: Lost City of the Desert	138
25	The Mogao Caves of Dunhuang	143
26	Singing Sands and Crescent Moon Lake	148
27	Shouhang Power Plant, Gansu	152
28	Jiayuguan Pass and Great Wall of China	155
29	Zhangye – The Sleeping Buddha Temple	160
30	Zhanghye's Rainbow Mountains	163
31	Lanzhou – Pizza Parlour Encounter and Zhongshan Bridge	167
32	Oodles of Noodles	171
33	How did Marco Polo cross the Yellow River?	174
34	Ningxia Vineyards	177
35	Helan Mountain Rock Paintings	181
36	Mimi's Magic Carpet and Zhenbeibu China West Film Studio	184

37	Genghis Khan Mausoleum	187
38	Mongolian Steppe Cowboys	193
39	Mongolian Wrestling	195
40	Mongolian Bows and Arrows	198
41	Xanadu I – 'In Xanadu did Kubla Khan'	201
42	Xanadu II – The Summer Palace	207
43	Highway 66 and the Grass Skyline Drive	215
44	The Great Wall: Juyong Pass	218
45	The Marco Polo Bridge	222
46	The Forbidden City	225
47	Departure	232

Postscript	236
Index	238
Other books by the author	246

ACKNOWLEDGEMENTS

I want to begin by acknowledging my debt to Tim Severin and Michael de Larrabeiti who set out with me in the summer of 1961 to follow Marco Polo's route from Venice to China. The first part of this book tells the story of that venture, relying on the notes I made at the time and the photos Michael took in Turkey, Iran and Afghanistan.

The second part of this book tells the story of the journey my son, Max, and I made in the summer of 2023 with the aim of completing the project that Tim, Michael and I had begun in 1961. Max and I planned to follow Marco Polo's route in China itself: from the High Pamirs, through Xinjiang, Gansu, Ningxia, and Inner Mongolia to Xanadu and Beijing.

From my point of view, the key moment in getting this idea off the ground was back in August 2021 when Sue Ayton of Knight Ayton Management introduced me to Dale Templar, CEO of OneTribeTV. Dale was enthusiastic, and the wheels soon began to turn.

Another key moment came when His Excellency Zheng Zeguang, the Ambassador of the People's Republic of China to the Court of St James, put us touch with China Central Television (CCTV). The Ambassador's continuing interest and support, together with that of his colleagues in London and Beijing, has been of critical importance. It gives me great pleasure to acknowledge that debt here.

We also owe a special debt to all those who worked so hard at the technical and practical level, as well as the scholarly and academic level, to make our trip a success. I was deeply impressed by the close and broad collaboration (which continues to this day) between the OneTribeTV team and their counterparts in China Central Television (CCTV). Max and I would like to record here our grateful thanks to our day-to-day 'travelling companions': Dale Templar, Owen Gay, Chen Dandan 陈丹丹, Ellen Xu 许倩倩, Peter Hayns, Mimi Templar-Gay, Charles Bush, Yang Ning 杨宁, Liao Xiaojie 廖晓洁, Cao Lei 曹雷, Lu Min 鲁敏, Wang Hang 王航, Jiang Xinyue 江心悦, Samuel Webb, Nadia Aleo, and Gang Yang 刚杨.

As a result of this brilliant collaboration, Max and I were able to spend almost eight weeks in China faithfully tracking Marco Polo's route in that country, while at the same time visiting places and people others are often unable to see.

Our journey would not have been possible without the generous support and encouragement of Dr Vishwajeet Rana, Founder and CEO of GEDU – Global Education, and of English Path Language Schools in particular, dedicated as that group is to strengthening the links between countries and peoples. I would like to express here my sincerest thanks to Dr Rana and his English Path team. This project simply would not have happened without him.

I would also like to express my warm thanks to Dr Jan Telensky, philanthropist, and entrepreneur, for his readiness to come to our aid at a crucial moment and for enabling this account of our trip to be published in its present form.

Finally, I want to want to acknowledge our debt to Marco Polo himself.

Marco Polo is probably the most famous example of the way the Silk Road flourished during that extraordinary period in the 13th and 14th Centuries AD when the Mongol Emperors, beginning with Genghis Khan himself, created a *Pax Mongolica* which enabled the interchange of goods, culture and ideas between East and West to flourish as never before.

Many of the people we met during our time in China spoke about Marco Polo's symbolic as well as historical importance. They see Marco Polo as a bridgebuilder between East and West. I would like to think that, in some small way, all of us who were engaged in this project were following Marco Polo's example.

PART ONE

TRACKING MARCO POLO, JUNE 1961 – MAY 2023

1

Oxford, England 1960–1961

Around the end of November 1960, during my fourth term at Oxford, a notice appeared in the Exeter College lodge. It read as follows: *'Gentlemen are reminded that, while the college encourages vacation travel, they should not forget the fact that at least ten weeks of study is expected from them during the Long Vacation.'*

This was an instruction that I was resolutely determined to ignore. At the end of the Easter term in the following year, 1961, I would be taking Mods. There would be seven full terms ahead of me before I would be taking Greats. Surely, I could take just one summer off?

A couple of days after that dispiriting notice appeared, there was a knock on my door. I was still living in college but had moved staircases and was no longer sharing a room.

'Come in!' I shouted.

A slim but rugged-looking individual entered.

'My name's Tim. I hear you're thinking of going to China in the next Long Vac. So am I. Perhaps we should join forces. I'm reading Geography at Keble.'

If you look for Tim Severin's publications on the Amazon website, you will find a list as long as your arm. After Marco Polo, he tracked St Brendan in his coracle, as well as Sinbad the Sailor and pursued Jason's quest for the Golden Fleece. He even retraced Ulysses' journey home from Troy to Ithaca. But all that was a long way ahead.

That first afternoon, over tea and toast in my room, we decided that we would try to follow Marco Polo's route from Venice to

Beijing. We would call our expedition the Marco Polo Route Project. I didn't know much about Marco Polo. My knowledge of history, ancient or modern, ended with the sack of Rome by Alaric the Hun in AD 479. But Tim seemed to have a lot of information at his fingertips.

'Marco Polo', he told me, 'set out in 1271 from Venice on a three-and-a-half-year journey to the court of the Great Khan in Cathay, which is modern-day Peking. He reopened the Old Silk Road which for centuries had been closed by ravaging hordes. He travelled through Turkey, Iran, Afghanistan, the High Pamirs and into China on a journey of, at times, incredible hardship, and danger.'

Tim made the whole thing sound irresistible.

'Count me in,' I said.

Tim came down to our family farm on Exmoor during the Christmas vacation for a few days of detailed planning. We established our base of operations in a room which we know as the Back Kitchen. We would appear at mealtimes but otherwise we remained closeted in front of the log fire, with papers spread out on a long oak table.'

My parents were intrigued by our preparations.

'How are you getting on?' my father asked.

'We need transport,' I replied. 'We need money, and we need visas, particularly Chinese visas. Otherwise, things are going splendidly.'

'Better get out one of the old Aladdin lamps and rub it!' my father laughed.

By then we had graduated from paraffin-filled Tilley and Aladdin lamps to our own electric generator. It was a four-kilowatt Lister Startamatic. This was something of a misnomer. To start it you had to go out to the engine shed, take the crank handle and whirl away while simultaneously trying to squirt Eezi-Start into the cylinder block. Once it was going it chugged away on the other side of the barn, filling the valley with a low thudding sound which we soon got used to.

My father had worked out a way of turning it off at night without having to go out to the engine shed. He had rigged a wire across the yard into the bathroom. The wire was attached to a stirrup. To shut the engine down, you pulled hard on the stirrup and held on until the lights faded before finally going out altogether. This took quite a time.

Once, when my father was still in the bath, my mother decided to try her hand at turning the engine off.

'Don't jerk on the wire!' my father instructed. 'Give it a long, firm pull.'

Inevitably, my mother yanked too hard on the stirrup. The wire broke and she fell into the bath on top of him. Meanwhile, the engine raced out of control and all the light bulbs exploded one by one. My father had to race naked across the yard and into the engine shed.

My father didn't want a repetition of the disaster. 'Don't bother to turn the engine off,' he would say as he headed for the pub. 'I'll do it when I get back.'

Even though he was seldom home before midnight, Tim and I were often still hard at it, planning the details of the Marco Polo Route Project, as we heard him drive into the yard in the ex-US Army Jeep which we had at that time.

Once he came through into the Back Kitchen to find us poring over maps. 'What are you going to do for a vehicle?' he asked.

We had already worked that one out. 'Marco Polo used camels,' Tim said. 'But he took three and a half years to get to Beijing. We've got only four months of the Long Vacation. We're going to go on motorcycles.'

In his youth my father was a keen motorcyclist. He had come down to the farm on his motorcycle on that first tour of inspection when, back in 1951, my parents decided to buy the farm which I still own today. While I was still at school, he bought me a 200cc

James Scrambler which I used around the farm and for journeys further afield.

'Motorcycles, eh? That's rather a good idea, actually.'

Acquiring transport, the first of the items on our checklist, proved more difficult than we anticipated. Since we didn't have enough money to buy our own vehicles, we knew we had to beg, borrow or steal. We wrote letters, we made visits and telephone calls, without nailing down a serious offer.

One day, early in the summer term with only a few weeks left before our planned departure date, I went to Birmingham where the Motorcycle Show was being held. In the early sixties, British motorcycles still led the world. Triumph, Norton, Enfield, BSA … these were household names.

I stood in front of the BSA stand, ogling the huge, gleaming machines. One in particular caught my eye. It was advertised as a 'BSA 500cc twin-cylinder Shooting Star'.

As far as I was concerned, it was love at first sight.

A man sat behind a desk.

'My friend and I are planning to follow Marco Polo's route to China this summer,' I said. 'Would BSA be ready to let us have a couple of motorcycles? We couldn't pay you anything, but it would be a good advertisement for you.'

The man looked me up and down. The Shooting Star was a big machine.

'Think you can handle it?' he asked.

In the end, after an exchange of letters, BSA loaned us one Shooting Star and Costain, the civil engineering firm, provided the second. Because of the amount of equipment we thought we needed, we decided to fit both bikes with sidecars, one a normal passenger sidecar, the other a box-type.

If the transport question had been solved, funding was still a problem. Though we planned to camp out throughout the journey, there would be fuel and food to buy. It all added up.

When the (newly launched) *Sunday Telegraph* offered £100 for 'exclusive rights' to our story, we thought we were in business. £100 went a long way in those days.

But we still hadn't managed to obtain Chinese visas. However often we presented ourselves at the Chinese Embassy in Portland Place, the result was always the same. Like the lady in the song, they wouldn't say yes, and they wouldn't say no. They just kept us waiting. I came to know one official in the Visa Section particularly well. His name was Chi.

'Hello, Mr Chi', "I would say.

'Please, no 'mister'. All people equal in Chinese People's Republic. No bourgeois titles. Just Chi, please.'

After half a dozen fruitless journeys to London from Oxford, we were at our wits' end.

Finally, I went to see Sir Cyril Hinshelwood, a Fellow of my own College, in his splendid rooms in the front quad. 'Hinsh', as he was widely known, was a scientist of immense distinction, probably the only person ever to have been simultaneously President of the Royal Society and the Classical Association. He had a Nobel Prize for Chemistry, too.

He served me China tea in a delicate porcelain teacup.

'How are you planning to enter China?' he asked.

I explained the route as far as we knew it. 'We plan to leave Afghanistan, as Marco Polo did, via the Pamir Corridor, that narrow tongue of land that today connects Afghanistan with China. After that, like Marco Polo, we'll have to cross the Gobi Desert.'

Hinsh looked puzzled. 'Is there a road through the Pamirs into China?'

I put my cards on the table. 'Frankly, we don't know for sure. But if the Chinese won't give us a visa, we'll never be able to find out.'

He took a sip of his tea. 'Have you tried Professor Needham in Cambridge? I'll give him a call.'

Two days later, I was on my way from Oxford to Cambridge in

a 1932 Sunbeam Talbot. This was a splendid vehicle, even then a collector's item. It had been used as the 'school car' at Ravenswood, my Devon prep school, during my time there in the late forties and early fifties. Later, Miss Nicholson, who taught us French, had acquired it. Miss Nicholson had left Ravenswood some years earlier, but we had kept in touch sporadically. One day, out of the blue, I received a letter offering me the Sunbeam Talbot.

'There's only one problem,' Miss Nicholson added as a PS: 'it's very difficult to find spare parts, if not impossible. If you do find them, they will be very expensive.'

I had written back to her. 'Delighted to inherit Sunbeam. As for spare parts, we'll cross that bridge when we come to it.'

This, then, was the lovely classic vehicle which I piloted from Oxford to Cambridge around the beginning of May 1961. I parked in front of the Rutherford Science Building, to be told that Professor Needham was in the lab.

That made sense. Professor Needham, I had by then established, was the author of the world-renowned publication, *The Science and Civilization of Ancient China*. He had already produced twelve volumes and was working on the thirteenth. More were planned.

He was also, crucially, the patron of the Anglo-Chinese Friendship Society.

One or two people, when I made my enquiries, tapped the sides of their noses meaningfully to indicate the Anglo-Chinese Friendship Society was probably a Communist front and that Needham himself might not be wholly kosher. That was the least of my concerns, I decided. He could be a fully-fledged member of the Comintern for all I cared. We just wanted his assistance.

When I eventually found him, wearing a brown beret behind a bank of scientific equipment in his laboratory, Needham was cautiously helpful. We went off to his office, and talked for half an hour about the difficulties we would certainly encounter if we did get into China.

'Are you sure you will find petrol for your motorcycles in the Gobi Desert, Mr. Johnson?'

'Not one hundred per cent, sir?'

'And what about Lop Nur? They won't want you to go anywhere near Lop Nur.'

'No, of course not.'

Tim and I had already found out about the Chinese nuclear testing site in the middle of the Gobi Desert and knew we would have to give it a wide berth.

In the end Professor Needham took me to his office. 'I'll give you a letter to take to the Chinese Ambassador in London.'

He introduced me to his secretary, an ancient Chinese lady.

'Dear Ambassador Xiang,' he dictated to his amanuensis, 'I do hope you will feel able to give Mr. Johnson and Mr. Severin every possible assistance. The historical-geographical research which they are expecting to undertake this summer in Asia, including in the People's Republic of China, will – I believe – contribute significantly to increased understanding between the people of Great Britain and China.'

When his secretary had finished, Needham signed the letter and handed it to me.

'Show it to the Visa Section at the Chinese Embassy as soon as you can. These things take weeks. You haven't much time. You'll have to leave as soon as the summer term ends if you're going to be back in time for First Week in October.'

Well, I thought, we could probably miss First Week and get away with it. Beyond that, we might be pushing it.

Back in the car, I slipped the letter in the glove compartment and checked my watch. If I put my foot on it, I could get to London before the Chinese Embassy closed for the day.

Everything was going swimmingly until, soon after Royston, I noticed a red light on the dashboard.

'Damn and blast!' I exclaimed. I knew what the red light meant.

The generator wasn't functioning. I pulled into the next garage. Maybe the fan belt was loose.

Unfortunately, the problem was not as simple as that. 'Generator's packed in, I'm afraid,' the mechanic told me. 'You're running on the battery. You can probably go a few more miles if you don't use the horn or turn the lights on?'

'Will it get me to London?'

'You can give it a go.'

I almost made it. I had reached Marble Arch when the engine finally died. I coasted to a stop next to an enormous hole in the ground. In those days, the area around Marble Arch was undergoing major reconstruction. A huge underground car park was being built and a new traffic system designed. The Conservative Minister in charge was Ernest Marples. Looking at the havoc he had created, wags had already christened the area 'Marple Arch'.

I remembered Miss Nicholson's warning about the difficulty and cost of obtaining spare parts. Getting a new generator for a 1932 Sunbeam Talbot might take weeks. It could be very expensive.

I took an instant decision. The car was blocking the highway. I needed to get rid of it. At once. *Instanter*.

I saw a bulldozer approaching, pushing a load of rubble into the enormous hole in front of me. I jumped out of the car and ran over to talk to the driver.

'Would you please push my car into the hole too?' I shouted.

'Come again?' The man had to throttle down before he could hear me properly.

When he finally understood what I was saying, he nodded: 'Cost you a fiver.'

For a fiver, it was cheap at the price. To be sure my money was spent as intended, I waited as the bulldozer pushed the car over the edge of the pit. When it hit the bottom, the car quivered for a moment and lay still. On its back, with its wheels in the air. Moments later, the bulldozer started filling up the hole with the rubble.

'Thanks.' I consoled myself with the thought of the joy archaeologists might feel, generations hence, when they came upon this unexpected treasure.

'Any time, mate.'

I just made it to the Chinese Embassy in Portland Place in time. At the reception, I asked to see Mr. Chi in person.

'Ah, Mr. Chi,' I began, when he came down to see me in the cavernous entrance hall.

He interrupted at once. 'Just Chi, please.'

'Sorry, Chi.' I wouldn't allow him to put me off my stroke. I felt supremely confident. 'I have a personal letter about our visas from Professor Needham for Chinese Ambassador Xiang.'

I put my hand into my inside breast pocket, and it came up empty. I tried all my pockets with a similar result.

'You have a personal letter about visas for Ambassador from Professor Needham?' At long last Chi sounded interested.

As he spoke, I had a dreadful sense of foreboding. I remembered that, to keep it from being crumpled or creased *en route* from Cambridge to London, I had put Needham's letter in the glove compartment of my Sunbeam Talbot, and it was now buried in and with the car about one hundred ft below the ground at Marble Arch. Buried, too, were our hopes of receiving formal permission from the Chinese authorities to enter their country from Afghanistan via the High Pamir mountains.

Chi shook his head sadly. 'No letter from Professor, no visa' he said.

We would just have to wing it when we reached the Chinese border.

2

Three Men on a Motorcycle

Before we left England, we had our two motorcycles modified for desert and high-altitude work. We loaded the box sidecar with polythene jerry cans for fuel and water. We also stowed tents, mattresses, sleeping bags, tools, spare parts, spare tires and quantities of vitamin tablets, dehydrated stews and curries.

The 'normal' sidecar served as a depository for 10,000 feet of cine film, two 16mm cameras, exposure meters and range finders. There was just enough space left for our cameraman, Michael de Larrabeiti.

How did Tim and I find Michael? Through the power of the press, of course. Never underestimate it.

Michael had seen an article about our proposed expedition in the London *Evening Standard* and had written offering his services. I still have the letter he wrote to us dated 25 May 1961, from Editorial Film Productions, 8 St Anne's Court, Wardour Street, London W.1.

Larrabeiti wrote, 'I don't know how factual the article in the Evening Standard was about your proposed trip to Peking, but it stated that you were looking for a professional cameraman.

'I have been engaged in the camera side of the documentary film industry for the last seven years as first assistant, operator, and finally as a cameraman. I have some experience of conditions in the East, having filmed last year in Singapore, Hong Kong and Gan.

'My work has not been limited to the film industry. I have taught English in Marrakesh, spent 18 months as the assistant manager of a hotel near Fréjus and six months with a band of Provençal Shepherds in the Alps.

'I assume that the trip will take place this summer and I'm free myself until the 23rd of October, when I go up to Trinity College, Dublin.

'If you are indeed looking for a cameraman, I could probably come up to Oxford to see you or perhaps meet you in London. In any event, I would appreciate a reply whether favourable or not.'

Michael de Larrabeiti had an unusual background, as well as an unusual name. He had been born and brought up in Battersea, had travelled around the world earning his living as a photographer and, at the age of twenty-seven, was now waiting to go up to Trinity College, Dublin. His sense of humour was inexhaustible. Already slightly bald, he tended to knot a bright yellow duster over his head.

As he mentioned in his letter, Michael had spent a season with the shepherds of Provence, walking with them and their flocks on the annual transhumance between mountain and plain. He would later write some moving tales about his time in France. He would also write several novels, including a classic children's book, *The Borribles*.

At the beginning of June 1961, we were ready to go. The Oxford term was about to end. We dressed up in our expedition uniforms of black jackboots, belted black jackets, dark green trousers and powder-blue helmets with the letters MPRP – for Marco Polo Route Project – inscribed on them (in little local difficulties MPRP could plausibly appear to stand for 'military police road patrol'). We threw a party in the Exeter College quadrangle for friends and supporters.

Tim Severin's parents came to Oxford for the occasion. Dr Kenneth Wheare, Rector of Exeter, emerged from his Lodgings to see what the noise was when we kick-started the machines and, just for fun, drove round the quad, keeping off the grass as best we could.

My father and mother had driven up from Exmoor in the jeep. My mother still had straw on the back of her coat. Did they – and Tim's parents – wonder whether this might be the last time they would see us? They certainly couldn't have expected to hear much from us over the next four months. Nor did we expect to hear much from them.

Once the champagne ran out, we headed for the coast.

Silver City Airways, dedicated to building bridges to Europe more than a decade before Britain signed the Treaty of Rome, 'comped' us a passage on their shuttle from Lydd to Le Touquet. We drove our spanking new machines with their spanking new sidecars up the ramp into the belly of the plane.

As I look back, that four-month motorcycle journey across Europe and Asia in the summer of 1961 was an utterly memorable experience. Ours was in every respect a supremely uncluttered existence. The task was simply to get from A to B each day. Sometimes, if we were lucky, we covered two or three hundred miles by nightfall. While our headlights were still working, we often drove after dark as well. Once, with our lights out of action owing to a collision with a herd of cows, we even drove by moonlight.

The wider world hardly impinged. We heard vaguely about the building of the Berlin Wall during that summer of 1961, as well as Iraq's first attempted invasion of Kuwait, but on the whole, we concentrated on finding the next petrol station or caravanserai.

In some respects, we were unbelievably incompetent. For example, at Temple's Garage in Oxford we had arranged for our newly acquired sidecars to be attached to the left-hand side of the motorcycles. This was fine when we were driving in England. But the moment we crossed the Channel, it was hopeless. If I wanted to overtake some slow-moving vehicle, I would pull out towards the crown of the road and wait till Michael signaled that the coast was clear. If it wasn't, he would use a rolled-up newspaper to beat me back.

By the end of the first day, this proved too hair-raising even for Michael's normally steady nerves. Thereafter he rode pillion.

Nor were we good motorcyclists. I had ridden my James scrambler for several years on Exmoor, so I wasn't a complete novice. But none of us had proper motorcycle-driving licenses though the Automobile Association sportingly gave us the international *'permis de conduire'*, which looked authoritative enough.

Our first two or three days were uneventful. After leaving Le Touquet, we spent hours in Paris riding round the Arc de Triomphe until Michael had the shot he wanted. Then we took the road south to Berne in Switzerland where my Turkish uncle, Zeki Kuneralp, whom I had last seen in Ankara two years earlier on a 'gap-year' visit to Turkey, was now installed as Ambassador.

Having been brought up in Switzerland, Zeki had the advantage of speaking Swiss German, the language of choice in the Bernese Oberland.

'Sometimes the good Swiss burghers don't realize I can understand everything they are saying,' Zeki told me with a twinkle in his eye.

Zeki and his wife, Neçla, welcomed us into their palatial residence. My Turkish cousins, Sinan and Selim, then ten and eight years old, were especially intrigued by our shiny new motorcycles.

Alas, they didn't stay shiny for long. After crossing a mountain pass in a rainstorm, I managed to crash the sidecar into a wall at the head of the Ticino valley. It took a day and a half to repair the damage.

We picked up Marco Polo's trail for the first time in Venice.

Nothing much is left of Marco Polo's house save one ornamental Byzantine arch, but there is a plaque on the wall which says: *'Qui furono le case di Marco Polo che viaggio le più lontane regioni dell'Asia e le descrisse.'*

Having spent time in Italy during my 'gap-year', I regarded myself as an expert at the language.

'Here was the house of Marco Polo who travelled through the farthest regions of Asia and described them,' I confidently translated.

'Can you ask for ice cream in Italian, too?' Michael asked. 'I could do with an ice cream.'

We paid our homage to the great explorer and then went on to visit the Mayor of Venice in his marble palace, the Doge's Palace. Our boots clomped across the floor. One steward produced a tray of drinks, and another brought out a leather-bound copy of *The Travels of Marco Polo* for the Mayor to present to us.

The mayor also gave us a voucher for 100 litres of petrol, which lasted us all the way to Istanbul via Yugoslavia and Bulgaria.

A long afternoon's driving finally took us into Turkey. A high watchtower, and the Turkish national emblem of a crescent moon and star carved on the hillside, denoted the border.

The Turkish customs officer, clearly intrigued by all our equipment, called us into his office. He dropped a lump of sugar into his tea and waited for it to dissolve. Then he dropped another lump in and waited for that to dissolve too. And a third. He spread out his hands and shrugged his shoulders.

'Ours is a poor country,' he said. 'Since we have no money for teaspoons, we must use more sugar.'

The customs officer in his way was a philosopher. He had the leisure to be one. There wasn't much traffic then between Bulgaria and Turkey.

'You are in a hurry, I can see,' he said. 'You people are always in a hurry. We Turks, in our centuries of empire, found that there is a place for negligence. We have not forgotten it today. The old Turkey of the Sultans seems to have disappeared. The fez has gone, purdah has gone, even the Arabic script has gone. But as people, in our hearts, we have not changed. The way we drink our tea is the way we are – slow and sweet. You last longer in the end.'

As a result of a chance encounter at a petrol station near Taksim square with Ergun, the oldest son, we stayed for a few days in

Istanbul with a wonderful Turkish family who befriended us as though we were close and much-loved relatives.

Then we headed east through Anatolia. By now we were well into our rhythm. We would wake at dawn, pack up our tents if we had used them (if it was a fine night we would sleep out in the open), kick-start the motorcycles, open the throttle and roar away.

Marco Polo himself did not pass through this part of Turkey. When he left Venice, he took ship for Acre, that extraordinary Crusader town which today sits almost on the border between Israel and Lebanon. If you visit the castle there, walk along the ramparts, or wander through the medieval bazaar, you are probably seeing the same sights Marco Polo saw.

Given the tightness of our schedule (we had to be back by the beginning of the Michaelmas term) we didn't have time to follow Marco Polo's detour through the Holy Land. Instead, we picked up his track again in Kayseri, in southern Turkey, and then followed his route into Greater Armenia, present day Turkey.

After Sivas, the city where Tamburlaine crushed a thousand children beneath his horses' feet, we left behind the distinctive features of the Anatolian plateau: peasants standing on the flat roofs of their houses winnowing grain in the wind; little girls scrambling in the dust, their black hair plaited with strings, then cross-threaded to form a mat against the sun; huge dogs that jumped at us as we passed; the conical stacks of dung for use as fuel; the donkeys trotting round the corn stacks, pulling thresher sledges.

We took the old road up into the mountains and twisted uphill into the afternoon.

By now we had jettisoned one sidecar and ruthlessly pruned our equipment. Each morning, before setting off, we tossed a coin to decide which motorcycle would take the lead. This was a matter of some moment. Because of the dust clouds the first motorcycle put up, the second had to follow several hundred yards behind. That left plenty of time for the villagers to arm themselves with sticks and stones. If it was your turn to bring up the rear, you had to keep your head down, gun the engine and hope for the best.

We spent a night with some nomads within sight of Mount Ararat. I am not sure what tribe they belonged to but for centuries they had moved with their tents and livestock across national frontiers without bothering about passports or other formalities. This way of life was now under threat as governments with 'blind arrogance' – as I wrote in my diary at the time – tried to 'settle' their pastoral peoples.

We took tea and yoghurt with the nomads in their yurts, smoked their pungent cigarettes and admired the horses and camels tethered outside and sometimes inside the tents.

Seeing Mount Ararat was exciting enough in itself. How many times had I sat in church or chapel listening to the story of the Flood and Noah's Ark? But we had a professional interest as well. Marco Polo, who passed this way, claimed to have seen 'some portions of the Ark' on the summit of the mountain.

We were ready to make our own reconnaissance of the area and even try to reach the top of the mountain but were warned off by the local military on the grounds that this borderland between Turkey, Persia and the (then) Soviet Union was a forbidden zone.

Contenting ourselves with a distant view of the mountain, we entered Persia along the road by which Xerxes, on his way to a massive defeat by the Greek navy at Salamis, had left it.

Today we call Persia Iran. We have managed to demonize it as a land of fanatic ayatollahs. That is not how we saw it then. After the harshness of eastern Turkey, we felt we had entered a country of fountains and gardens and walled enclosures, of delicacy and colour. We looked for wine and bread and found them in abundance. We drank bowls of syrup with iced noodles. As we rested cross-legged beneath the trees, boys brought us tender cucumbers and yoghurt to dip them into flat bread for us to tear and eat. Goats nibbled, water flowed, apricots and peaches climbed and clung in the sun.

It was too good to last. Outside Tabriz, the front fork on one of the motorcycles snapped. It was a major mishap.

While I went on to Teheran, having succeeded in loading our damaged vehicle onto a passing lorry, Tim and Michael headed north on the remaining machine to explore the Valley of the Assassins.

Marco Polo's account of the Old Man of the Mountains, a great tyrant who held sway in a remote region south of the Caspian Sea, is one of his most vivid tales. In a secret valley, the Old Man founded a cult. His emissaries went forth, captured and drugged young men, who were then brought back to the valley where they found themselves surrounded by all manner of good things, by fountains and flowing water, by pavilions and wine, by green pastures and delightful women. Paradise on earth, in other words. After suitable indoctrination, these young men were then sent out to murder rival potentates. The unlucky victims included a Shah of Persia, a Grand Vizier of Egypt, two Caliphs of Baghdad, Raymond, Count of Tripoli, and Conrad, King of Jerusalem. Edward I of England, when heir to the throne, was almost killed by the Old Man's envoys in Acre in 1272, soon after Marco Polo left that city.

The fanatics were called 'Assassins' after the drug 'hashish', which the Old Man used when he first had them kidnapped.

Tim and Michael had failed to penetrate the secret Valley of the Assassins though they came tantalizingly close. On the way back, Tim broke a bone in his foot as the motorcycle skidded on rough ground.

It was clear that we couldn't wait for his foot to heal. Michael and I headed off to track Marco Polo through southern Persia and on into Afghanistan. Tim planned to join us in Kabul.

From a professional point of view, we had some serious historical research to do on our way through Persia. Among other things, we were looking, however improbably, for traces of the Three Wise Men, the Magi. Marco Polo had described how *'in the city of Saba ...*

the three Magi are buried, in three large and very beautiful monuments side by side and above them is a square building, carefully kept. The bodies are still entire with their hair and beards remaining.'

He goes on to say that though all three Magi were buried at Saba, only one was native to that town, the other two coming from Kala' Atishparastan and from Ava.

Scholars had visited Saba and no traces of the Magi had been found. Kala' Atishparastan, though known to be in Persia, had never been precisely located. But Ava apparently had. Nowadays, it is known as Aveh. We were even able to find it on the map, about eighty miles south-west of Teheran.

Mike and I turned off the main road from Teheran to Qum at Baqilabad and plunged onto the caked and salt-encrusted mud of the desert. We drove from oasis to little oasis, stopping from time to time to rest from the heat and the dust by the wall of some village house.

In the end we found Ava/Aveh. We followed a flock of sheep into the central square of the village. Here, exhausted and oblivious of the steady stream of women who came with pitchers on their heads to draw water from a deep brick well, we flung ourselves down. Night fell. Camels padded softly by, and donkeys trotted with tinkling bells.

It wasn't hard to imagine the Magi surveying the sky on a night such as this, seeing a strange bright star in the east and deciding to set out on the long journey to Bethlehem.

Did we find any convincing evidence that Marco Polo was right and that the Magi, or at least one of them, had come from Ava or Aveh? No, of course, we didn't. Given our total inability to communicate in Persian, I doubt whether the villagers of Aveh even understood what we were looking for. They certainly didn't leap up to show us the embalmed body of Gaspar, Melchior or Balthazaar.

Some months later, after we had returned to England, the *Sunday Telegraph* printed my account of our journey into the Persian desert under the headline 'Village of the Magi.' I spun the story as best I could, but frankly there was no telling for sure whether we had hit upon the right village.

Our trip to Aveh had convinced us that we could manage with just one motorcycle. When I crashed one of our machines comprehensively outside Qum, we realized the time had come for a major reorganization. We had huge camel-hide panniers fitted to the remaining machine and strengthened the pillion to carry the additional weight.

'Lean and mean!' Michael, as always, looked on the bright side.

His enthusiasm was infectious. We had had our setbacks, but we would keep going.

Two days later I woke up in the desert outside Isfahan on the morning of my 21st birthday. A mile away, I could see the great Sheikh Lotfollah Mosque silhouetted against the sky. The first rays of the sun caught the top of the minaret, then caressed the giant curve of the dome.

The donkeys brayed frostily into the morning air. Michael lay on the ground beside me, wrapped in his sleeping bag. The first flies of the day were beginning to bother him and from time to time he moved his head in his sleep, trying to avoid them.

As I sat cross-legged taking in the scene (when would I have a 21st birthday again?), an old man emerged from nowhere to offer me a small green apple.

'*Hoob?*' the old man enquired as I took a bite.

'*Hoob*' was one of the few Persian words I knew. It meant 'good'.

'*Hoob*,' I replied.

Michael woke up at this point. 'Time for nosh, then, is it?'

Then he remembered: 'Happy birthday, Stan!'

3

'Mango Juice, Sahib?'

We followed Marco Polo's route in Persia from Yazd, which Marco Polo describes as a *'very fine and splendid city,'* to Kerman whose people, Polo says, are *'skilled craftsmen, who make the full range of equipment for mounted soldiers: bridles, saddles and spears, swords, bows and quivers, and every sort of armour used in these parts.'*

In Kerman we had two choices. We could either try to head north across Persia's great central desert – the Dasht-i-Lut – and enter Afghanistan via Meshed (which was the route Marco Polo is thought to have taken), or we could take the road through Pakistan.

Whenever we stopped at a *chai-khaneh* (teahouse) or caravan-serai, we tried to get a reading on the problem. Was there a track across the desert to Meshed, we asked? Could we make it on a motorcycle?

Our spirits rose one day when, in one of the local teahouses, we discovered a brightly coloured map pinned to the grimy wall. The map was crowned with a smiling picture of the Shah of Persia and his bride, the whole being garlanded with a laurel wreath. What interested us was the broad slash of red running through the centre of the map, across the heart of the Dasht-i-Lut and denoting a broad new highway between Kerman and Meshed.

As we sipped our sweet tea in the little clear glasses we had come to know so well, we interrogated our fellow travellers.

'Road Kerman–Meshed? *Hoob? Vroom-vroom?*' we asked.

Alas, we soon discovered that the Kerman–Meshed highway was a totally fictional project and that the map was more an endearing expression of future road-building hopes than a statement of current realities.

In the end we had no choice but to swing south and east through Pakistan before heading north into Afghanistan.

It might not have been as bad as the Dasht-i-Lut but the road from Kerman to Zahadan still runs through a most pernicious desert most of the way. Red dust swirled persistently. The sun beat down through the haze. You pass the bleached carcass of a camel or the wreck of a truck that has caught fire by the roadside and you thank your lucky stars that you still have fuel and water. The corrugations were the worst, jarring the spine in the most fearsome way. Occasionally we would meet seasoned travellers who would blithely advise us to 'just keep going at around forty miles an hour and you'll find you'll ride the bumps – or coruscations – without feeling them'. Try as we might, we never found the knack. If we did reach the magic speed, there was always a dried-up wadi to negotiate just round the corner.

Michael and I fell off more times than I can count. Once, as we sprawled in the road, there was a loud honking behind us. The driver of an oil tanker had witnessed our latest accident and took pity on us.

He offered us a lift in his cab, which we gladly accepted. Somehow, we managed to lift the motorcycle onto the back of the tanker and lash it in place.

That unscheduled lift through the southern Persian desert to Zahadan was a lifesaver. Refreshed and reinvigorated, we said goodbye to our kindly driver and belted on to Nok Kundi, Iran's border post with Pakistan, seventy-five miles away.

After that it was – for a while at least – plain sailing. As we rode on through Baluchistan towards Quetta, we stopped from time to time at the 'dak' bungalows and guest houses which still survived in that part of the world. There we savoured briefly and uncritically the traces that remained of the old life.

'Mango juice, sahib?'

'Yes please, bearer, with ice.' And an easy chair on the veranda, looking at the stars through the palm trees and waiting for the water in the swimming pool to cool from the heat of the day.

'Curry and rice, sahib?' Yes, and the first clean white linen tablecloth we had seen for weeks.

The soft voice of the proprietor enquires in perfect English (he has been educated in an English school in Quetta) what time we will take breakfast in the morning and whether we will have one fried egg or two. Then we swim in the pool, while the dhobi man washes our clothes.

'We better make the most of this,' I said to Michael. 'It won't be like this in Afghanistan.'

It wasn't.

Actually, at this point we weren't really sure we would be allowed into Afghanistan at all. We had Afghan visas all right, but we had never received permission to take our camera equipment into the country.

Happily, we reached the frontier post between Pakistan and Afghanistan, high up on the Bolan Pass, just as the sun was setting. No one appeared to be guarding the border. Then we noticed. Around the base of the flagpole, fifty yards away, we could see a group of soldiers at prayer. Their backsides rose into the air together whenever they put their heads to the ground.

'Why don't I just unhook the chain?' Michael suggested. 'They may not notice, and even if they do, they won't be able to stop us, since they're occupied with higher things!'

He nipped off the bike. Half-expecting to hear a volley of shots behind us, we rode on towards Kandahar.

Nowadays, we read about Kandahar as a 'Taliban heartland'. This is where British troops in Afghanistan suffered the largest number of casualties. My memories of Kandahar are, on the contrary, of a city given over to dancing and merriment.

As we rode into town on our motorcycle, we found the three-day festival of Jeshyn in full swing. The streets swayed with colour; the national flags hung in their thousands, fluttering over the flowing robes and tough brown faces of the tribesmen who might have walked through the hills for a month to reach the big city. Horse taxis, gaily decorated with yellow or purple plumes, dashed past, shafts shifting and groaning under the weight of whole families. Everywhere there were huge portraits of the King and the Prime Minister.

Jeshyn, we discovered, meant 'independence'.

'Who are they celebrating being independent from?' Michael asked.

I'd done my homework. 'The British, actually. They nearly wiped us out in two Afghan wars in the last century.'

'Did they indeed?' Michael looked around. 'They do seem a tough lot, don't they?'

Jeshyn was still being celebrated when we arrived in Kabul. Kandahar's local feast had been transmuted into a World Fair, with Russians and Americans competing for effect.

The Russians had already put a man in space. From an enormous globe on top of the Russian pavilion a huge rocket appeared to erupt into the sky, blasting past the smiling faces of Nikita Krushchev and Yuri Gagarin.

The American offering was less spectacular. The emphasis, as I remember, was on education, roads and dams. They were obviously making an impact. The road from Kandahar to Kabul, which we had just travelled, had been newly built through American aid. The first traffic lights in Kabul had been installed in the city thanks to a US-financed highway project.

Of course, we weren't in Afghanistan to make a political report. We were tracking Marco Polo.

The day after we reached Kabul Tim joined us, having flown in from Herat. Still hobbling, he undertook to make a last round of the ministries and embassies to see whether the Afghans would give us permission to enter the Wakhan Corridor which debouched into Xinjiang, China's westernmost province, and whether the Chinese would actually allow us to enter Xinjiang through the Wakhan Corridor.

In the meantime, Michael and I headed north on our motorcycle into the Hindu Kush mountains. If we couldn't enter China, then at least we could see the great Buddhist statues at Bamiyan, surely one of the wonders of the ancient world.

When, in early 2001, I heard how the Taliban had ordered the Bamiyan monuments to be blown up, I felt a real pang of grief. We saw many extraordinary sights during our journeys that summer of 1961 but the Buddhist statues in the Hindu Kush certainly came at the top of the list.

We left Kabul one morning and followed the Chardeh River as it flowed north through gorges and rapids. Sheep-and-goat paths climbed obliquely up the hillsides. Tribesmen moved among the rocks, most of them carrying rifles. Peasants crouched in pocket-sized fields, plucking the mountain hay by hand. We ate stews of grey, fatty mutton and smelt hashish in the tea parlours.

The road seemed to get narrower all the time. As the driver of the motorcycle, I constantly had to make fine judgements. If you found yourself stuck behind a slow-moving lorry, you ran the risk of being blinded or suffocated by the dust. On the other hand, if you tried to overtake, the lorry driver would almost certainly pull over to try to push you off the road. Good, clean fun from his point of view, but a life-or-death matter from ours.

The secret was to wait for a moment when the lorry driver was otherwise occupied – on a hairpin bend, for example. If I spotted a gap, I'd ram the motorcycle into a lower gear, shout to Michael to 'hold on tight' and try to cut through on the inside.

I won't say we were quivering wrecks by the time we reached Bamiyan, but we were not far off.

We parked the now horribly scarred and battered BSA Shooting Star at the foot of the cliff to gaze up at the gigantic sandstone gods.

'Ozymandias, eat your heart out!' Michael exclaimed.

Here are the notes I wrote at the time: "The valley of Banyan is of red sandstone. The river widens out between the valley walls, and along the banks of this river are meadows and fields of considerable fertility. Bamiyan is famous for its Buddhas, two of them, carved as Colossi in more than half-relief out of the hill itself. They are gigantic, the largest being 165 feet in height. It stands in a hollowed recess in the cliff walk, dominating the valley. Beneath it extends a large square area, and here the Buddhists, who lived in Bamiyan at the time of the early spread of Buddhism from India into China, came to pray to their God. Thousands of them lived in hollows and caves in the hillside.

"This big Buddha is not artistic: but he is magnificent. Great chips have been torn away from his face and body; the rolls of fat on the neck, to be seen in so many statues of Buddha, preface a face without a nose, with only one ear, and no eyes. Somehow, he is still magnificent.

'A staircase twists up inside the sandstone. Every so often a window is let into it, and one has a glimpse of a thigh, waist, trunk, and finally the head of the great Buddha himself. After this, the staircase comes right out on the top of his head, on top of the very Godhead.

'The roof of the hollow in the cliff that has been made for his head is decorated with crumbling frescoes. The cliff, arching down on either side, frames the valley below. Lying flat on my stomach on top of the Buddha's head, with Michael holding tight to my ankles, I looked down to the Buddha's gigantic toes so far below. It was rather a weird feeling.'

'Alexander the Great passed this way,' I told Michael when I got back onto my feet.

'I wonder if he scratched his name on the rock up here!'

Michael made to pull out his penknife, but I slapped his hand down.

'Only joking!' He gave me a wry smile.

Michael was certainly an older and a wiser man now than he had been when he first joined us. There were moments, for example, on one of those hairpin bends – with the lorry ahead of us refusing to give way – when he probably wished he hadn't thrown his lot in with two callow Oxford undergraduates.

But you couldn't keep him down for long. He was like one of those rubber toys. If you knocked him over, he bounced back up.

We thought of turning back after Bamiyan but decided against it. To the north lay the multi-coloured lakes of Band-e Amir, among the highest in the world. We simply had to see them.

The road grew steeper all the time; the motorcycle laboured with the altitude. At a 12,500-ft pass, we paused and looked north, towards the Oxus and Russia, and north-east, towards the Pamirs and China. We saw that we were too late to try to tackle the Wakhan Corridor into China. The snows had already fallen on the land ahead. Even if we received all the permits we needed, we would never make it.

'This is probably as far as the Marco Polo Route Project is going to go, Michael,' I admitted. Sometimes you just had to face reality. I was desperately disappointed.

Michael still had his cameras. Whatever else we threw away, he hung on to those. He took a photograph of me, with the Band-e Amir Lake in the background, lighting a cigarette with a match from a Bryant and May matchbox. (Bryant and May were one of our expedition's sponsors.)

Not long ago my second son, Leo, was going through some photographs of that Marco Polo trip. He found the 'Bryant and May' snapshot and had it enlarged.

It now sits on top of 'Grandpa's bookcase' at Nethercote. This intriguing piece of furniture is made from the Lincoln College boat, the one which famously won Torpids at Oxford in 1898, making four 'bumps' in three days. (The victorious boat was apparently sawn up into pieces after the event and each oarsman received a section. Grandpa got the bow)

Leo's interest in my Afghan experiences arises, among other things, from the fact that he has married an Afghan: Taies. Though Taies' family happily escaped to the United States when the Russians took over Afghanistan in 1979, their links with the country remain strong and several members of the family have visited the country following the 'defeat' of the Taliban in 2003. The re-emergence of the Taliban in 2021 as the rulers of that benighted country has been a bitter blow.

I little expected during the memorable weeks I spent in Afghanistan in the late summer of 1961 that I would in due course have two part-Afghan grandchildren (both girls). It would be good one day to go back to Afghanistan to join in a great family reunion in Kabul, with Afghan exiles (like Taies' parents and siblings) flying in from all over the world.

Given today's headlines, it looks as though that happy day may still be some way off. Still, we must live in hope.

We left Kabul at the beginning of September (1961). I wouldn't say we departed with our tails between our legs, as it were, but we certainly hadn't achieved what we set out to achieve.

On our last night in the city, I was sitting alone in a teahouse, writing up my notes, when a man came over and joined me at my table. We talked for a while in the all-purpose language in which we were now quite proficient. I gathered he was suggesting I should come to his house and drink some whisky. I accepted with pleasure.

His chauffeur was outside. Feeling a bit uneasy, I got in. My feeling of uneasiness increased when we drove at speed into the mountains outside the city.

As I have already indicated I was younger and thinner then, and possibly blonder too. It didn't take me long to realize what the man had in mind. I needed to get out of there. There were a couple of his mates in the vehicle too. They looked tough and determined.

I did the only thing I could think of. I pretended to be violently sick. The car stopped. The man got out. I hit him hard on the jaw. It wasn't a good blow, more of a haymaker than anything else. I bruised my right thumb badly and to this day it still has a swollen appearance.

Seconds later, I had to throw myself off the road into a ditch as the car roared past.

A few weeks later, after we had returned to England, Peter Fleming interviewed Tim and me for the BBC's Home Service. Peter Fleming was already a world-renowned explorer. He had searched for Colonel Fawcett in the Amazon and had travelled in Tartary with only a camel for company.

It was scheduled to be quite a long piece, more than thirty minutes, with a part-replay foreseen for *Pick of the Week*.

Fleming turned to me towards the end of our time on air: 'Tell me, Stanley, what was the worst thing that happened to you during your journey in the steps of Marco Polo?'

I wanted to say that I had almost been raped by an Afghan, but then I thought of all the little old ladies glued to their wirelesses.

'I was kidnapped one evening in Kabul,' I replied. 'They wanted to steal my British passport.'

'Would that have been worth a lot?'

'About one hundred pounds on the black market. Maybe more.'

When we were having a drink afterwards in the BBC's hospitality room in their Langham Place headquarters, I told the great explorer that, as far as the passport story was concerned, I had been – as Lord Armstrong would later put it – 'economical with the truth'.

'Quite right,' Fleming said briskly. 'You should never shock your audience. Bad manners.'

Fleming didn't stay long that evening. Given his own war record (he had headed 'D' division in charge of military deception in South-East Asia), I think he thought we were a fairly raffish couple of adventurers. He checked his watch and quickly downed his drink.

'Does anyone want a lift to the War Office?' he asked.

4

The Grand Trunk Road, Calcutta, Bombay and Home

The journey back to Oxford from Afghanistan was considerably longer than on the way out.

Just in case we never made it to China, we had arranged a fallback return route from Bombay (now Mumbai) in India. P & O, the shipping company, was one of the sponsors of the Trevelyan scholarships and their representative had been present at a black-tie Trevelyan Scholars dinner held a month or so before our departure date.

I was sitting next to one of P & O's directors. Over the port, I had explained our predicament.

'Problem is,' I said, 'if we can't get into China, we shall have to go on into India and come back from there. There would be three of us and our motorcycles. Do you think P & O might be able to help?'

'I'll have a word with Sir Donald,' the man obligingly replied.

In the event, Sir Donald Anderson, P & O's chairman, couldn't have been more helpful. P & O would find us berths on a ship leaving Bombay for the UK. They might not be able to offer us first-class accommodation, but they would certainly do better than steerage.

Before we left Kabul, we spread out a map of the subcontinent on the floor of one of the city's many *chai-khanehs*, where men (and only men) gather to sit cross-legged on well-worn carpets, smoke tobacco and drink those endless glasses of hot, sweet tea.

'We've still got a bit of time,' I said. 'Why don't we take the Grand Trunk Road down to Calcutta and then put the bike on the train to Bombay in time to catch the boat?'

And this was precisely what we did. We left Kabul for the Khyber Pass, then wound our way through the Jalalabad defile down onto the plains.

It was an eerie experience. If you looked up at the Khyber's towering cliffs, you saw riflemen all around. Watchtowers bristled with guns. This was the place, I remembered, where, halfway through the nineteenth century, a British army had been totally wiped out. More than 9000 soldiers had been massacred. The sole survivor, Dr Brydon, had stumbled into Peshawar to tell the tale.

Like Dr Brydon, we almost didn't make it to Peshawar. Our papers were checked at the frontier post. Tim's were in order, but Michael's and mine definitely were not.

'Where is your entry stamp?' the official asked me brusquely when I showed him my passport. 'Why is there no entry stamp? We cannot give you a stamp to leave Afghanistan if you have not entered the country.'

Of course, I remembered why we had no entry stamp. We had simply gunned our motorcycle past the border post north of Chaman while the guards were at prayer.

'But we *have* entered the country,' I explained patiently. 'You can *see* we are here.'

The official seemed unconvinced. I had a strong sensation that our luck might have run out.

Happily, Michael, quick-witted as ever, came up with the answer. He slipped a ten-dollar note inside his passport. 'Surely the solution, 'ossifer' – he always called 'officers' 'ossifers' as a matter of principle – 'is not to stamp our passports at all. We were never here. Simple as that.'

When we finally unloaded the bike in Peshawar, feeling we had earned a break before beginning the long journey to Calcutta, we decided to spend the night at the Peshawar Club.

It was another of those blissful interludes. We had a bath, then dinner in the dining room. On the ceiling, high above the chandeliers, we could see that names and regimental details had been scribbled on the ceiling.

'Even the ladies are writing their names on ladies' night,' the turbaned Sikh bearer told us. His moustache bristled with disapproval. 'It is not at all a graceful thing for ladies to be climbing up chandeliers, even with petticoat.'

Next morning, one of the Club's stewards, Roshan Khan, a member of the famous squash-playing family and himself a former world champion, gave me a game in one on the Club's courts but I failed to win a single point.

The last few weeks of the Marco Polo Route Project were one continuous blur of movement.

When we left Peshawar, Tim and Michael both climbed onto the motorcycle behind me. For the next several hundred miles – in fact all the way to Calcutta – I had not one but two pillion passengers. Driving was more fun than being driven, I'm sure. There are some advantages in being one of nature's prop forwards.

We still carried the camel-hide bags we had fitted in Persia, as well as jerry cans for fuel. As we careered down the Grand Trunk, or 'GT', Road, we must have looked like some multi-limbed Hindu god.

Michael took to crooning a home-made lyric in my ear as we ate up the miles.

'*Magni intrepidi,*' he sang in Gregorian plain chant,
'*Three on one motorcycle*
Viri fortissimi,
Stanley, Tim and Michael!'

We entered India at Amritsar, the town where in 1919 General Dyer had famously ordered his men to fire on the crowd – with devastating effect. We paid a lightning visit to the Golden Temple, then pressed on to Delhi, with a side trip to Agra and the Taj Mahal. I was already quite familiar with the Taj Mahal in the Turl in Oxford. In those days, you could have a lamb curry for two shillings and sixpence. But it was good to see the real thing.

Then we rattled on down through the great Indo-Gangetic plain. Lucknow, Cawnpore, Benares … of course most of the names have changed now.

I remember we stopped in Benares (now Varanasi) overnight. We went down to the ghats and watched pilgrims who had come from all over India bathe in the sacred waters of 'Mother Ganga'. We saw the funeral pyres at the water's edge and the flower petals floating on the scummy surface of the river.

Over the years I would go back to India many times, but those first impressions will always stay with me. We might not have made it to China but in our brief stay in India that summer we found a worthy consolation prize.

We rested for a couple of days in the Tollygunge Club in Calcutta. The Club Secretary was the father of a boy who had been at school with me. Bill Pool took it on the chin when we rolled into his grand establishment one night with our tenuous claim to his hospitality.

'I expect you chaps could do with a bath,' he told us.

We would have loved to have lingered in those sumptuous surroundings, but time was running out. At Calcutta's Howrah railway station, finding no room for our motorcycle in the guard's van, we lifted the battered machine bodily into one of the compartments. Thirty hours later, having crossed the country from east to west via the great Deccan Plateau, we rode out of the station in Bombay.

A telegram awaited us in Bombay's Central Post Office: 'SS *Stratheden* sailing 9 a.m. 20 September. Three cabin class berths reserved.'

It was the news we wanted to hear.

With two nights to spend in Bombay before sailing, we needed some cheap, preferably clean, accommodation.

I must have told Tim at some point about my Exmoor-born ancestor, Sir George Williams, the founder of the YMCA, because he suggested we should seek a room there at the Y.

'Tell them about your great-great grandpa.' Tim advised. 'Maybe they'll give us a room for free.'

We weren't, I promise, scroungers at heart. But by then we were truly at the limit of our resources.

We drove round to the Y on the bike. Tim and Michael stayed outside while I went in to negotiate.

'No point in scaring them off,' Michael said.

My spirits rose when I saw a huge, framed portrait hanging in the hall. I recognized the picture immediately. The high forehead, the earnest stare and the long white beard were unmistakable.

'I say,' I pointed at the painting, 'that's my great-great-grandfather hanging on the wall, looking as though he were alive. I'm his great-great-grandson. What about a free room and some fried eggs for myself and my two friends?'

The man looked wearily at me. 'I am hearing that story about the ancestor only last week.'

We stayed at the Y anyway, even without a concession. It was a convenient base. For a couple of days, we rode around Bombay, still three-up, on the motorcycle. I have a photograph of the three of us in front of the Gateway of India.

Tim and Michael, sitting behind me, are both wearing the Marco Polo Route Project (MPRP) crash helmets. I am bareheaded. I had given up my crash helmet some time earlier. Michael and I had cadged some mutton stew from some nomads on our way up to Bamiyan in Afghanistan. Lacking a convenient receptacle, we had used my helmet instead.

When we left them the next day, we had given the nomads the still gooey item as a keepsake since I didn't feel like putting it back on my head. It's probably still there, up in the mountains somewhere.

Those short trips around Bombay were the last time the three of us rode together as a team. One day we stopped at a shoe shop in the bazaar. Our motorcycling boots had seen better days and anyway we would need something to wear on the boat.

'Something smart but casual, please, dear,' Michael requested.

We all bought shoes. Since this was a proper cobbler, where they made shoes on the spot, I decided to order a last as well. They could keep it on the shelf for me. I had visions of sending telegrams to Bombay over the coming years, asking for a new pair of brogues or whatever to be dispatched – dirt-cheap, of course.

A well-dressed Indian gentleman, clearly another a customer, intervened to congratulate me on my decision.

'I am always buying my lasts here,' he told me.

This puzzled me. I thought you bought a last and that was it for the rest of your life.

'Why do you need more than one last?'

'The shape of your foot is changing all the time,' the man explained.

'Oh, is it? So how long did your last last last?' I asked.

As we approached the entrance to the Suez Canal, a week or so later, I persuaded Tim and Mike that there was just time for one more adventure before the clouds of academia descended and we had to 'hit the books' to make up for all the time we had spent not studying during our Long Vacation.

'Why don't we jump ship in Suez and make a beeline for Cairo while the ship passes through the Canal. We could get back on board in Port Said – at the northern end – having spent a full day in Cairo while the ship goes through the Canal.'

Tim and Mike were easily persuaded. That mad day, as I remember, we not only visited the National Museum and saw the golden mask of Tutankhamun. We saw the Pyramids too.

It was, as the Duke of Wellington once famously said, 'a damned close-run thing.' We had to sprint up the gangplank as SS Stratheden's hooter was sounding.

In due course, the SS *Stratheden* docked at Marseilles. Leaving the motorcycle on board so that it could be taken on to Southampton where we could collect it, we dashed for the overnight train to Paris.

Twelve hours later we were back in Oxford.

Jack, the College Porter, winked at me when I came into the Lodge.

'Bit late for term, aren't we, sir?'

'Only three days late, Jack. Might have been three months.'

My eye fell on the notice board. The notice about the Long Vacation was still there. '*Gentlemen are reminded…*'

'Isn't it about time you took that notice down?' I said.

5

Newdigate Poetry Prize Debt to Marco Polo

Towards the end of my last summer term, I heard that I had been awarded a Harkness Fellowship.

This meant two years travel and study in the United States. My chosen field of study was creative writing, and the destination was the State University of Iowa where one of the most famous of America's 'writers' workshops' was to be found.

I have often wondered why I was awarded a Harkness Fellowship. After all, I hadn't got a first in Greats, hadn't edited *Isis*, hadn't been President of the Union, hadn't got a Blue in a major sport like Cricket or Rugby. These were my ambitions when I first went up and I had failed on every count.

Looking back on it now, I am convinced that the real reason why I was awarded a Harkness Fellowship in the Spring of 1963, was that had won Oxford's Newdigate prize for English Verse.

The year I entered the Newdigate Prize poetry contest, the poet and author Robert Graves was chairman of the judges, and the selected topic was 'May Morning'. You had to stick to the general theme denoted by the title, but after that the form, content and length of the poem was up to you. Robert Graves wrote me a letter from his home in Majorca, saying my entry was 'the only one which made poetic sense.' Praise indeed from a fine poet, and the author of 'Goodbye to All That', as well as the Emperor Claudius novels.

It remains something of a mystery to me why I entered for the prize at all. When I was at Sherborne, I had had a couple of poems published in *The Shirburnian* but that was largely because I was the

Editor at the time. Editors always printed their own poems. It was one of the perks of the job. But by no stretch of the imagination did I consider myself a poet.

That said, I've always liked a challenge, and winning the Newdigate, or at least putting in for it, seemed like a good idea.

They didn't award the Newdigate very often. If the entries weren't good enough, the prize went unclaimed. When people asked me, as they did, who else had won the Newdigate, I would pause and scratch my head.

'Let me see. John Ruskin, Matthew Arnold, Laurence Binyon …' I would allow my voice to trail off, to make it clear that to win the Newdigate was to join a very select band indeed.

The main, indeed the only task, of the Newdigate Prizewinner was to recite his or her prize-winning entry at the Encaenia, the annual ceremony at which Oxford awarded honorary degrees. That year Encaenia took place on June 27, 1962, and it was a big deal. The list of honorands included some real A-list figures, such as Charlie Chaplin, Yehudi Menuhin, Graham Sutherland, Eugene Black, and Dean Rusk.

A few days before the ceremony I received a letter, in Latin, from the Public Orator, Mr Bryan-Brown, suggesting that, in view of the pressures of time, I might like to limit my recitation to a brief extract from my poem. The full 98 lines would be far too long, even if recited at breakneck speed. *Celerissime.*

I wrote back by return, also in Latin. 'The *'tempus'* might be *'breve'*,' I protested, 'but the *'ars'* was *'longa'*.'

'Vel totum vel nihil,' I concluded. As far as I was concerned, it was all or nothing.

Quick as a flash, the Public Orator sent back the message: *'Tunc nihil.'* Then, nothing!

If I wanted to play hardball, he could play hardball too.

In the end we compromised. I was allowed to choose seven out of the fourteen stanzas, or forty-nine lines altogether.

I remember that morning so well. The Sheldonian was being refurbished so the Encaenia was being held in the Town Hall instead. Normally Harold Macmillan, the then Prime Minister who was Chancellor of the University, would have presided but he was indisposed that day so the Pro-Chancellor, Professor A. P. Norrington, stood in.

I was seated, with other University prize-winners, in the front row of the gallery, wearing my subfusc (dark suit, white shirt and white bow tie) and a peony that Helena Wills – then widely considered to be the most beautiful undergraduate in Oxford – had very kindly brought round to my lodgings in St John Street that morning. Down below us, every seat in the Town Hall was taken.

As the clock in the tower of the University Church, St Mary the Virgin, struck eleven, Norrington lifted his mortar board.

'*Ite! Petite!*' he said to the Senior Proctor which, being translated literally from Latin, means 'Go and seek!'

'*Ite! Petite!*' The Senior Proctor in turn urged the bulldogs and a small procession set off into the High Street to bring in all the honorands, those great and good men who lingered on the pavement outside, waiting to be inducted into one of Oxford's most arcane rites.

To the delight of those present, Charlie Chaplin gave us an ironic version of his famous waddling walk as he proceeded up the aisle to take his seat in front of the Pro-Chancellor. Dean Rusk, the US Secretary of State, looked solemn, as well he might with all the problems the US was then experiencing in South-East Asia. Yehudi Menuhin, who was about to receive an honorary doctorate in music, looked particularly splendid in the LL. D gown.

When they were all in place, Norrington once again took off his mortar board. This time he waved it, not at the Senior Proctor, but in the direction of the balcony.

He gabbled away in Latin. After studying the language for so many years, I ought to have picked it up straightaway.

'Newdigatus poema ... scholaris Exoniensis ... Stanleius Patricius Johnsonius ...' Norrington intoned. It sounded like one of those pseudo-Latin sketches in *Private Eye*.

In the body of the Town Hall, some of the faces looked up in my direction.

'Newdigato premio laureatus Stanleius Johnsonius!' Norrington waved his mortar board more vigorously.

A hand twitched my scholar's gown and the winner of the Gaisford Greek Verse Prize sitting behind me whispered urgently, 'It's your turn now! Off you go!'

I have never suffered from stage fright. I have always appreciated these full-dress performances. You have a strange sense of power. There they all were, about a thousand people in the body of the hall, all in their finery, waiting for me to spout away.

Spout away I did. In a funny way, truncating the poem seemed to improve it. Of course, I kept in the classical allusions, the references to Troy, Agamemnon and 'Hellenic signatories' and so on. But I also retained some of the – dare I say it? – more lyrical passages as well, passages which were inspired – to a large extent – by my Marco Polo experiences.

Mr Bryan Brown had kindly allowed me to keep the last stanza, so I boomed away from the balcony in the crowded Town Hall that morning:

'So once in Mykonos at dusk
I thought May Morning came.
And once upon a Persian mosque
I felt I knew some name
Of God when in the tiles of Holy Writ
It circled one whole minaret.
And streamed to heaven again.'

Winning the Newdigate Prize for Poetry certainly helped with the Harkness. I'm sure of that. Particularly since I had applied to do Creative Writing at the State University of Iowa. Most Harkness

Fellows in those days headed for Harvard or Stanford or Johns Hopkins. But there was more to it than that.

Michael had taken a photo one day, which showed me showed me sitting on the ground, surrounded by villagers. I appear to be oblivious of my surroundings. I have papers on my knee and a pen in in my hand.

I'm pretty sure we were in Iran, or maybe Afghanistan, when he took that picture. Anyway, it did the trick. I stapled it to my Harkness application form. Thank you, Marco Polo!

6

To China – at Last! 1975

I left Washington in May 1968, where I had been working for the World Bank, to go to New York. I had been appointed Project Director of a blue-ribbon National Policy Panel set by the United Nations Association of the USA. The aim of the Panel, chaired by John D. Rockefeller 3rd, was to produce a report urging the UN to set up a body to take action to deal with the world's unprecedented population growth (i.e. the 'population explosion' and related problems.)

The UNA-USA Report was published in May 1969, and it was well received. The United Nations Fund for Population Activities (UNFPA) was established before the end of the year and is still going strong today, though its focus has evolved, as the world's demographic situation has itself evolved.

Later that summer, I signed up to study demography at the LSE in London, under Professor David Glass, while also moonlighting as the first ever Environment Officer in the Conservative Research Department. I also wrote my first non-fiction book, called '*Life Without Birth, a Journey through the Third World in Search of the Population Explosion*'. This was largely based on my own personal observations when, with the UNA-USA's Panel support and guidance, I undertook a first whistle-stop world tour of ten countries in Asia, Africa and Latin America, which were already trying to put in place population and family planning programmes to deal with demographic and/or health and welfare issues. Those countries/regions were Brazil, Chile, Japan, Taiwan, Hong Kong, Singapore, Indonesia, Thailand, India, Pakistan and Kenya.

I didn't visit China in 1969. The Kissinger-Nixon US-China *démarche* was still two or more years ahead. But I did include a chapter about China's demographic policies in the book.

I pointed out that China, with (then) a population as much as 850–900 million, already comprised a quarter of mankind. I wrote: 'In modern times. Chinese demographic situation has an impact outside her borders as well as within. China's population problem is Asia's population problem and Asia's is the world's. It is one of the paradoxes of our age that this country, through her distinctive political and social organisations as a non-revisionist state subscribing to Marxism, Leninism and Maoism, is probably better able to solve her population problem through family planning measures than any other nation similarly placed. Yet, by the very same token she has – so it seems- effectively forsworn such solutions.'

China's position on birth control would dramatically change in 1979, when the Chinese Government confronted with ineluctable population pressures, advocated the practice of 'One couple, one child' with a view to keeping China's population below 1200 million by the year 2000.

I had the good fortune to be present at the World Population Conference held in Mexico City in August 1984. My old friend, Rafael Salas, Secretary-General of the Conference and head of UNFPA, made a brilliant opening speech. *'Our goal is the stabilization of global population before the end of the next century. The combination of rapid population growth, slowly growing incomes and inadequate level of technology continues to widen the disparities in international levels of living and frustrate the efforts of developing countries to improve the quality of life for their people.'*

'Stabilisation of global population'! When did we last hear a world leader speak such good sense? How distant that prospect still seems.

Sitting in my seat in Mexico City's magnificent Palacio de Bellas Artes, where the Conference was being held, I was astounded and delighted when China's delegate, Mr Wang Wei, took the floor to stress that China 'as a developing socialist country' had been making unremitting efforts to develop her economy while controlling rapid population growth. The natural population growth rate had dropped to 1.154 per cent in 1983 from 2.089 per cent in 1973.

'All this has proved' Mr Wang Wei said, 'that the policy decision of promoting family planning to control population growth along with planned economic development is a correct one.'

Back in 1969, of course, when I wrote that book, China's remarkable *volte-face* on population and family planning was still some way ahead. Further ahead still were the substantial tweaks to the country's demographic policy which we have seen in recent years.

In the summer of 1975, I finally had an opportunity to visit China.

As I have already described, in September 1961, almost 14 years earlier, Michael de Larrabeiti and I had come within striking distance of the Chinese border, as we pushed north on our BSA motorcycle from Kabul in Afghanistan, following Marco Polo's route towards the Wakhan Corridor, that narrow tongue of land running through the High Pamir mountains, which in Marco Polo's day had been one of the Old Silk Road's routes from Europe into China.

But that project failed to reach its destination. China remained a closed book to me – and indeed to most of the rest of the world. In 1975, though Mao – the self-styled 'Great Helmsman' – was still nominally in charge, he was a sick man. The Gang of Four ran the show, creating chaos and mayhem on a grand scale.

Of course, there were some straws in the wind, presaging the end of China's isolation. President Nixon's visit to Beijing took place in February 1972, following several reconnaissance missions by Dr Henry Kissinger.

Britain's Prime Minister Edward Heath had visited China in 1974 and had returned with two giant pandas, called Ching-Ching and Chia-Chia, which he presented to the London Zoo.

A year later, when I was working for the European Commission in Brussels, I heard that a group of Commission officials was planning an 'informal' visit to China, I quickly presented my credentials. The trip, I learned from the group's Italian leader, Corrado Pirzio-Biroli, would be an extended affair. After visiting Beijing, we would first go north to Manchuria, then south to Jinan, Nanking, Wusi and Shanghai, before heading for Canton, Hong Kong and home.

Most of the other members of the group came from the Commission's development cooperation department, known then as DG 8. There were around a dozen of us altogether, mainly French, Italian or German.

We weren't an official EEC delegation. We were just a group of individuals from the EEC on a private trip. But we knew, right from the start, that our Chinese hosts didn't really see it that way. Wherever we went there were great red and gold banners: 'WELCOME TO HONORABLE EEC DELEGATION!' 'LONG LIVE ETERNAL FRIENDSHIP BETWEEN EEC AND CHINA!'

I don't blame the Chinese for the efforts they made. The interest they expressed at our arrival was understandable. At the time, China's distrust of both the United States and the Soviet Union was profound. The EEC could prove a valuable trading and political partner.

I reproduce here part of the entry in my diary for Tuesday 29 July 1975, the first day of the Manchurian leg of our journey.

'Shenyang is in Liaoning province. The Manchu Emperor made his capital here. In later years, it was also the capital of the Japanese puppet government. It is an industrial town, in fact one of the key industrial towns of China. On arrival, by overnight train from Peking, we went straight to the hotel, which is off the main square, facing an enormous red statue of President Mao exhorting the people forward in their glorious tasks. A quick breakfast and, by 8.30, we are on our way to see a machine tool factory.

'There is a sign outside the entrance to the factory painted in big bold two-feet high Chinese characters which, we are told, says WELCOME TO STAFF MEMBERS OF BELGIAN COMMON MARKET TO OUR FACTORY.

'The factory was built in 1935 under Japanese imperialism in order to squeeze resources out of China. At the time it was run on a small scale with low-level equipment. It was severely damaged during the Kuomintang regime, which also stole and sold the equipment. Then it was liberated and brought within the people's hands.

'Now the factory has 421 teams for the study of the work of Lenin, Marx and Mao. There are 4,000 members in these groups and 1,000 activists to study Marxism, Leninism and to criticize bourgeois ideas. All the workers are full of confidence that they can fulfil the State Plan and the goal set down in the Fourth People's Congress regarding full modernization.'

Rereading this, I realized that I must have scribbled down what we were told virtually verbatim. My notes cover 110 (double-spaced) A4 pages and much of it reads like the extracts given above. Our Chinese hosts showed us what they wanted to show us. We lapped it all up and panted for more.

Of course, it wasn't all an unrelieved diet of propaganda. On 31 July, for example, we visited the Institute of Traditional Chinese Medicine in Anchang. My diary records:

'First, we go to see how to remove teeth without anaesthetic. An old man, maybe 60 or 70 years old, sits in the dental chair. We crowded round him and watched as the doctor pushed the man's head back and pressed hard, it seemed, on his cheekbones and the side of his mouth. He did this for maybe 30 seconds and then took out a tool and whipped out two teeth from the bottom jaw …'

'We also watch an operation to treat tonsillitis using the burning as opposed to the cutting method. There are long instruments with arrow-shaped heads, and these are heated in the flames. Children then say 'aagh' in their throat and, as they say 'aagh', the doctor puts in the arrow-shaped tool and burns away at the infected tonsil for a few seconds. He treats it point by point. We can see the two children undergoing this treatment and it was apparent to me that they were not suffering in any way …'

We worked hard during those few weeks. If the days were full of official visits, the evenings were also packed with entertainments in which the propaganda element was at best thinly disguised.

Here is another extract from my notebook:

'In the evening, we go to see another performance by acrobats. This time it is the Shenyang municipal troop who, a year or two ago, apparently toured the United States with great success. It is even better than the performance in Peking. There are the usual scenes with bicycles, chairs, plates and mock lions. As we enter to take our seats two minutes before the curtain there is applause from the audience. They all stand up to clap us and we sit down in one of the best rows a few yards from the front. When it is time for the interval, we are ushered into a special reception room, and we sit with tea and cigarettes until it is time to go back in.

'The last item of the programme is a conjuring trick. There is a large Chinese bowl which is empty, and which the audience can clearly see is empty, but all sorts of things sprout and grow in this bowl by magic. Flowers, ducks, aquariums filled with goldfish; there seems absolutely no limit to the contents of the bowl. Nobody knows how the things get into the bowl or how the trick is done. In the end the lid is taken off for the last time and we see a quantity of red material inside. The girl pulls one end, and another girl pulls the other end and they run round the stage and the material still pours out of the bowl and finally they stand at either end of the stage and stretch out the huge banner between them and of course it is a revolutionary banner with a revolutionary slogan which incites the people to: 'UNITE TO WIN STILL GREATER VICTORY!' So that's the end. Everybody claps – more vigorously than they ever did in Peking – and we all go home.'

We went to the opera too. On 2 August, for example, we were in Jinan, a large city on the Yellow River. We spent the morning visiting a thermos factory and the afternoon at a museum, returned to our hotel for a twenty-minute break, then headed back into the city centre.

I wrote in my diary: 'In the evening we go into town to see a Chinese opera called *The Two Heroic Sisters of the Steppe*. As we get off the bus and walk into the opera building, the people line up on every side and clap us. It takes me back to my school days and running onto the rugger field for the First XV at Sherborne. The whole school had to watch.'

With all the visits to factories, communes, conjuring displays and operas, we still managed to do our share of sightseeing: the Forbidden City and the Temple of Heaven in Beijing, the Ming Tombs and the Great Wall of China, the Mausoleum of Sun Yat Sen in Nanking, the canals and lakes of Wusi, the Bund in Shanghai.

I got into trouble in Wusi for jumping off the deck of the boat into the lake while we were going for a cruise. I just felt I needed a swim. That evening our guides, Mr Chen and Mr Chou (they stayed with us throughout), called the group together and, looking at me pointedly, scolded us about the need to have 'a correct revolutionary attitude' at all times.

On 14 August 1975, we left Canton (now Guangzhou) for Hong Kong. It was a two-hour train journey in an air-conditioned coach, blissfully comfortable. Mr Chen and Mr Chou came with us on this last leg too.

As always, the music of the Internationale was piped in an endless loop into our compartment. There was no escaping it, short of wearing earplugs, so we made the most of it, singing lustily along with Chen and Chou as the train passed through the paddy fields of southern China.

'Arise ye prisoners of starvation.

Arise ye wretched of the earth.

For justice thunders condemnation

A better world's in birth …'

When the chorus came, we turned up the volume, like the prisoners released from the dungeon in Beethoven's Fidelio.

''Tis the final conflict

Let each stand in his place

The Internationale shall be the human race!'

At the border station, we climbed down out of the train, went through the Chinese border posts, changed all our Chinese money into Hong Kong dollars, had the currency form stamped, gathered our hand luggage together and finally walked a hundred yards or so up the road which ran alongside the railway track to the bridge. At the far end of the bridge the Union Jack hung limply in the soggy air.

7

Looking Ahead

My third novel, published by Macmillan in Britain as *The Urbane Guerrilla* and by Doubleday in the US as *God Bless America*, had not been a blistering success. But the China trip gave my literary career a boost. Twelve months or so after I got back from China, I had completed a thriller called *The Doomsday Deposit*, where much of the action takes place on the Sino-Soviet border. Toby Eady arranged a large advance from Dutton in New York (US $20,000 in those days seemed large to me, at least) and Felicity Bryan, a friend from Washington days who was now a literary agent in London, elicited £5000 from Charles Pick, Heinemann's managing director.

The Doomsday Deposit was an 'alternate' Book of the Month Club choice in America. I was very pleased about this. I felt it was something to write home about.

By coincidence, the other 'alternate choice' that month was Rachel Billington's *A Woman's Age*. As the authors of the 'alternate choices', Rachel Billington and I found ourselves promoting our respective works in New York at the same time. Our publishers both gave parties for us. The next day, when I picked up the *New York Times*, I could find no mention of *The Doomsday Deposit*. Instead, I read the neatly alliterative banner headline: 'Last of literary Longfords lionized'.

I knew then that an 'alternate choice' was not really a big deal and that my literary career still had a long way to go.

My letters to my parents, still on the farm on Exmoor, I am ashamed to say, became less frequent than they once had been.

Telephoning was not so good. My father did not enjoy talking on the telephone and my mother was increasingly deaf. But I remember one day writing home along the following lines.

'Dear Mummy and Daddy,' I began. 'We are enjoying life in Brussels. Alexander [aka Boris] and Rachel are both doing well at the European School, and so is Leo. Jo is a delight and soon he will go to a nursery school. Charlotte's painting is going extremely well. She has just had an exhibition in a gallery in Brussels. Lots of our friends came and she sold almost all her paintings. Apart from people who work in the Commission, and the journalistic community, we are lucky to have many Belgian friends too. They all came to the Sablon, which is where the gallery is, and had a good time.

'My new novel about China, *The Doomsday Deposit*, is an alternate Book Club selection in New York. I do hope you enjoy it, now we've sorted out the problems with the dog!'

I need to explain my reference to 'the dog.'

I had sent my mother the galleys of the American version of my novel. My mother enjoyed proof reading. I suspect she got a real kick from finding a typo or, better still, a grammatical error. As it turned out, after she had bumped down the Nethercote track in her battered VW Beetle to pick up the parcel I had sent her from Brussels, she really hit the jackpot.

The hero of *The Doomsday Deposit* is a steely American, John McGrath. And McGrath has a dog, a Labrador. That was what got me into trouble.

A few days after I had sent the parcel of proofs to Nethercote, I received a stinging letter.

'I cannot believe that a son of mine,' my mother witheringly began, 'can write about a Golden Labrador! You either have a Yellow Labrador or you have a Golden Retriever!'

Ouch! In those pre-email days, I had to send a full-rate telegram to E. P. Dutton in New York: 'For Golden Labrador please read Yellow Labrador *passim*'.

The Latin word *passim* – as any competent proofreader should know, I imagined – means 'throughout' or 'wherever and whenever it occurs'. I thought I had made my meaning abundantly clear.

How wrong I was! When the page proofs arrived, McGrath's dog had acquired a new name: Passim!

I sent another full-rate telegram to New York: 'Please delete Passim *passim*!'

Even if my mother enjoyed finding howlers, she enjoyed – even more – feeling useful and needed. She always wanted to help. To the end of her life, my mother retained an almost unquenchable optimism, even when, in her declining years, she sometimes had good reason to be despondent.

She came out to stay with us several times in Brussels and her visits were always a joy.

My father, I have to say, was always more reserved than my mother. Enthusiasm was not his default mode. But perhaps because his own early life, in Canada and Egypt, had been full of adventures (though he didn't talk much about it), he was quite excited about my efforts to write a decent thriller. He appreciated a good story.

I remember my father saying one day at supper: 'Maybe they'll make a film of one of your books, Stan, like Ian Fleming and James Bond.'

I laughed at the idea at the time. But they *did* make a film of one of my books. In 1987 Century Hutchinson published *The Commissioner*, a thriller set in Brussels. I wrote the novel soon after returning to work in Brussels in the mid-eighties, once again for the European Commission, after a five-year stint as a member of the European Parliament (MEP).

As a matter of fact, I didn't *write* the novel – I dictated it in twenty-minute bursts as I drove to work in the morning. Whereas in my earlier incarnation as a *fonctionnaire* I usually cycled to work, ten years later – I must admit – I most often drove to the office (still the same lovely *trajet* through the leafy beech woods where Wellington's troops bivouacked on the eve of Waterloo).

Every week I used to send a collection of the tapes off to a typing agency in England and after a while a bulky typescript would plop through the letterbox at 3 Avenue Boesdael.

I was agreeably surprised at how well the first draft turned out. Occasionally, I muddled up the names of key characters and once one of them inadvertently changed sex halfway through. But as soon as I had the complete text in front of me, I was able to sort out the minor blips. More to the point, the book seemed to ring true. I suspect the real reason *The Commissioner* worked was that I was writing about a world in which I was deeply involved on a personal basis. Roy Jenkins, the Commission's former President who had left Brussels to 'break the mould of British politics' by co-founding the SDP, gave me a splendid puff for the jacket. '*Strong on authentic detail*,' Roy wrote. And I think he meant it.

The film rights were sold to a German company, and in due course a film of *The Commissioner* was made, with John Hurt playing the lead role.

One day I was invited to attend a morning's shooting. They had taken over a Brussels café. I sat in a corner watching the action. At one point, John Hurt called out in an irritated voice: 'Stop! Stanley is in my eye-line!'

Before it went on release in Europe (it had been co-financed by Canal Plus) *The Commissioner* was shown in the competition section of the Berlin Film Festival in 1998. Walking onto the stage in the giant Zoo Palast Cinema on the Kurfürstendamm to shouts of 'author, author!' was certainly a moment to be treasured.

We were quite a party of Johnsons in Berlin that night. Jenny and I arrived with our two children, Julia and Max, and made our way to the posh hotel where reservations had been made (and paid for!) by the Film Festival organizers. As we took the lift to the seventh floor, we noticed that *The Commissioner* posters were stuck on the doors and walls. The corridor leading to our suite was also lined with posters.

Julia and Max guessed immediately. 'Leo is here already!' they pronounced.

'Leo!' I exclaimed. 'Surely not!' Leo was in Washington, working for the International Finance Corporation, part of the World Bank Group.

As we were debating the point, Leo emerged laughing from behind a pillar. Having flown in that morning, he had visited the Film Festival offices and grabbed a huge bundle of posters which he had put up all around our hotel.

Jo, too, flew in from Paris where he was working for the *Financial Times*, so that was a double bonus. Okay, so it wasn't a full house as far as the Johnson children were concerned. But when you have six children, as I do, a two-thirds turnout is certainly a quorum.

I am particularly sorry that my father wasn't still alive at the time of the 1997 Berlin Film Festival. He didn't have much time for my political ambitions, believing that all politicians were scoundrels. And I don't think he had a great deal of sympathy for my work as a civil servant, given the amount of 'paper-pushing' he imagined was involved, although I think he appreciated the case for action on the environmental front. But I would have liked to have taken him with us to Berlin. I think he would have enjoyed, as I did, seeing the credit 'based on the novel by Stanley Johnson' roll up on the giant screen. It would probably have rated a 'Good show, Stan' which, from him, would have been high praise indeed.

As I say, my father liked a good story, and *The Commissioner* had a good plot line, full of sex, scandal and intrigue. Just like everyday life in the European Commission's huge starfish-shaped Berlaymont building in Brussels.

My second stint in Brussels, working for the European Commission, lasted six years, from 1984 to 1990.

It was an astonishingly invigorating time. The Commission,

under the Treaty, had – and still has – the sole right of initiative and, boy, did we make use of it! I spent a lot of time shuttling between the Commission, Council and Parliament buildings, defending the Commission's environmental proposals.

But there were many forays further afield as well.

Each year we had formal meetings with the United States Environmental Protection Agency (established by President Richard Nixon in 1969). We didn't always agree on a common approach, but at least we discovered what our differences were. We learned from them. Maybe they learned from us too.

We also went to Japan. Here our principal interlocutor was the Ministry of International Trade and Investment, mighty MITI.

On one of those trips to Tokyo, I decided I would call in on Tom Mori, my Japanese literary agent. Two of my early novels, viz. *The Doomsday Deposit* and *The Marburg Virus*, had, thanks to Tom, been translated into Japanese. *The Commissioner* was about to be launched upon the world, and I hoped that Tuttle-Mori, Tom's firm, would engineer a lucrative sale of the Japanese rights for that book too.

I arranged the RV with Tom at 4 p.m. on the day of my arrival in Japan. He sent me a fax with the address of his agency, and I printed it off.

Things began to go wrong as soon as I landed at Tokyo's Narita Airport after the long flight from Europe. The traffic into the city was horrendous, the taxi ride took over two hours and cost an arm and a leg. When we reached central Tokyo, the driver was totally at a loss. The avenues and cross streets are not conveniently numbered. There was no discernible pattern. The meter mounted as the minutes passed. Quite obviously, we were nowhere near our destination. I grew increasingly agitated. Tom Mori was still waiting for me to arrive. It was long past his going-home time.

Suddenly I had had enough. I had been travelling for more than twelve hours on the plane, and now another two or more in the taxi.

I waved the piece of paper with Tom Mori's address on and shouted at the driver. 'Stop, I'm going to ask directions. Here's a place. I'll try here.'

We had pulled up in front of some kind of tea shop. I burst into the room and, raising my voice, cried: 'For heaven's sake, can't somebody tell me where the Tuttle-effing-Mori Literary Agency is? It's meant to be in Chobe-Shinjuku block 361 or something. Is that anywhere near here?'

The man behind the counter looked at me. I don't know if he understood everything, I was saying but he realized perfectly that I was just another 'gaijin' or 'foreigner' who didn't know how to behave.

He didn't raise his voice but, as far as I was concerned, he could have held a foghorn to his lips.

'You not king here,' he said. 'In Japan, politeness is all.'

I crawled back into the taxi, totally deflated and ashamed. *You not king here. Politeness is all.* I have never forgotten that quiet ticking off. It seared the soul.

I found Tom Mori in the end. Everyone else in his office had gone home – lots of people who worked in Tokyo commuted three hours each way from outlying regions – but Tom was still there waiting for me. *(Politeness is all!)* Tom was the man who had brought Jeffrey Archer, Frederick Forsyth, and John Grisham to Japan, and the Japanese reading masses had been duly grateful. Of course, I wasn't in the Archer-Forsyth-Grisham league, not by a million miles. But I had been travelling about twenty hours and I felt I deserved a drink,

Happily, Mori was only too ready to oblige. He was a large, ebullient man. I had been told that at the Frankfurt Book Fair he gave legendary parties. He certainly didn't stint on the hospitality that evening. In Japan, even in those days, Johnny Walker Black Label whisky cost about £80 a bottle. He poured us both a generous glass, put a huge arm round my shoulder, holding the other arm out in front of us, and took a photo with a Polaroid camera. Nowadays that's called a 'selfie'.

I told Tom that evening that I was looking forward not only to a Japanese version of *The Commissioner* (which duly appeared) but also to the publication, in Tokyo, of *Dragon River*, another novel which I had planned.

'It's mainly set in China,' I explained. 'There's talk about building a giant dam on the Yangtze. It's another disaster novel.'

Tom Mori poured me another drink. 'Your books have not been a disaster in Japan. They have done very well.'

'I mean it's *about* a disaster. The Chinese build the dam all right, but there's a fatal flaw. The dam is in an earthquake zone and the pressure of the water in the reservoir triggers a seismic shock. That happens on the very day the new dam is being opened by the Chinese Premier. A crack appears in the dam wall and the water begins to seep through. The trickle becomes a torrent! Three hundred million people live downstream in the Yangtze valley! The flood could wipe them out!'

Tom Mori's attention was fully engaged.

'And does the dam actually fail?' he asked hopefully. Overall, the Japanese don't seem not very keen on the Chinese. I suspect the feeling is mutual.

'I'm afraid I had to leave the reader in suspense, Tom,' I replied.

'Pity!' He roared with laughter.

8

Returning to China, December 1986

It was perfectly clear to me that, to make real progress with the plot I had outlined to Tom Mori that evening in Tokyo, I needed to revisit China. As I have noted, more than a decade had elapsed since our little group of keen Brussels-based Sinophiles had dutifully recorded the glorious achievements of China under Chairman Mao. Now a different regime was in place under Deng Xiaoping. China was in the throes of the Four Modernizations. The construction of the Three Gorges Dam, as I had explained to Tom Mori that evening in Tokyo, was to be one of the centrepieces in the transformation of China, producing – so it was hoped – over 16 Gigawatts of electricity.

'Sixteen Gigawatts, Tom!' I had explained. 'That's equivalent to the output of sixteen nuclear power stations.'

At the time that I was working up the plot for *Dragon River*, the construction of the Three Gorges on China's mighty Yangtze River was by no means a done deal. The basic financing, for example, was not in the bag, the World Bank having announced that it was not ready to support the project.

What interested me most of all were the engineering considerations. Was the dam really safe? Who had done the original research?

Digging around as best I could, I discovered that the US Army Corps of Engineers, with an amazing track record of building dams in America in the 1930s (including the great Hoover Dam in Colorado), had been based in Chungking, capital of China's

Szechuan Province, during the Second World War and had produced the first proposals for a dam on the Yangtze.

In the London Library I found a copy of Madame Chiang Kai-shek's memoirs. Madame Chiang, aka Mayling Soong (one of the three famous Soong sisters), vividly describes the nightly Japanese bombing raids on Chungking. Since Chungking was situated at the junction of the Jialing and Yangtze Rivers, on moonlit nights the Japanese simply had to fly up through the Three Gorges from Yichang till they saw the silver gleam of the confluence.

I also discovered that 'Vinegar Jo' Stillwell, commander of the US forces in Chungking, hated Chiang Kai-shek, whom he called 'the Peanut', a slighting reference to the shape of the Generalissimo's head. Meanwhile the wily Chou En-Lai, probably the cleverest Communist of them all, was lurking in the background, just waiting for the moment when the Nationalists and the Communists, with the war against Japan behind them, could concentrate on ripping each other apart.

As a setting, Chungking sounded irresistible. Location, location, location!

I found a little Sino-Belgian tourist agency in one of the grimmer parts of Brussels. Could they please organize my trip to Chungking, where I hoped to catch a boat down through the Three Gorges to Yichang, the most likely construction site for the Three Gorges Dam?

'*Vous serez combien de personnes dans votre groupe, monsieur? Seulement les groupes sont permis.*'

Only groups permitted! This was a cosh-blow. But then I had a brilliant idea.

'*Je suis un groupe d'une personne!*' A group of one!

The nice young Belgo-Chinese travel agent, though hesitant at first, sent off a cable to Peking, now Beijing, and quite soon we received an answer that, with the favourable evolution of events under the Four Modernizations, 'groups of one' were now being permitted to travel in China, as long as they were accompanied by a guide.

Well, I don't remember the guide. I don't think we ever met up. All I remember is walking down that immense flight of steps at Chungking, getting on the boat at the quayside, finding a berth in a primitive cabin at water level (the river lapped at the porthole) and spending four days and nights cruising down the Yangtze to Wuhan.

It certainly wasn't the kind of luxury Three Gorges Cruise you can sign up for nowadays. The food basically consisted of a bucket of rice dumped on deck. As far as I could see I was the only foreigner on board, but that certainly didn't guarantee me any privileged treatment. I was issued with a spoon, and I waited in line to scoop up a plateful of the glutinous substance. Occasionally, you could find a bit of fish lurking at the bottom of the bucket, an eyeball perhaps or a piece of gelatinous fin, or a scaly yellow chicken claw.

But as a means of firing the imagination, that trip down the Yangtze was ideal. I worked out the plot of *Dragon River* in detail and when I disembarked at Wuhan, I found a fax machine at the airport and whizzed off the outline to my editor at Century Hutchinson.

As it turned out, I had a lot of time at the airport.

I was standing in line waiting to check in for the flight to Hong Kong when the announcement was made: 'China Airways flight to Hong Kong is delayed for three days due to technical problems.'

I could probably have tweaked the outline a bit.

Since that trip to research my novel about the Three Gorges Dam, I have visited China quite regularly. In May 2001, for example, Jenny and I visited our daughter Julia, then teaching English in Hangchow during her gap year. And when Max was living in Beijing and Hong Kong, we visited both places on several different occasions.

Whenever I went to China, Marco Polo was in the back of my mind. How good it would be, I thought, one day to pick up where

In the Footsteps of Marco Polo

we left off way back in 1961 and retrace Marco Polo's footsteps from the Chinese border out in the West, on the Pamir Plateau, all the way to Beijing along the route of Old Silk Road.

9

Visits to the Chinese Embassy: January–February 2020

One day in early January 2020, my old friend Tony Samuels, then Chairman of Surrey County Council, rang me to tell me he had been invited to the Chinese Embassy to celebrate the Chinese New Year.

'I didn't know you were involved with China,' I said

'Oh, I am! I'm trying to twin Surrey with Liaoning Province in China. I've been out there a couple of times. They're tremendously keen. My problem is trying to persuade Surrey! Would you like to come along? Should be a fun evening. If you can, I'll let them know. It's the Year of the Rat, by the way!'

My son, Max, was visiting London at the time. Tony was only too pleased to have Max as an addition to the party.

'Max speaks Mandarin, too, doesn't he?' Tony asked.

'He does indeed.' Having got an MBA at Tsinghua University in Beijing and having spent several years working both in Beijing and Hong Kong, Max was fluent in Mandarin.

The Chinese New Year is a big deal. In China itself the festivities last days, if not weeks. The airports and railway stations are packed with travellers off to meet relatives in the far-flung corners of the country. The New Year festival is also taken very seriously by overseas Chinese and of course by China's own embassies, 'corners of a foreign field' that are forever China.

The party was already in full swing when we arrived at the Embassy in Portland Place. A band was playing. There was a chorus of dancing girls. A good time was clearly being had by all.

As a long-standing environmentalist, I had been following closely the preparations being made for two big international events, both of which were to take place in the latter part of the year. The first was the meeting of the parties to the UN's Convention on Biological Diversity (CBD) which was due to take place on Kunming, China, in November, with China in the Chair. A month later the 26th meeting of the parties to the UN's Framework Convention on Climate Change – known as COP 26 – was to take place in Glasgow, Scotland with the UK in the Chair.

As the band played and the guests mingled, I sought out the Ambassador. I had to speak up to make myself heard above the noise. After the usual pleasantries, I came to the point.

'China has such a key role to play this year, Ambassador. If China, as Chair of the Biodiversity Conference, manages to get a strong commitment to nature protection, you will be creating a vital plank for the climate work too.'

I went on in that vein for a minute or so.

The best way to ruin a good case is to plug it too hard. Other guests were queuing up to shake the Ambassador's hand.

A few days later I received an invitation to meet the Ambassador at the Embassy to discuss some of the points I had raised.

Mike Clarke, at the time the CEO of the Royal Society for the Protection of Birds, (RSPB) came with me to the Chinese Embassy in Portland Place, London, on Feb 4, 2020.

In the course of a long discussion about biodiversity and climate change, Mike mentioned the great work that China was already doing in protecting and restoring the wetlands near Shanghai. He spoke about the real on-the-ground help some UK NGOs were giving.

'The carbon-absorptive capacity of wetland mud is many times higher than that of tropical rainforest.'

The Ambassador was intrigued. 'Mud?'

'Yes, mud' Mike confirmed.

We were sitting on either side of the Ambassador in a conference room. Tea had been served, and cups refilled. When the Ambassador relaxed, the staff did too.

I thought it was time to strike a lighter note. The Chinese New Year festivities had after all only just ended.

'Do you remember the Flanders and Swan song, Your Excellency?' I volunteered. 'Mud, mud glorious mud?'

The Ambassador shook his head.

'I'll sing it for you' I said.

If the Ambassador was surprised, he didn't show it. In that solemn hall, with its backdrop of colossal Ming vases and huge hanging tapestries, featuring mountains and fountains, lakes and crags, Mike and I gave our audience an impromptu rendition of the famous song.

We tried to get the Ambassador's staff to join in.

'Mud, mud glorious mud,
There's nothing quite like it for cooling the blood,
So, follow me follow, down to the hollow
And there let us wallow in glorious mud!'

I won't say the result was especially musical, but this little choral interlude cracked the ice very effectively. Seizing the moment, I told the Ambassador that the very first time I had visited his splendid establishment in Portland Place had been way back in the early summer of 1961 when I was in quest of a visa. When I mentioned Ambassador Xiang by name, who had been *en poste* at that time in London, Ambassador Liu nodded thoughtfully.

'Ah, yes. Ambassador Xiang Hua. One of my predecessors. Very distinguished man.'

I explained that I had hoped to present to Ambassador Xiang a letter of endorsement from Dr Needham.

'Professor Joseph Needham?'

'The same.'

Ambassador Liu was clearly impressed. 'Professor Needham

is still much respected in China today. Why did you not present Needham's letter to Ambassador Xiang?'

'I'm afraid it was mislaid.'

'Mislaid?'

'Well, lost. It was buried somewhere beneath Marble Arch in the glove compartment of a 1932 Sunbeam Talbot.'

I went on to explain more fully how my lovely antique car came to its undignified end.

Later that afternoon I received an email from the Ambassador's office. I was happy to learn that the Ambassador had been pleased to meet us. Apparently, my story about Dr Needham's letter and the car had been much appreciated.

I took that as a good sign. Maybe Professor's Needham's message had, in some mysterious way, been received by the Chinese Embassy after all. Better late than never I thought.

10

OneTribeTV Comes on Board

Inevitably, during Covid, the Marco Polo project had to be put on the backburner, but by mid-2021 there was light at the end of the test-tube. Lockdown was being relaxed. Real life would resume.

On August 11, 2021, my agent, Sue Ayton of Knight Ayton Management, organized a zoom call with Dale Templar, who ran a TV and film production company called One-Tribe TV.

'You'll love Dale' she told me before the call. 'You'll hit it off. She has filmed all over the world. Done a big wildlife series in China.'

Sue was right. Dale liked the idea of filming my planned trip to China. 'What a great scheme' she enthused 'to finish off a journey you started sixty years ago.'

Next day August 12, 2021, I sent Dale, an email:

'Dear Dale,

'Great to talk. Max very keen.

'Maybe we should drive a car, rather than two motorcycles. More time to talk, also safer! But ready to do motorcycles too. Triumphs? Nortons? A British Model would be good. We had BSAs in 1961. We would need to get international motorcycle licenses or at least a nationally valid one!

'Re the route, let's start in Kashgar and end in Beijing. Around 3000 miles or a bit more. Marco Polo mentions Dunhuang (Suchow) and Xian, so those places ought to be on the itinerary.

'Happy to fix lunch with Chinese Ambassador or his delegate to discuss this, or alternative project (e.g. the China environment film we discussed).

'Jenny and I much looking forward to seeing you on Aug 28. All best, Stanley'

After that, things really started to move. The fact that my fourth son, Max, was ready to join the party was a tremendous bonus. Not only would he be co-presenter of the TV series Dale envisaged. As a fluent Mandarin speaker, who for years had lived and worked in China and Hong Kong, he would play a key role.

One-Tribe TV, based in Bath, produced a promotional brochure, entitled: 'The Johnsons in the Footsteps of Marco Polo.' It went on to explain which Johnsons, out of the great pool of Johnsons who inhabit this planet, would be involved.

Yes, it would be a 'father-and-son road trip'!

At 81 years old (as I was at the time), I was described a 'charismatic polymath and statesman' (thank you, Dale!).

Max was described as a 'charismatic character who was educated at Eton and Oxford.' As the brochure put it: 'Max went on to do higher studies in China and set up an investment company. He has lived in China and Hong Kong for more than 10 years and speaks fluent Mandarin, Russian, French and Polish. He is also a Black Belt in Taekwondo.'

One Tribe TV didn't duck the political issue. 'If the COVID-19 pandemic proves anything, it is that you need your neighbours. If you refuse to talk to or even boycott China, where do you go next? As they follow in the footsteps of Marco Polo, they'll be exploring much of China we never get to see in the West. Along with the spectacular backdrops, wilderness adventures and the rich history of Old China, they will be spending time with 21st century Chinese people to celebrate not only our differences, but the many things we have in common.'

Dale's people obviously thought that the interaction between Max and me on what was likely to be a long trip might produce some good tele-visual material. They wrote: 'father and son – as you would expect from two strongly opinionated individuals – have a spiky relationship. The tough conditions along their route, their various vehicles, and the challenges they will face, will only add spark to that relationship'.

Spiky relationship! Where did they get that from? I wondered. Events might prove me wrong, but from my point of view, Max's decision to join me as a co-presenter was a definite and unadulterated plus.

The brochure continued. 'Stanley Johnson is on a mission to clear up some unfinished business. 60 years ago, he and two friends from Oxford University decided to follow explorer Marco Polo's Silk Route Journey from Venice to China. On motorbikes they got as far as the Afghan-China border, but a mix-up over visas meant they never got to complete the route. And most importantly, never got into China. Now Stanley is determined to finish the job. This time his travelling companion is his son Max. They pick up the famous explorer and trader's journey on the Chinese side of the border. Using eco-friendly 4-wheel drive vehicles, camels and even getting 81-year-old Stanley back onto a motorcycle, they follow in Polo's footsteps. It is an adventure that takes them across stunning landscapes, visiting places ancient and modern and meeting remarkable people in the world's most populous and arguably most powerful nation. They're heading towards Xanadu or Shangdu as it was called – the legendary summer capital of Emperor Kublai Khan – before concluding their journey in Beijing.'

Well, I said to myself as I put it down, it's great having a glossy brochure. Not so great being reminded in that same brochure that my earlier venture came unstuck. Not least owing to the lack of Chinese visas. Would the situation in 2021 be any better than the situation in 1961 had been?

I have already mentioned a few straws in the wind, hopeful omens, but what we needed was some concrete indication from China that the scheme, ambitions though it was, was at least worth considering. It shouldn't be written off as some far-fetched fantasy, best pitched straight into the dustbin of entertaining but unworkable ideas.

The key thing now was to get going.

As an Ambassador for the Conservative Environment Network (CEN), with the task of helping CEN members interested in two key international issues: climate change and the protection of the world's biodiversity, I greatly welcomed the regular contacts I had with the new Chinese Ambassador, Zheng Zeguang, since China was clearly a key player, as far as both issues were concerned.

And at a personal level our relationship flourished too. The Ambassador and his wife, Hua Mei, came to lunch with Jenny and me at our London home.

We in turn had a delightful lunch with the Ambassador and his charming wife at their residence in Hampstead.

All in all, I was convinced that the Ambassador's support would be crucial not only in ensuring that Chinese visas would be forthcoming when we needed them but also in convincing his colleagues in Beijing that the revived Marco Polo Route Project could and should be helped in a practical way too, in terms of transport, accommodation, and general logistical back-up.

The next vital step, as I saw it, was to find a financial backer for the project. Back in 1961, Tim Severin and I had basically winged it as far as financing that first Marco Polo venture was concerned.

Well, that was then. This was now. It wasn't just a question of three men and a couple of motorcycles. Now that One-Tribe was involved, with plans to produce four 45-minute TV programmes and a 90-minute film, we were – as they say – in a whole new ballgame.

Would some *deus ex machina* appear on the scene to help turn the dream into a reality?

In the Footsteps of Marco Polo

Tim Severin, Afghanistan, August 1961.

Marco Polo's travels, 1271–1296.

In the Footsteps of Marco Polo

Michael de Larrabeiti, Afghanistan, September 1961.

Departure, Exeter College, Oxford, June 1961.

We dressed up to call on the Mayor of Venice.

In the Footsteps of Marco Polo

Being received by the Mayor of Venice, June 1961.

With our Turkish 'family'. Istanbul, June 1961.

In the Footsteps of Marco Polo

Refuelling on the Anatolian plateau, June 1961.

Isfahan, Iran, August 1961.

In the Footsteps of Marco Polo

Buddha Statue, Bamiyan,
Afghanistan, September 1961.

Author, Afghanistan,
September 1961.

In the Footsteps of Marco Polo

EEC Group visiting a health centre, Anchang, China, August 1975.

In the Footsteps of Marco Polo

Lunch *chez nous* with the Chinese Ambassador, HE Zheng Zeguang, his wife Hua Mei, Dale Templar, Owen Gay, Prof William Sutherland, Nicola Crockford, Stanley and Jenny Johnson.

With Dr Rana and his wife, Tatiana, in the Dubai Desert Conservation Reserve, November 13, 2021. With the stars overhead, the three of us had dinner together in the desert.

In London, April 27, 2023. Dr Jan Telensky with Boris Johnson and bust of the author.

My first 'Piece to Camera' in China, on the Chinese side of the China-Pakistan border.

In the Footsteps of Marco Polo

Author on yak, Pamir Plateau, Xinjiang, China.

Dale Templar, OneTribeTV CEO, on the Panlong Ancient Highway, Xinjiang.

Max with a Kyrgyz photographer.

In the Footsteps of Marco Polo

Lake Baisha, Xinjiang

In the Footsteps of Marco Polo

In front of the Gate, Kashgar, Xianjiang.

He put my Australian bush-hat on his head and nodded proudly. I wore the traditional 'doppa' as I made one final attempt to make a recognizable piece of pottery.

In the Footsteps of Marco Polo

Id Kah Mosque, Kashgar, Xinjiang: the largest mosque in China.

With Imam Abasi at Id Kah Mosque, Kashgar.

In the Footsteps of Marco Polo

Max and I headed for one of the little food-stalls that offered refreshments to hungry traders.

Max and I stood in front of a huge statue of Chairman Mao Zedong.

In the Footsteps of Marco Polo

Muqam musicians, Yarkant, Xinjiang

In the Footsteps of Marco Polo

Hotan's jade market

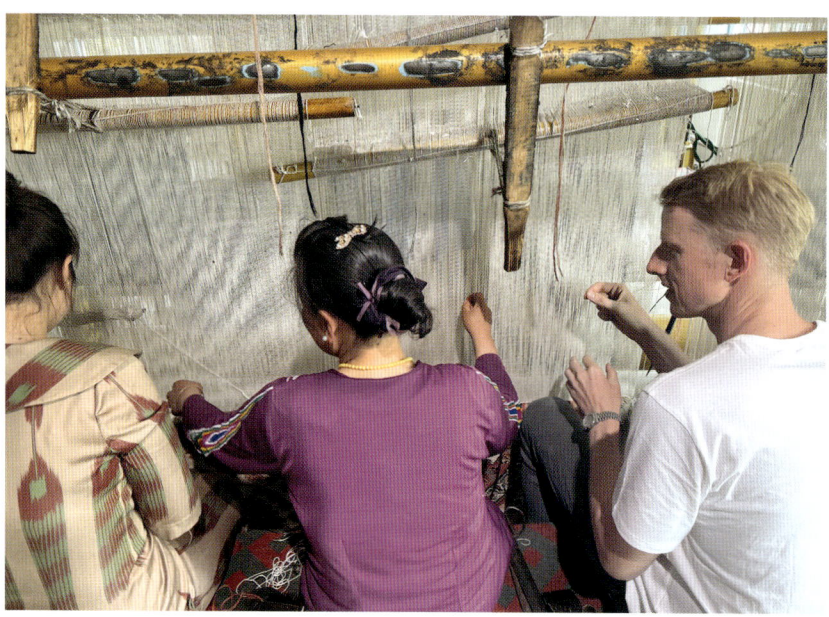

Room at the loom for Max in a 'carpet factory' in Hotan.

11

Enter Dr Rana

In early November 2021 I flew from COP 26 in Glasgow to Dubai to meet Dr Vishwajeet Rana, founder and chief inspiration of the Global Banking School, and an associated world-wide network of educational establishments grouped under the banner of GEDU: Global Education.

GBS already had nine campuses in the UK offering a range of course in finance, management and healthcare.

For the last few years, I had had the honour of serving as Chairman of the GEDU Advisory Board. A few weeks earlier Dr Rana had called me to invite me to open GBS' new Dubai campus, an important step in GBS' expansion overseas.

'Delighted', I said. I realized I would have to go straight from COP 26 in Glasgow to Dubai, but it was doable.

A huge back Mercedes whisked me from Dubai airport into town.

'They've booked you a room at the Burj Al-Arab' the driver said.

That was an understatement. I didn't just have one room at the hotel. I had a whole suite of rooms. A bedroom, a spare bedroom, a sitting room, kitchen, two or three bathrooms and, yes, a dining room with a table for eight already laid.

I woke up from a brief nap with a start. It was 3:20 pm. The driver would be picking me up in 10 minutes. I reckoned I still had plenty of time, but I was wrong. I couldn't find my shoes and I'd only brought one pair with me, having flown direct from Glasgow. That pair had vanished. Could someone have entered the room while I was asleep and removed my shoes? Maybe some kind soul thought they needed polishing. Maybe I'd find them outside the door.

No such luck. The suite I was staying not only had a large number of rooms, but it was also a duplex. The upper floor was linked to the lower floor by a splendid circular staircase. I spent the next few minutes rushing up and down stairs from one room to another, with an increasing sense of panic. What would all the dignitaries think if I showed up in bare feet?

With about a minute to go before my RV at 3:30 with the driver I rang the front desk. 'Please can you send somebody up to help me find my shoes?'

The Burj Al-Arab rose to the occasion. Two athletic young men in flowing desert robes arrived almost instantly. They started searching. They went from room to room. No luck. The clock went on ticking. Then, as I stood there biting my nails, one of the young men emerged with a pair of black shoes in his hand. My shoes.

'They were in the dining room,' he said.

'I looked there.'

'They were on a chair, and the chair was pushed under the table.'

I still have no idea why I put my only pair of shoes on a chair in the dining room.

Dr Rana and His Excellency Sheikh Saqer Bin Mohammed Al Qasimi were waiting for me at the new campus, with an entourage of other dignitaries, staff and students. The red ribbon was in place across the entrance to the foyer. I was handed a super-large pair of scissors, the Sheikh had another. We synchronised our snips perfectly; the red ribbon fluttered to the floor. A spanking new campus had been added to Dr Rana's ever-growing portfolio.

Next day, Dr Rana invited me to drive with him and his wife, Tatiana, into the desert to visit Dubai's famous wild oryx reserve, an excursion I thoroughly recommend. We must have seen twenty or thirty of those magnificent animals, brought back from the brink of extinction.

With the stars overhead, the three of us had dinner together in the desert.

Talking of stars, I started to reminisce about the time Michael de Larrabeiti, and I had ridden off on our motorcycles trying to track the little Persian village where the Three Wise Men saw the Star in the East and began their long journey to Bethlehem.

'We were trying to follow in the footsteps of Marco Polo' I explained. 'We didn't finish the Marco Polo journey then, but – sixty years later – I aim to finish it now.'

I told him about OneTribeTV and our plans to make a film and TV series.

Dr Rana listened carefully, very carefully. 'Maybe I can help' he said.

'I can put you in touch with Dale Templar' I said. 'She's the one who's getting it all together.'

'I would very much like to talk to Dale Templar', Dr Rana said.

A week or two later, when Dr Rana arrived in London, Dale came up from Bath, where OneTribe TV was based, to meet him.

Dr Rana is not a successful entrepreneur for nothing. His people looked at all the facts and figures which Dale got together: particularly, of course, the projected costs versus the projected revenues.

I remember him ringing me once. He thought Dale's budget might be a bit generous here and there. What did I think?

I ducked that one. 'I think we had better leave that to the experts' I said.

The good news was that in due course Dale's people and Rana's people found common ground. English Path, part of GEDU, agreed to sponsor the project.

Dr Rana and I had a quiet lunch together before he left town. 'You ought to know, Stanley, that if I say I'll do something, I'll do it. I'm with you on this one.'

I held out my hand. 'See you in Beijing' I said.

12

False Start

'Chengdu!' I exclaimed. 'Why are we flying to Chengdu? Marco Polo didn't enter China at Chengdu. He came in from Afghanistan through the Wakhan Corridor in the High Pamirs. If we can't come in over the mountains, can't we at least fly to Kashgar, and then head west as far as we can till we come to the place where Marco Polo entered China?'

Dale shook her head. She poured herself another cup of tea. (She had taken the train to London from Bath, and we were meeting in the Frontline Club near Paddington.)

'Chengdu is what they are offering. We don't really have a choice. Actually, I'm amazed they've come up with anything at all. China is still in lockdown. We are lucky to get anywhere under the present circumstances.'

'Lucky' was, of course, a relative concept. Dale and her team had been engaged in almost daily zoom discussions with their Chinese counterparts, looking at the detailed questions of transport and accommodation, as well as the filming programme itself.

'Chengdu seems to be free of Covid for the moment' Dale said, 'but restrictions are still in force. When we get there, we will have to quarantine, maybe for as much as ten days, before moving on to start filming.'

Up to 10 days quarantine! That was a bit of a shock. I don't think any of us fully understood just how seriously China was taking Covid.

We left London on August 23, 2022, to fly via Athens to Chengdu, a city of around twenty million people and the capital of

Sichuan Province in Western China. The plan was that Max, who was already in Asia, would join us there. When I spoke to him on the phone before we left, I warned him that he faced quarantine when he got to Chengdu.

Max was basically sceptical. Living in Asia, he possibly had a clearer idea than we did about the extent of China's Covid provisions and of the way in which the whole country been shut down under the country's rigorous and comprehensive policy for dealing with the pandemic.

'I'll wait to hear from you,' he said. 'I can join you when you get going.'

We landed at Chengdu airport early on the morning of August 25, to be met by masked and gowned officials in HazMat gear, before being whisked on a bus to the hotel in the city centre.

As far as I could see, we were the only guests staying in the Serengeti Hotel. Each member of the OneTribe team had his/her individual room, with strict instructions not to leave it. The only means of contact would be via WeChat, the Chinese version of WhatsApp.

From my room on the 20th floor, I could catch a glimpse of distant mountains, presumably the peaks of the Tibetan or, as it was now called, the Qinghai-Xizang Plateau. Nearer at hand, but quite some way below, I could see the roof terrace of a block of flats. Once or twice today, a woman appeared with a pile of clothes in a basket which she hung up to dry.

Beyond the apartment block was a small park which was largely deserted except once when I saw a group of children playing football. There was no traffic on the street, nor any other sign of movement. Chengdu was a city of over 20 million people, but it was like a ghost town.

I was able to open my window a crack but not enough to throw myself out.

OneTribe technical experts had kindly downloaded some films

to my laptop. During my time in the Serengeti Hotel, I remember watching the Godfather Parts I, II and III, as well as the Shawshank Redemption.

On our last day of quarantine Dale called a WeChat meeting.

'First, the good news' she said. 'Our time in quarantine is almost over. Well done everyone!'

'And what's the bad news?' Peter Hayns, our chief cameraman and Director of Photography, asked.

'The bad news is that the authorities in Kashgar don't want to have us when we leave here. There's been another outbreak of Covid here in Chengdu. We'd have to do another seven or even ten days quarantine in Kashgar before we can start filming.'

We didn't need to take a vote. None of us could face another ten days in solitary confinement.

That evening, when I put my tray out into the corridor for collection before turning in for the night, I thought I'd take a gentle stroll in the corridor. Against the rules, of course, but this was our last night. We were flying back to Europe the next day.

I took my plastic key with me and stepped out into the corridor. As it happened, Dale who had the room next to mine put her tray out at the same time. It was the first time we had met in almost 10 days. I mouthed a greeting. She mouthed one back and quickly disappeared into her room. We were still in quarantine. Any human contact was strictly *verboten*.

I decided I would forget about strolling down the corridor. Just too risky. The cameras would spot me and there could be hell to pay.

I had my plastic key in my hand, so I tried to get back into my room. It didn't work, of course.

I swore under my breath. Why hadn't I realized that we had all been issued with a 'one-time key'? You can use the key to get into the room that first time, but if you don't prop the door open when you pop your tray out, you'll never get back in again!

I stood in the corridor in my pyjamas, waiting for someone to come and pick up the trays. They would have a master key surely. But no one came. I waited. I waved at the ceiling and at the walls. Still, no-one arrived.

In the end, I walked along the corridor to find the lift. I planned to go down to Reception to explain what had happened.

I find the lift, all right. Press the button. Doors open. Completely dark inside, but the doors shut anyway. I fumble with the buttons, press the lowest one I can find. Hope it's not the basement button. I don't want to be stuck in the basement.

The lift jolts into action. Twenty seconds later it jerks to a stop. Still pitch-black inside. Not a glimmer of light anywhere.

I couldn't help wondering whether my dehydrated corpse would be found weeks, or even months, later on the floor of the lift. Would my fingernails have left tell-tale scratch marks on the walls?

I look around for the emergency telephone. I start banging on the doors. What a fiasco!

Even ten minutes can seem a long time when you're stuck in a darkened lift in China.

The old music hall lyric plays in my head:

Oh dear, what can the matter be?/Three old ladies stuck in a lavatory/They'll be there from Monday to Saturday/Because nobody knows they are there.

Suddenly, I hear a sound outside. Someone is trying to get the lift door open. Moments later a female figure appears. At least I think it's female. Hard to tell since she or he is clothed in regulation hazmat kit. Plastic facemask, hood, rubber gloves and breathing tube: the whole shebang.

S/he shines a heavy-duty torch at me and nods sternly. Meaning is clear. Follow me and take your punishment like a man.

The lights come on in the corridor and, yes, it is a woman. She glares at me from behind the mask.

I'm a bit shaken. 'Forgot my key didn't work. Tried to go down to Reception.'

'Oh, key does not work?'

She produces her own key and lets me back into my room.

'No leave room' she says.

Next morning, with our official quarantine finally over, we all head to the airport to catch an Air Sichuan plane to Cairo, with connections to the UK.

Less than two hours after we left, Sichuan was hit by a major earthquake. We hear the news when we arrive in Egypt.

'We can thank our lucky stars' Dale said, 'If we hadn't left when we did, we could have been stuck in that hotel for another month.'

Max was still in Mongolia, having delayed his arrival in China until our precise itinerary post-Chengdu was clear. I sent him a message. 'Sorry we didn't manage to meet up in China. Just as well you didn't join us. Would have been a wasted journey. Will keep you posted. Dale is determined to try again. So am I.'

13

Dr Jan Telensky Commissions a Bust

As we left our quarantine quarters in Chengdu, I had – on September 3, 2022 – written confidently to Ambassador Zheng that we were 'looking to come back to China in the spring or early summer, very much hoping of course by then the Covid issue will be more manageable than it has proved to be this time.'

Little did I know that, less than three months later, in a sudden reversal of policy, most of China's Covid rules would be binned. On Dec 7, 2022, the BBC reported

By Frances Mao
BBC News

China is lifting its most severe Covid policies – including forcing people into quarantine camps – just a week after landmark protests against the strict controls.

People with Covid can now isolate at home rather than in state facilities if they have mild or no symptoms.

They also no longer need to show tests for most venues and can travel more freely inside the country.

Citizens have expressed relief but also concern about the sudden changes.

'Finally! I will no longer worry about getting infected or being taken away as a close contact,' one person wrote on Chinese social media.

Another said: 'Can anyone explain to me what's happening? Why is the change all of a sudden and so major?'

The sweeping changes indicate China is finally moving away from its zero-Covid policy and looking to 'live with the virus' like the rest of the world.

I telephoned Dale. Dale took soundings. She called back. 'Yes', she said, 'It really is true. I'm getting the team back together.'

If this was the good news, the bad news was that September's aborted trip – where we had got no further than the 20th floor of the Serengeti Hotel in Chengdu – had taken a hefty chunk out of our budget.

'Basically' Dale explained, 'we didn't get a green light until the last minute and by then airfares to China had shot through the roof'.

I am sure that Dr Rana would have done his best to help. He was – and is – that kind of a man. As it happened, quite by chance, another brilliant benefactor appeared on the scene at precisely the moment when we needed that last vital push to get us over the line, from a financial point of view at least.

In the old days – I'm talking about Imperial Rome 2,000 years ago – you usually had to be dead before you qualified for a bust. Dr Jan Telensky, philanthropist and entrepreneur, thought otherwise. He came up to me at a party almost three years ago at the Czech Embassy.

He took out his phone. 'Let me show you some pictures.'

I'd always thought the Czech Embassy was a genteel, respectable place. What did he think I had in mind? *Feelthy* pictures? I didn't know what to expect.

I had met Dr Telensky for the first time that day. His wife, Alenka, and I had both just been awarded the Jan Mazaryk Medal by the then Czech Ambassador, Libor Sečka.

I clutched my medal and the accompanying citation while Dr Telensky showed me a series of photos. 'These are some of Jakub Vlcek's recent pieces. He's a young Czech sculptor, one of the most brilliant sculptors in Europe.'

Telensky sized me up, first from the front, then from the side.

'I'm going to ask Jakub to sculpt you. A proper Roman bust.'

'Laurels and all?' I asked.

'Laurels are optional. You've still got plenty of hair.'

Covid intervened and I rather forgot about Telensky's surprising offer. But Telensky hadn't forgotten. Early one morning two years later, I drove up to Luton for my first sitting.

Why Luton? The answer is simple. In 1968, when Russian tanks invaded what was then Czechoslovakia, 20-year-old resistance-fighter, Jan Telensky, escaped with his life and came as a refugee to Luton with exactly £2 in his pocket. Luton welcomed him with open arms and over the years Telensky had returned the compliment in spades, launching a series of successful business ventures, which it would take too long to describe here. Suffice it to say that in 2022 he won the FIRST Award for Responsible Capitalism.

Vlcek, who had flown in the previous evening from Prague, was waiting for me in a studio in one of the buildings Dr Telensky owns in the town. I sat in the chair while Vlcek coaxed a likeness from the clay.

He worked for three hours that morning.

For me, it was a strangely peaceful experience. There was no need to talk and not much point in it anyway since I don't speak Czech and Jakub doesn't speak much English.

Telensky came down to the studio a couple of times that first morning to see how things were going, and we went out for lunch to a little Thai restaurant down the street. People smiled at him as we passed.

Six weeks later, Jakub flew in again from Prague and I drove to Luton for a second, longer sitting.

In artistic terms, this was a crucial moment. Vlcek had obviously done more work on the bust.

Telensky was as impressed as I was. 'I told you: the man is a genius,' he said.

I only had one slight reservation at that stage. 'I don't mind looking Roman, but I don't want to look *too* Roman if you see what I mean. Could Jakub get the hint of a smile in there somewhere, do you think?'

Telensky took the point. 'You mean a bit more quizzical?'

'That kind of thing.'

I didn't see the finished work until the actual official 'unveiling' in April 2023.

Dr Telensky is not a man who does things by halves. Ambassadors were invited. Friends and family were alerted. He hired the Churchill Room of the splendid Luton Hoo Hotel with its 1000-acre grounds. This is the place, Telensky told his guests, where 'the great Winston himself' had addressed an audience of over 100,000 people at the end of the Second World War.

I don't think any of us that night really knew what was in store. Yes, Telensky informed us in his opening speech that they were to see, as he put it, the presentation of a new work by renowned Czech sculptor, Jakub Vlcek. Yes, he revealed that the recipient of that 'new work' was to be – 'wait for it, ladies and gentlemen, Stanley Johnson, in recognition of his long-standing commitment to Europe, the environment and animal welfare'.

But he didn't in those opening remarks reveal the nature of the item which stood shrouded in silk on a plinth beneath a magnificent portrait of Winston Churchill himself.

When he had finished his speech, it was my turn. I rambled on a bit because Leo (my second son) was driving down from Leeds from a business meeting 'up North' and said he might be late. I played for time. He finally arrived just as I was running out of steam.

Of course, I am prejudiced. I must declare an interest. Full transparency. I admit to all of that. But I truly mean it when I say that, as I looked for the first time at the finished work, at the detail of the carving (if that's the right word), as I took in the lustrous texture of the bronze, and – yes – the way Jakub had indeed caught the quizzical look, I was totally staggered.

When it was all over, and the captains and the kings had departed, Leo loaded the 50kg+ bronze bust into our car. Then he went back for the plinth. We waited patiently. It had been a long but great evening.

'One day my plinth will come,' I said as it started to rain.

My wife, Jenny, and I drove back down the M1 to London with my youngest daughter, Julia, and the sculpture sitting together on the rear seat.

The rain got worse. Visibility was bad. Drivers ahead of us were jamming on their brakes suddenly and unpredictably. Julia had her seatbelt fastened, but the bronze didn't.

How ironic it would be, I thought, if I too had to stop suddenly with the bronze bust being flung forward through the windscreen decapitating the driver on its way!

A few days later, Dr Telensky and his wife came to our house in London to see the bust in situ. He had brought with him a second copy of the bust.

'I want to present one to Boris' he said. Which he duly did.

That evening Jenny and I invited Jan Telensky and his wife, Alenka, to dinner down the road. Inevitably we talked about China. Dr Telensky is passionate about the country. He is a Confucius addict. He has visited Confucius' birthplace in Zou, in modern Shandong Province. He has even lectured in China itself about Confucius's Analects.

'I predicted ten years ago that China would by now be the world's third economic power' he said at dinner. 'I was wrong. It's already the second!'

Next day, Dale rang me. 'Guess what?'

'What?'

'I just heard from Dr Telensky's office. He wants to plug the gap, make sure we can buy all the tickets now. We're looking into the flights as I speak.'

'Phew!' I said.

'Double-phew!' Dale replied.

PART TWO

TRACKING MARCO POLO IN CHINA, MAY–JUNE 2023

14

Leaving England – High Pamirs

As it happened, the best available flights to China were on May 6, 2023: Coronation Day.

'Have you noticed' I said to Dale as we boarded the Air China plane at Heathrow, 'that some of the commentators, even people who should know better, say the King is going to be 'coronated' today, rather than 'crowned'?

'Either way, we're going to miss it.' Dale replied. 'I'm sorry about that, but the airline came through with the tickets and at a good price. I felt we had to say snap.'

Dale was right, of course. We caught the plane, but we missed the Coronation.

It's hard to describe the excitement I felt that first day in the Pamir Mountains. Here I was – on a brilliant early afternoon in May – surrounded by some of the highest peaks in the world and about to set off on the journey of a lifetime. My precise location? The Khunjerab Pass, at 4706 metres above sea-level the highest point of the famous Karakoram highway.

Dandan, CCTV's senior series producer, bustled over. 'Do you want oxygen, Stanley? Oxygen level here is only 52% of that of the plains.' She proffered a flask. 'Just take a gulp. It will do you good.'

Right from the start, Dandan was worried about my welfare. I don't think she trusted me to look after myself, as far as health and safety were concerned. If there was a step in the road, or some obstacle to negotiate, she would take me by the arm. Her English was perfect. She knew all sorts of ways of warning me to take care. 'Watch out, take care, mind your step, please be careful …'

At first, I assumed – perhaps cynically – that she was mainly worried about the implications for the 'In the Footsteps of Marco Polo' project, if I broke a leg, suffered altitude sickness, had a heart attack or whatever. The CCTV's team was as committed as OneTribeTV to the success of this venture. An accident to one of the principals would be highly unfortunate and could be expensive.

But I realized quite soon that Dandan's concern was, at heart, cultural rather than commercial. Here I was, only a few weeks away from my 83rd birthday. Clearly an 'oldie'. I am not an expert. I haven't seen the evidence from social surveys. But on the whole, I have the feeling that Dandan and her peer group didn't expect people of my age to take avoidable risks. Sometimes when she was pursuing me over some health and safety issue, I was reminded of that recorded voice you sometimes hear at airports. 'YOU ARE APPROACHING THE END OF THE CONVEYOR BELT. PLEASE TAKE CARE.'

After a few days, I learned to accept Dandan's admonitions in the spirit in which they were offered. If a young Chinese woman is brought up to believe that 80-year-olds need special care and attention, then you must accept that's an important part of the culture. Of course, I found this 'hyper-concern' irritating at times, but it had its compensations. Right at the end of our trip, when I was climbing about 100 steep steps in Beijing's famous Bell Tower, a young man behind me put both hands on my backside and literally propelled me 'onwards and upwards.'

I have no idea who he was but at the time I bowed my thanks. He bowed back and said something in Mandarin. Probably 'Only too happy to help, grandpa!'

It was not just Dandan who went out of her way to treat me with concern and, yes, respect. Within a few days of our arrival in China, I felt I had got to know my Chinese colleagues quite well. There was Dandan Chen herself, series producer. Hard working, totally dedicated, and a brilliant linguist. There was Ellen Xu, Chinese Line Producer. Like Dandan, competent and dedicated. Fang Liu, Producer, could always be relied on to fix whatever needed to be fixed. She was infinitely resourceful. Then there was Yang Gang, the Sound Recordist, whom everyone called 'Cino'.

Cino would stalk me with his mike, saying 'Can I stick this up your jumper', and when, at the end, you walked off with the mike still attached, he would run after you and grab it back, not in the least put out.

Looking back, I would say that working together with our Chinese colleagues on this joint project was one of the most satisfying aspects of the whole adventure.

After a long day in the field, the team would most often gather round two huge round 'Lazy Susan' tables in the dining-room of whatever hotel we happened to be in. All the food, in plates and bowls, would be in the middle of the table. I never really worked out what we were eating. When we were in Xinjiang, Gansu and Inner Mongolia mutton – and toothpicks – featured quite prominently. As we travelled east, the rice to noodle ratio seemed to shift in favour of rice. There were of course all sorts of other offerings on the table: fish, flesh or fowl, fruit and veg, nuts and nuggets of whatever kind. The trick was to grab whatever you wanted as it passed in front of you.

Of course, you could put out a hand and stop the table from moving, but that meant putting others off their stroke. So, basically, stopping the table or even slowing it down, was bad form. If you missed your moment, you were meant to wait till the dish came round again. The risk, of course, was that someone else – on the far side of the table, for example – might have raided the bank ahead of you.

The key thing was knowing how to use the chopsticks. Though no-one else seemed to have any problems, I had great difficulty in mastering the technique. You had to get the chopsticks ready at the right moment, then – as the table circulated – be ready to aim at, and hit, what was literally, a moving target.

Even though in all other respects, Chinese and UK colleagues worked closely and happily together, when it came to stuffing our faces – and we did a lot of that after a long day in the field – I would say that the home side had a definite advantage. They knew the terrain. They were diving in for second helpings when I, for one, hadn't yet managed to spear a single solitary prawn!

Joking aside, in all essential respects we were a joint OneTribe-CCTV team, and we worked together as a team. Dale and Dandan had been 'zooming' together for months. Now they were face to face, running the show as joint team captains. We could not have been better served.

That first morning in the mountains saw the whole China-UK team in action for the first time and it was an eye-opener. I already recognized how much we owed our Chinese colleagues in terms of setting up what looked set to be a very full programme extending over six or seven weeks. Now it was clear to me too that they were absolutely on top of the details on a day-to-day basis.

One major problem, that first morning was how could we 'arrive' in China, when we were already in 'China'.

Dandan was absolutely firm. 'China's borders must be respected. You can leave China, but they may not let you back in. Beijing may say it's okay. But the border guards here sometimes feel they don't have to take too much notice of what Beijing says. Beijing is more than 4000 kilometres away!'

'Can't you try?' Dale asked.

Dale went off to the Chinese frontier-post. I could see her engaged in a vigorous discussion with officials.

Maybe her peaked cap saying 'In the Footsteps of Marco Polo' gave her a sufficient of authority. Or maybe she just had that air of authority naturally. Anyway, she came back with a smile on her face. She poked her head through the window of the Toyota Prado Land-Cruiser 'They'll let us pass the frontier post' she said.

'Will they let us back?'

'Let's hope so, otherwise our journey is over before it has begun.'

In a way, it was a kind of philosophical question of the 'when is an egg not an egg?' variety.

'How can you be 'not' in China, when you're 'in' China?' I pressed her.

'Wait and see' Dandan replied, heading for her own vehicle. 'Let's get going before they change their mind.'

My driver gunned the machine into action. Dandan led the way. We drove past the guards over the peak of the pass, till we could see the highway swooping down into Pakistan.

Dandan called me on the intercom. 'We're in Noman's land now; we haven't reached the Pakistan frontier post. Normally there's no turning back once you've gone past the guards. But this time they're going to let us do a U-turn in 200 yards and come back.'

As she spoke, my driver swung the wheel and moments later we were heading back the way we had come.

We drove past the great symbolic frontier arch, as big as the Arc de Triomphe in Paris it seemed to me, eyes blinded by the sun. We were safe on Chinese soil without being shot to pieces by the frontier guards.

I jumped out of the car with my already tattered volume of Marco Polo's '*Travels*' held tight in my hand.

Peter, the lead cameraman, was all set up. He positioned me neatly with the Arch behind me and the mountain peaks in the distance. Ideal beginning, surely, I thought, as long as I didn't fluff it.

The guards were eying us suspiciously. We couldn't take all morning.

'Are you ready for your first PTC?' Pete asked. He sounded solicitous. 'I'm sure you'll nail it in one.'

'What's a PTC?' I asked.

If Pete the Camera, as I came to call him, was amazed that I didn't know what a PTC was, he showed no sign of it.

'Piece To Camera 'of course''

'Of course.'

Piece to Camera. Piece of Cake? Well, not exactly.

Over the weeks that followed. I had to do quite a few PTCs, but this was my first.

I didn't get it right the first time. 'Close, but there was a bit of hesitation at the end' Pete said.

I didn't get it right the second time. 'We're getting there' Pete said. 'You said Marco Polo's 'troubles' not 'travels.

'Oh, f**k!' I said.

'Don't worry. I'm not recording' Pete said. He knew how to tickle trout from a chalk stream. 'You're doing fine.'

Holding *The Travels* in one hand, while gesticulating with the other, I tried again.

'I can't believe I'm actually here' I began. 'After more than 60 years thinking about this moment, it has finally arrived. Here I am at an altitude of almost 5000 m, standing literally on the Roof of the World, just as Marco Polo did when he passed through this great mountain range, the High Pamirs,'

I paused to consult the actual words Marco Polo had used, holding the book up to camera as I recited the key passage. '*The plain is called Pamir, and you ride across it for twelve days together, finding nothing but a desert without habitations or any green thing, so that travellers are obliged to carry with them whatever they have need of. The region is so lofty and cold that you do not even see any birds flying.*'

Then I continued: 'Just a few miles south-west is K2, the second highest mountain in the world. A few miles north Afghanistan's Wakhan Corridor debouches into China. So we are almost at that very spot where Marco Polo began his long journey through China, though Xinjiang, Gansu, Ningxia and Inner Mongolia to Xanadu

– the Court of the Great Khan – and finally Beijing. That's exactly where we are going too. Please stay with us on our journey.'

I knew I had done okay that third time, because Pete said 'You nailed it! 'As he began to pack up his gear, I offered to help. Least I could do. There was a lot of gear too. Boxes of lenses, tripod, cameras etc. But Pete turned my offer down.

'Thanks for asking. Always carry my own gear. Do you know how much that stuff costs?'

As he spoke, I saw another Toyota Prado Land-Cruiser, virtually identical to my own vehicle, pull into the empty space in front of the Arc de Triomphe. Out stepped Max, tall as ever. God he was tall!

Max gave me a huge hug. 'Where on earth did you come from?' I asked.

I gave him a huge hug back, standing on tiptoe so I could come up to his shoulder.

'Wonderful to have you here.'

It was indeed wonderful to have Max as co-presenter and so much else and it stayed that way for the whole of our trip. Max was cheerful, he was resourceful, he was inventive. When we walked in the streets at night or during the day, as we often did, the girls crowded around him. They certainly weren't looking at me.

Best of all, he was fluent in Mandarin. If you need an icebreaker, Max was your man. He not only broke the ice; he dissolved it on the spot into large puddles!

The last time I had seen him properly was during lockdown when he and his wife, Gabriela, had spent a few months on our farm on Exmoor. At the end of that period Gabriela had a baby girl, Ayla, and the baby had been christened in the local church. They had gone back to Asia after lockdown ended and it had been more than a year since I had seen them.

I knew there would be plenty of time to catch up later. My job then was to finish my PTC, so we could get moving.

Pete lined up the camera again. I wasn't going to fluff this one. My heart was in it. This is what I said to camera with Max standing by my side.

'Quite wonderful to have Max here today. It's going to be an amazing journey and I can't tell you how pleased and delighted I am that Max has somehow popped up out of nowhere to share that journey with me.'

Dale joined us and gave Max another big hug. 'Fantastic, you made it. We missed you in Chengdu!'

Max gave a hollow laugh. I don't think he ever believed, six months earlier, that we would really be leaving. He was living out there in Asia. He had a pretty good grasp of the situation. If President Xi hadn't had that sudden and total rethink about lockdown, the barriers might still be up.

Dandan came over and most of the crew. Everyone was hi-fiving everyone else.

'We had better get going' she said.

15

Buzkashi

Max and I boarded the Prado Landcruiser, which apparently would be ours for the duration, unless we were mounted otherwise. We spent a good deal of time over the next weeks in the back of this vehicle and, frankly, I can't believe any other car would have done the job better. It was tough, it was durable, it was comfortable. With over 4000 kilometres to travel, through mountains and deserts, plain and prairie, when we weren't filming, eating, or sleeping, we would quite likely be sitting in the rear seats of the car. With the air conditioning on at full blast on a hot day, it wasn't a bad place to be.

The distance between the Khunjerab Pass and Tashkurgan, China's most westerly town, where we were due to spend that first night, is around 120 klm. We had gone about 10 k when Dale came through on the intercom. She was riding ahead of us in the other Prado.

Dale was her usual cheery self. 'How are things? All good? Are you guys ready for your first in-car chat? You are? Switch the camera on then. Just chat naturally.'

In practice, our vehicle was fitted out with three cameras. One aimed at Max, one aimed at me, with a third providing a wide-angle view of the both the vehicle and the passing terrain. Because their battery-life was limited, they had to be switched on by hand.

Max and I were just getting into it, when Dale intervened. 'Hold it, please. Have you got your seat belts fastened? It doesn't look as though you have.'

Well, of course we hadn't, so we had to start our impromptu chat all over again.

We saw the yurt around 3.30 pm. Totally thrilling. I've seen yurts in different parts of the world. I've even lived in one for a week in the Tian Shan mountains in Kyrgyzstan while tracking snow-leopards. But this was my very first Chinese yurt.

Behind it, the snow-clad peaks of the High Pamirs caught the late sunlight. In the foreground, the Chinese flag flew atop a tall pole. Men and yaks were beginning to gather.

'What's going on?' Max asked, as we slowed to a halt.

'We're going to see a buzkashi match.'

I knew what I was talking about. Though I hadn't in fact seen any snow leopards in Kyrgyzstan, I had witnessed a ferocious game of buzkashi played out between two rival teams up in the Tian Shan mountains.

I explained to Max: 'Basically, the tribesmen were mounted on horses, the 'ball' was the carcass of a goat, and the object was to score a goal by depositing the goat beside a pole set at one end of the ground.'

'I don't see any horses here' Max said, as we walked over to join the crowd.

'Maybe they are going to ride their yaks.'

By then Ellen Xu, Dandan's principal lieutenant, had joined us. She seemed up to speed, as far as the yaks versus horses' argument was concerned. Her English was as good as Dandan's.

'Horses can't run at these high altitudes. Not above 4500 metres anyway. Yaks can. They've got the lungs for it,'

Legend has it that the 'game' of Buzkashi was first invented centuries ago when Afghan tribes would gallop up on horseback to steal a rival tribe's goats. The game spread across Asia. It became a popular sporting event at many traditional Tajik festivals. Up here in the mountains more than 90% of the population were Tajiks so buzkashi was in their blood. If your daughter is going to get married, you might want to sponsor an afternoon's Buzkashi.

I'm not sure whose daughter was getting married that afternoon.

Maybe it was just a practice match. In any case, the game we watched was fast and furious.

I wouldn't say I grasped all the finer points, but I got the general drift.

In Kyrgyzstan, they had used a headless goat as the 'ball'. Here, they had the carcass of a sheep. I am not quite sure how they distinguished one side from another, since they all seemed to join in pell-mell trying to grab the sheep, then either run for goal themselves, or else pass it to some better-placed colleague.

Buzhashi is a rough sport. And not just for the participants. You can be standing by as an innocent spectator and suddenly find yourself directly in the path of a horde of mounted men, concentrating on one thing – and one thing only – how to grasp a dead sheep and head for goal.

'The Reds will try to block the Yellows' an athletic young man called Bijiang explained from the saddle, before swinging his mount towards the throng gathering in the field.

I was busy taking some photos when I suddenly found Max himself in my viewfinder. Max on a Yak! He absolutely looked the part. I was green with envy. Why hadn't anyone offered me a ride? I felt miffed. Some health and safety rubbish, no doubt. No yak-riding if you are over 80.

I looked around. The teams were still out there on the plain, galloping hither and yon, in so far as yaks may be said to gallop. Dandan was consulting her phone and not looking in my direction.

'Quick' I shouted, 'A yak, a yak, my kingdom for a yak!'

One of the tribesmen brought a yak over to me. The animal was still puffing from its exertions on the field. The stirrups were too short, 'Please bring a stool' I shouted amid the hubbub. 'Or give me a leg up.'

Wow, it was fun! I grabbed the rope in one hand and held a switch in the other and away I went. If the name of the game was

Whack-a-Yak, I played it with a vengeance that afternoon. 'Yebbo! Yebbo!' I cried, cracking the whip.

By then, Pete the Camera had cottoned on to the fact that I was playing truant. He hot-footed it over to the scene, camera whirring.

Perhaps I overdid the whip or the 'Yebboing' Just as I was thinking about jumping off my trusty steed in the manner of Frankie Dettori jumping off his latest Gold Cup winner, my yak suddenly stopped. He (or she) had decided she had had enough. I slithered to the ground.

'Pure gold!' Pete beamed.

If I have one special memory of those first days on the road in China, it would be riding a yak on the Pamir Plateau, surrounded by Tajik herdsmen, urging me – and the poor animal I was sitting on – to go further and faster.

Citius, altius, fortius! Faster, higher, braver! They should make buzkashi an Olympic sport. At the very least, it would be worthwhile for UNESCO or some similar august body to look into the cultural significance of buzkashi in these regions of Western China, Afghanistan, Pakistan and Central Asia where that remarkable sport is an integral part of the way of life.

For my money, another candidate for some kind of cultural recognition would be the Tajik Eagle Flute and Eagle Dance. We'd heard the flutes already that afternoon, before the races began. Having done my homework, I knew the story too.

According to Tajik legend, an eagle dies in the effort to save a man from an evil spirit. In her last breath she asks the man to make a flute out of one of her bones so that he can fill the world with joy after her death. I knew that today the favourite musical instrument of Tajik herdsmen is a short flute called a 'nayi' or 'nay', a kind of piccolo made of eagle wing bones. I had learned, too, that the best Eagle Flute is apparently made from the Crested Serpent eagle.

But even if I knew about the Eagle Flute, having done my homework, I didn't know about the Eagle Dance.

I was soon to find out.

I was taking a momentary break behind the yurt after my exertions with the yak when Ellen found me.

'Why don't you and Max join in the Eagle Dance?' she said. One of the Tajiks had taken out his 'eagle flute'. The 'eagle dance' was about to begin.

I got up a shade reluctantly. 'What do we do?' I asked.

'Just pretend you're eagles about to fly. Start slowly with open arms. Like two eagles soaring.' Ellen mimicked the motions.

Some twenty or thirty people, men and women, were already dancing when we joined the party. The man with the flute increased the tempo. The eagles swooped and soared.

My own attempt to imitate an eagle in flight was clumsy to say the least, but Max's vision of a soaring eagle had both energy and grace.

That first day on the road was totally memorable. First, the border crossing at Khunjerab Pass and the excitement of Max's arrival. Next, that first glimpse of Tajik life on the Pamir Plateau and the extraordinary game of buzkashi. which I felt privileged to have been able to witness.

That evening, we had dinner in a local hotpot restaurant. The owner of the restaurant, Dildar, is a young Tajik who went to university in Shanghai. He speaks very good English. He explains that his wife is a primary school teacher in Tashkurgan, and his home is in Dafsar, some 50 km from where we are.

About four years previously, Dildar and his friend Zang E graduated from university. At the time they were working for a media company in Shanghai. They quickly became good friends because they were the same age and had similar interests.

What fascinated me, as I listened to Dildar, was his entrepreneurial spirit. Back in 1975, when I made that first extended trip to China with the delegation from the European Commission in Brussels, I felt that the said entrepreneurial spirit was fairly dormant. It took President Deng Xiaoping to revive it.

In those pre-Covid days, Dildar and his friend Zhang E spotted that tourism was growing in Xinjiang. They came back from Shanghai to Dildar's home and started a business which in due course led to this 'yak hotpot' restaurant called 'Guests of the Glaciers' where we now were.

We sat in an alcove around three sides of a square table. Dildar ushered us to our seats in the middle. 'Tajik tradition is that guests sit at the top of the table. Please have a seat.'

The hotpot itself was built into the middle of the table. Whatever was in the hotpot was bubbling away. There was obviously some source of heat below. I imagined some electrical current, or perhaps burning coals.

There was some kind of divider in the pot. 'This side is spicy, and this side is not' Dildar said.

'How spicy is spicy?' Max asked.

'Not very spicy, I promise you'

I was intrigued. I wondered what we were eating. Mutton, goat, chicken?

'What is the main ingredient here?' I asked.

'This day we are eating yak hotpot' Dildar replied.

'Yak! Max exclaimed.

Dildar explained: 'Actually this is our traditional food. You can find it in everything. Hot Pot is the best way to eat yak. Yak meat is much tougher than other meat, so it requires a long time boiling to make it soft and tender.'

Before we left, Max asked Dildar whether he himself played buzkashi.

'No' Dildar replied. 'It's a very dangerous game for me. My generation, you know, we don't play anymore. It's too dangerous.'

I didn't quite know what to make of that. Dildar was a tough athletic guy. I could well imagine him galloping onto the Buzkashi field of play and tossing a dead sheep 20 yards through the air without batting an eyelid.

16

Tashkurgan

We arrived at our hotel in Tashkurgan, China's most westerly town, in time for bed. It had been a long day. Next day, Max and I went for an early morning stroll.

Tashkurgan today is a modern town with an abundance of concrete block buildings which reminded me of other towns in formerly Soviet Central Asia. Its population is around 9000, almost all Tajiks. Tajik County, formally known as Tashkurgan County, is the only Tajik Autonomous County in China, with Tajiks accounting for around 93% (33,718) of the total population of around 40,999.

With only around 50,000 Tajiks altogether living in China, Tajiks – in terms of numbers at least – are quite a long way down China's official list of minority ethnic groups.

The key landmark in the town is a traffic roundabout where a vast pillar has been erected – a bit like Nelson's Column in Trafalgar Square in London – topped by a huge eagle in flight.

Having heard the sweet sounds of the Eagle Flute and having done my best to learn the key steps of the Eagle Dance the previous day, I gazed up at the bird's outstretched wings with a new understanding.

Though we had lost more than a thousand metres in altitude since leaving the Khunjerab Pass, Tashkurgan is still 3000 metres above sea-level. Outside the car, it was best to keep your jacket zipped.

We were back from our stroll in time for breakfast and a quick briefing by Dale.

'You're going to be interviewing Ai Tao at the Stone Fortress. He's the leader of the archaeological team working there. He has been in Xinjiang since 2008.'

An hour later, I was standing at the foot of the wide stone steps which lead up to the entrance of the Stone Fortress.

Soon I was declaiming to camera. 'The old city, the Stone City with its Stone Fortress, has a history going back 2000 years. Some scholars believe that Tashkurgan is the 'Stone Tower' mentioned by Ptolemy in his famous treatise 'Geography' of 150 AD which is said to have marked the mid-way point between Europe and China on the Old Silk Road.

'This is the truly spectacular ancient fort on the edge of this modern town which we're here to see.

'Once a thriving city at a crucial crossroads … it was home to royal palaces and a haven in a war-torn land …

'Behind me you'll see the steps leading up to the Tashkurgan stone fortress – 'Tash' means 'stone', 'kurgan' means 'fortress.' It was built to keep the people and their livestock safe from invading forces … that's where we're going now.'

Ai Tao, Deputy Researcher at the Xinjiang Institute of Cultural Relics, was waiting for us at the top of the stairs. We walked with him to a vantage point where we could see the immense plain below us, and the towering mountains behind.

Ai Tao was the first of our 'interviewees' He had made a special journey from Urumqi to Tashkurgan to meet us. He was lively and entertaining and, as far as I could see, more than intrigued by our interest in Marco Polo.

Some way into the interview, Max in fluent Mandarin posed the question which had intrigued us both for some time.

'Mr Ai Tao, you have led the excavations of this vast site painstakingly over the years: First thing we need to know – why is there a fort in what seems like the middle of nowhere?'

Ai Tao spread his arms like an eagle in flight (where had he learned that?) and swivelled on his feet to encompass the fort and the mountains.

'The stone fortress' he told us 'is located in a very important site on the Pamir plateau. To the north is Uzbekistan and Kazakhstan … to the south, India and Pakistan. To the west is Afghanistan and Iran and to the east is present-day China.

'Centuries ago, this was at the crossroads of transport, culture, economics and geography. Tashkurgan was a pivotal point between East and West on the ancient Silk Road.'

Artefacts, he went on to say, dating back 10,000 years, had been found here but this walled city was at its most prosperous during the Tang Dynasty, about 1400 years ago.

Over the centuries, it had been attacked, rebuilt and abandoned numerous times.

'We are following the track of Marco Polo' I said, 'He definitely came through the Wakhan Corridor. Do you think it's possible that he came near or through this particular plateau?'

As far I was concerned, Ai Tao hit the jackpot when he answered: 'As you said, Marco Polo travelled through the Wakhan corridor from what today is Afghanistan, heading towards Kashgar. Whichever way he crossed the mountains, this was the main road to Kashgar. Other routes would have been more difficult so he must have passed this way.'

'Well,' I exclaimed. 'This is fantastic news from our point of view … we're following Marco Polo, and you tell us he was definitely here'.

'Why do you think Marco Polo doesn't mention he came here in his *Travels*?' Max asked.

Ai To replied: 'We haven't found any traces from the Song and Yuan dynasties during our archaeological excavations. So we think that when Marco Polo reached this ancient city, it may have been abandoned at that time.'

Throughout our trip. I carried round with me a single page

crib-sheet entitled 'Chronology of Dynastic China.' You couldn't afford to get your Mings and Qings muddled up.

So I took a quick peek at it as Ai Tao was speaking. The Northern Song dynasty, I saw, lasted from 960 to 1127. The Yuan Dynasty was 1206 to 1368. Since Marco Polo left Venice for China in 1271, he was smack in the middle of the Yuan – or Mongol – dynasty.'

'I see what you're getting at' I said to Ai Tao. 'If Marco Polo didn't mention Tashkurgan, maybe the reason is that there was nothing to see. Maybe, thanks to the universal good order brought by the Mongols and the Yuan Dynasty, the main traffic on the Silk Road had shifted to the now safer northern route round the Taklamakan Desert, so places like Tashkurgan withered on the vine.'

I could see Danda n, standing off to one side, looking a bit worried. Maybe it wasn't such a good idea to bang on about the wonderful Mongols. Not now anyway. So, I piped down. But I still think it was largely thanks to the *Pax Mongolica* that Marco Polo was able to reach his destination in one piece.

Would we reach *our* destination in one piece?

17

Panlong Ancient Highway

We don't know for sure that Marco Polo visited Tashkurgan since he doesn't name the place in his book. But we do know he visited Kashgar and the route to Kashgar from the Wakhan Corridor would almost certainly have included a stretch of one of the most spectacular highways the world has ever seen.

When Dale, back in England, first showed me the photos I was staggered. I've seen switchback and hairpin roads in my time, but this was something else.

'208 hairpins in 35 kilometres!' Dale explained. 'You're losing 1000 metres in height in a matter of minutes.'

I felt dizzy just thinking about it. 'Has this road got a name?' I asked.

'It has. It's called the Panlong Ancient Road. And it really is ancient. 2000 years old.'

Reality often disappoints. This time it didn't. Panlong, I learned, meant 'coiled dragon' with 'pan' meaning 'coiled' and 'long' meaning 'dragon'. I can't think of an apter name.

We left Tashkurgan straight after breakfast. By 10 a.m. we had reached Wugeliyate Pass which – at 4261 metres in altitude – is only 430 metres lower than Khunjerab Pass where our journey had begun. Time for a pit-stop before the slalom!

Others obviously had the same idea, since there were half-a-dozen vehicles parked by the roadside.

One of them, I noticed, was a makeshift camper van. A youngish man was crouched by a camping gas-stove, cooking up some kind of stew. A young boy, around 6 years old, I guess, and a long-haired husky type dog made up the party.

Max wandered over and greeted the man. They got chatting. The man, Max learned, had decided to take some time off and visit parts of China he had never visited before. It turned out he came from Jinhua, a city in Eastern China, 5000 kilometres away. He, his son, and the dog had even visited Lhasa in Tibet *en route* to Xinjiang.

'Ask him what he's cooking?' I said to Max. Was this another yak-hot pot?

'What are you cooking?' he asked.

'Mutton, carrot and leeks. Would you like some?' He held out a bowl.

Max looked at me, I looked at Max. We looked at the road below us, zigzagging towards infinity. Besides, we had had breakfast not so long ago.

'Thanks, but no thanks!' Max said. Except he said it in Mandarin.

The man gave the stew another prod. It was bubbling away, but it didn't seem really hot. I remembered Marco Polo's comment: *'because of this great cold, fires burn less well and with a different hue to other places and food does not cook so well.'*

Had he had a thermometer Marco Polo would have noticed that up at 4000 metres in altitude water boiled at 85 or 86 degrees C, rather than 100°C. But he got the point anyway. His comment was clearly evidence-based, to use that trendy term.

We learned that the man was called Guo Hongwei, and his six-year-old son was called Jiaxing. I didn't catch the name of the dog, but all three of them were obviously on the trip of a lifetime.

It was time to go. We didn't need Dale to remind us to buckle up. We hung on for dear life. I started to count the number of switchbacks but gave up soon after a hundred.

I haven't felt car sick since I was eight years old, but I have to admit that by the time we had reached ground level, at 3000 metres, I was feeling distinctly queasy.

At one point we overtook Dale's car. It was parked in a lay-by. Dale had got out and was standing by the safety-rail. I think she was feeling queasy too.

When you reach the bottom, there's another rest area and a big board with a notice saying, in Mandarin, 'You have gone through all the detours of life. From now on, it's all smooth.'

Travellers who have made it all the way to the bottom gathered round that sign to have their photos taken. We did the same.

18

A Short Walk in the Cryosphere

At 7546 metres Muztagh Ata is one of three highest mountains in the Eastern Pamir/Kunlun range which forms the northern edge of the Tibetan or Qinghai-Xizang plateau. Though Eric Shipton, Britain's Consul-General in Kashgar after the war, made an attempt on the summit in 1947, getting as far as the summit 'dome', it wasn't until 1956 that a Chinese expedition 'conquered' Muztagh Ata.

There are fewer than 50 mountains over 7500 metres high and Muztagh Ata is one of them, so for me the chance of seeing one 'up close and personal' was too good to miss. It can take weeks to get to the base camp of Mt Everest. All we needed to do that day was to swing right off the G314 to Kashgar onto an unpaved road, go pass a yurt or two, and there we were, literally, already on the lower slopes of one of the great 'seven-thousanders.'

I took out my camera for a close-up of the three almost parallel glaciers which had cleaved massive tracks of rock and ice down the side of the mountain. How far had those glaciers retreated? How much ice had they already lost to global warming? This Hindu Kush-Himalaya region, I knew, harboured more ice than anywhere else in the world, outside the Arctic and Antartica. They called it the Third Pole. 250 million people live in the region and the glaciers are a critical waterstore. 1.65 billion people rely on the great rivers that rise in these moutains and flow from the peaks into India, China, Pakistan and a half-a-dozen other nations.

With the mountain behind me I did another Piece to Camera. 'Since the 1970s, 15% of the ice in this region has disappeared. If we manage to keep temperature rise to below 1.5°C, we will still lose a third of the glaciers in this region. If the global rise in temperature in 2°C or more, half the glaciers may disappear by the end of the century. People talk about the need for countries like China to play their part in cutting emissions. China, I am sure, is determined to do just that. If the ice and glaciers in the Himalayan region disappear as a result of global warming, China itself and hundreds of millions of Chinese people will suffer the consequences.'

When I got back to England at the end of June (2023), I found that I had if anything understated the problem. The International Centre for Integrated Mountain Development (ICIMOD), based in Kathmandu with eight regional members – Afghanistan, Bangladesh, Bhutan, China, India, Myanmar, Nepal, and Pakistan – had just published a new report. Glaciers in the Hindu Kush-Himalaya region could lose up to 80% of their current volume by the end of the century, on current greenhouse gas emissions trajectories. Snow cover was projected to fall by up to a quarter under high emissions scenarios – drastically reducing freshwater for major rivers such as the Amu Darya, where it contributes up to 74% of river flow, the Indus (40%) and Helmand (77%).

Scientists predicted devastating consequences for water and food security, energy sources, ecosystems, and the lives and livelihoods of hundreds of millions of people across Asia, in circumstances which for many if not most would be beyond the limits of adaptation.

Izabella Koziell, ICIMOD's Deputy Director General, said, 'Climate scientists are reeling from observations in the Arctic and the anomalies we are seeing elsewhere in the cryosphere. The glaciers of the Hindu Kush Himalaya are a major component of the Earth system. With two billion people in Asia reliant on the water that glaciers and snow here hold, the consequences of losing this cryosphere are too vast to contemplate. We need leaders to act now to prevent catastrophe.'

In late September 2023, a couple of months after our Marco Polo expedition was over, I had to return to China for an international environmental conference being held in Yancheng with a view to creating a World Coastal Forum.

That conference coincided with the release of the English version of the 2023 Blue Book of China's Ecological Conservation Redlines (ERLs). I was encouraged to hear Mr Feng Wenli, President of the Land Surveying and Planning Institute, confirm that a total of 296,500 km² ERLs had been delineated for Qianhai province, the largest province in China, bordering Gansu on the northeast, Xinjiang on the northwest, Sichuan on the southeast and the Tibet Autonomous Region on the southwest.

I found Feng Wenli's remarks particularly interesting since, only a few weeks earlier I had traversed both Xinjiang and Gansu in the 'footsteps of Marco Polo'.

The Blue Book states: 'Dubbed 'Chinas water tower' and 'source of rivers' Qinghai is the hinterland of aquatic lifelines in the whole country and even Asia and the key area of biodiversity of great global significance … According to the results of the third national land survey, the glacier area on the Qinghai-Xizang Plateau has retreated by 10% in the last 10 years.'

The Blue Book goes on to describes Qinghai as an 'ecological regulatory region with the greatest impact on the global atmosphere and water cycle, a key ecological barrier in the whole country and Southeast Asia, the start-up area and regulatory region of climate change in the Northern Hemisphere, a key wetland ecosystem in high altitude areas of the world, and biological germplasm resource gene bank for plateaus.'

And it concludes that 'Qinghai plays an irreplaceable and special role in maintaining the national ecological conservation pattern and building a national ecological security barrier.'

It became clear to me, from conversations I had while I was in Yancheng in September 2023, that these ERLs – Ecological Conservation Redlines – whether in Qinghai or elsewhere are not going to be 'paper parks.' Far from it. Fully implemented, they will help

China deliver its own national goals under its 'New Development Philosophy.' They are also going to help China meet international commitments including – most recently – the commitments made at the China-chaired Biodiversity Conference in Montreal in December 2022 (CBD COP 15).

I attended that CBD Conference in Montreal on behalf of the International Conservation Caucus Foundation. I applauded, as many others in that vast Conference Hall did, when the Conference adopted the crucial Kunming-Montreal Global Biodiversity Framework with its Target 3 for 30% protection of both land and sea area to be achieved by 2030 – now more succinctly described as the 30:30 target.

Why do I believe that China will reach targets that other countries with similar goals may fail to reach? Part of the answer, I suppose, is that China has a political system which makes it easier to stick to both short-term and long-term goals, without being distracted by other pressures.

As I have already mentioned, I carried with me – almost without fail – a copy of my personal bible: Marco Polo's *Travels*. When, towards the end of his life people accused him of making things up, Marco Polo querulously replied: 'I have not told half of it'. I tend to side with Polo on this one. If anything, he understated rather than overstated.

Back in 1961, as I have already mentioned, Tim Severin, Michael de Larrabeiti and I had attempted to 'verify' some of Marco Polo's observations. Did he really find the Persian village where the Three Wise Men came from? We did our best to find a likely village. Did he really visit the Valley of the Assassins in Persia? That kind of thing.

Well, that was then. This was now. We were, at last, in China. What did Marco Polo have to say about the extraordinary region where we now found ourselves?

Leaving the great mountain Muztagh Ata behind us, we headed north-east. I picked up *The Travels*.

'I'm sure we're on the right track' I said to Max. 'This is what Polo says: *'The Traveller heads for three days towards the north-east across a series of mountains, climbing so high that it is said this is the most elevated place in the world. When he reaches these heights, he finds a plain between two mountains with a great lake that feeds are very fine river.'*

'Lake Baisha?' Max asked.

'Exactly.'

To say we were stunned by the beauty of the place would be an understatement. We had just been up on the glacier. Glacial meltwaters, from Muztagh Ata and other peaks, feed Lake Baisha. The lake returns the compliment. On a calm day, when there are no surface ripples, the peaks of the surrounding mountain are reflected perfectly on the surface of the lake.

Lake Baisha is a major tourist attraction as we could see from the crowds of people who arrived in busloads at the site while we were there. Many of these were Kyrgyz. There are over 2 00,000 Kyrgyz people living in China, and many of them are to be found here in this border area between China's Xinjiang Province, Tajikistan, Kazakhstan and Kyrgyzstan.

Max and I had a lovely interview with Aly, a Kyrgyz photographer.

'We Kyrgyz' Aly said 'love living beneath blue skies, on green plains and by clear lakes. We herd animals, mainly yaks and sheep. We use the sheep wool to make yurts and hats like mine.'

He pointed to his hat. 'The white part of this hat represents snowy mountains, and the black part symbolizes the vast lakes in this part of the world. Our cows and sheep graze here and drink spring water and provide delicious meat and milk. We have always lived in a totally natural environment.

By the time we had finished talking to Aly, the wind had got up and ripples were appearing on the surface of the lake.

19

Kashgar I

We left our hotel early our first morning in Kashgar. Setting up for filming always takes time. There's the gear to be unpacked, camera angles to be decided, lenses to be polished or whatever.

Leaving such details aside, for me this was a very special moment. Back in 1961, when Tim Severin and I were planning the original 'In the footsteps of Marco Polo' expedition, I had marked Kashgar with a double asterisk in our itinerary. The first asterisk would have been to celebrate our arrival in China from the other side of the world. The second would have been to recognise the exceptional importance of Kashgar itself as one of the oldest cities in the world. Old even in mediaeval times when Marco Polo was here. And a vitally important oasis on the Silk Road between China, the Middle East and Europe.

My first piece to camera (PTC) in Kashgar was to be right in front of the city's historic gateway.

Dale's instructions were very clear. She motioned to the spot where Pete Hayns, Director of Photography, was already positioned, camera primed and ready to go.

'As you can see, Pete's camera is pointing at the Great Gate' Dale continued. 'You're going to come in from the left, Pete's left. I want you to walk right in front of the gate, but not looking at it, then pivot 90 degrees right to face the camera so you have your back to the Gate, pause for a second, then away you go with your PTC, so you are speaking to camera with the Gate directly behind you. What are you planning to say?'

My usual instinct, when confronted in normal everyday life with that kind of direct question, is to give an evasive response. Need to know principle. Mind's a blank. That kind of thing.

But on this occasion, my PTC had already been written, far more eloquently than any text my poor brain could produce.

'My text this morning' I told Dale, 'is taken from the *Travels of Marco Polo*, Chapter 3, the Road to Cathay, beginning at page 53, fourth para. That is where Marco Polo describes his arrival in Kashgar. I simply plan to repeat some of his own words.'

By now a small crowd had gathered. I opened the book to read out the passage I had just cited: *'Kashgar was once a kingdom, but nowadays it is subject to the Great Khan. The people worship Muhammad. There are many towns and cities of which the largest and finest is Kashgar.'*

'Great!' Dale enthused. 'As soon as you have said the 'largest and finest is Kashgar', put the book down, turn completely round and begin to walk towards the Great Gate itself as though you are about to enter the city. Is that clear?'

Pete Hayns, the cameraman, added: 'Look the camera in the eye – don't look at me!'

'Can I hold the Polo book up to the camera, Pete? Look like I've done my homework. A touch of verisimilitude?'

'Very what?' Pete asked.

No matter how experienced you are, your heart is always in your mouth, while you're waiting to hear the dreaded word 'action'.

But I shoved my heart back down my throat, walked back fifteen paces, turned round, and then, on Dale's shout of 'action' started back along the way I had just come. I had Marco Polo's book – my vital 'prop'- grasped firmly in my right hand.

Well, having the book with me for that morning's PTC turned out not to be such a good idea after all. Just before I was about to stop, pivot to my right, look at the camera, then start talking, I was seized by a moment of panic. Did Marco Polo say Kashgar was 'the largest and finest' of the world's towns and cities, or did he say, 'finest and largest?' There was bound to be some Marco Polo buff out there who would write a letter to the Daily Telegraph if I got it wrong,

I am convinced that this was the moment when I blundered. There I am, closing in for the kill. But instead of looking where I am going, I'm thinking about whether the quote I'm about to use is strictly accurate. Net result: I fail to see a small uncharted downward step ahead of me. I stumble. I almost hit the ground walking. The book flies skywards from my grasp, disappearing into the ether. Seconds later, while I'm still trying to recover my balance, Marco Polo's *Travels* falls from the sky like the discarded shell of a space-rocket and hits me on the back of the head!

OneTribe TV has a splendid video of the whole event because Pete of course kept filming. Who wouldn't? Certainly not Pete Hayns (DOP), who's a professional to his fingertips.

Well, I made it through the Gate in the end, my PTC finally in the can. Max, who had once visited Kashgar when he was hiking as a student across Central Asia, wanted to look for a café he remembered. He strode off, camera crew in tow.

The streets were filling up. On our journey so far, we had met Tajiks and Kyrgyzs, but here in Kashgar we were in the heart of Uygur territory. The population of Kashgar Prefecture is over 4.6 million, and over 90% are Uyghur. Many of them lived in Kashgar itself where the population was predominantly Uyghur.

I wasn't sure how I would get on without Max to act as guide and interpreter (apart from being fluent in Mandarin, he seemed to have picked up quite a bit of Uyghur in the few days we had been in Xinjiang). Happily, English Path's Nadia – also fluent in Mandarin – was able to come with me. We set off together. I didn't know how she would get on with Uyghur, but time would tell.

Halfway along the main drag, with fruiterers, cobblers and other merchants lining both sides of the road, we stopped in front of a shop selling pottery of every kind and description. Every surface was piled high with goods, ranging in size from two-foot tall amphoras to tiny teacups.

Two men stood behind one of the tables. One, the younger of the two, was bare headed. The other wore a traditional Uyghur hat.

'Not sure if they speak Mandarin' Nadia said, 'but I'll try.'

We were in luck. The older man – his name was Zuli – did speak Mandarin and he told us he made all the goods we saw in front of us. He was a potter and practised a craft which had been passed down in his family through generations.

Ten minutes later Zuli had set up his wheel on the pavement and was showing me how to knead the clay to make a perfect pot.

The key thing, as I understood it, was to put your two thumbs in the middle of the ball of clay, creating a first inner space, while using the palms of both hands to mould the shape of the vase or urn or whatever else you are trying to create.

And all the while, you must control the speed at which the wheel is rotating by pressing the pedal with your foot. Take your foot off the accelerator and the wheel slows down.

Amazingly after a couple of failed attempts, I produced something which resembled a blancmange with a big hole in the middle.

'I've cracked it!' I cried. 'Cracked' was *le mot juste*. As I tried to lift my masterpiece off the turntable, the whole thing disintegrated. I recalled Job's lament. 'Can the pot say to the potter, why hast thou made me thus?'

Making pots was hard work. I took off my Australian bush-hat to wipe the sweat off my brow. I looked at Zuli's hat, the traditional 'doppa' worn by the Uyghur and other Central Asian people. Maybe I'd make a better pot if I was wearing traditional headgear.

I asked Nadia: 'Do you think Zuli would lend me his hat for my next effort?'

She seemed doubtful. 'I could ask him. He might not want to be without his hat.'

'Why don't you tell him that in England, we have an ancient hat-swapping custom, a way of welcoming strangers!'

I'm not sure what Nadia said but, whatever it was, Zuli seemed delighted. He put my Australian bush-hat on his head and nodded proudly. I wore the traditional 'doppa' as I made one final attempt to make a recognizable piece of pottery.

Nadia relayed Zuli's instructions. 'You need more water. The clay crumbles if it's too dry.'

'I am already using two hands, and one foot. How can I pour water as well?'

'Zuli says he'll help you'.

And he did, pouring water into the hole that I had made – and was now enlarging – with my juxtaposed thumbs. I could feel the pot emerging from the clay. Early Minoan, perhaps?

Nadia and I boarded a little low-slung electric bus and cruised gently back through the now-crowded streets towards the Gate. We saw our first camel of the trip, tethered and – presumably – waiting for customers. Though Western tourists were few and far between, China's 'domestic' tourist industry was fast rebounding from Covid.

We found Max not in a café, but in a teahouse. He had already made friends with the owner, Mairedan, a young Uyghur entrepreneur who would not have looked out of place in the King's Road, Chelsea.

'Mairedan' Max asked him, 'please tell my father why you decided to set up a café instead of a teahouse?'

'People were confused about this when I was planning to open the café', the young man replied. 'They said there are lots of teahouses in Kashgar, why don't you open a teahouse? I said I'm opening a coffee shop because there are plenty of coffee shops in the West but very few here. We want visitors from all over the world who come to Kashgar, to this place on the edge of China, to able to drink a cup of coffee.'

Mairedan's teahouse didn't do lunch, so we went on to a restaurant not far from the gate, then headed to China's biggest and oldest mosque, Id Kah, in Kashgar's central square.

There are 12 million Muslims – mostly Uyghurs – living in Xinjiang. Kashgar's total Muslim population must be well over half a million, possibly as many as 700,000. For practitioners, Id Kah – the largest mosque in China – is the focal point and place of worship.

This was certainly a Muslim city back in the 13th Century, when Marco Polo travelled through Xinjiang. As I recalled in my Kashgar Gate PTC as finally delivered, Marco Polo states bluntly that 'The people worship Muhammad.'

At the appointed hour, Max and I were ushered through the garden into the prayer hall. A few minutes later the mosque's Deputy Imam, Abasi Mamati, arrived.

'Salam alaykum!' Max and I said in perfect unison.

'Salaam' said the Imam.

The Imam, soul of politeness, showed us around. We were meeting in the Outer Hall of the mosque. Poplar-wood pillars – 140 of them altogether, we were told – each one seven metres high, exquisitely carved and painted, supported the roof.

Max and I knew we didn't have long. As we arrived the crowds were already gathering for evening prayers. The Imam clearly had other duties to attend to.

The ice having been broken, I plunged straight in. I wasn't quite sure what the correct form of address might be, when talking to a high cleric in the Muslim faith. Marco Polo called everyone 'idolaters' unless they were Christians, but I wasn't sure that addressing the Imam as an 'idolater' or 'Your Idolatry' would go down well. It sounded pejorative, even though it was simply Marco Polo's shorthand for 'not one of us. (Check the index in *The Travels*, Penguin edition, and you will find two full double-column pages of entries under the heading 'idolaters')

'Holy Father' had already been bagged by the Catholics. The diplomatic world would be up in arms if I plumped for 'Your Excellency.'

Inspiration dawned. I remembered the story of the Turkish imam, who swooned with pleasure when presented with a whole aubergine stuffed with onion, garlic and tomatoes, and simmered in olive oil. Ever since, that dish – so my wife, Jenny, once told me – has been named 'Imam Bayildi'.

'Imam Abasi' I began 'We are tremendously honoured to be here today. As you may have been informed, my son, Max, and I are trying to follow Marco Polo's route as he travelled across China at the end of the 13th century. He spoke then about the worshippers of Muhammad in Kashgar. Were there mosques here in Kashgar even before this mosque was built? Was this already a thriving Muslim community?'

Imam Abasi nodded: 'This mosque had not been built then but there were other mosques.'

Max had a follow-up question. 'And on a Friday, which is the Jummah, how many people on average come to pray here?'

Imam Abasi obviously didn't want to be pinned down to an exact number.

'Praying is held every Friday' he said, 'we don't usually count the numbers of people who come here. Sometimes there are a lot of people, sometimes not so many.'

That evening we had dinner in the open air, at a street café, in the shadow of the Kashgar Gate. As a matter of fact, there wasn't just one café. There was a whole row of them on the wide pavement, some of them offering music and dancing as well as food.

I headed off for the hotel early, but I think some of the younger members of the crew – Chinese as well as UK – stayed up quite late.

'Got to keep up with the locals' Charlie Bush, Camera Operator, said at breakfast next morning, looking a trifle bleary-eyed.

20

Kashgar II

Having been brought up on an Exmoor farm where cattle and sheep auctions are a vital part of the farming calendar, I was very keen to see Kashgar's livestock market, reputedly one of the largest in Asia.

This market used to be part of the great Bazaar in the heart of the old city, but in recent years it has moved to another part of town, further out, where there is more space.

Sunday morning apparently was the time to go, By half-past ten the market was in full swing. Ellen Xu kitted us out with walky-talkies in case we got lost in the crush.

Poultry, sheep, goats, cows, bulls, horses etc were all on offer. You had to wend your way through crowds of Uyghurs, many of them – literally – leading their prize bulls to the auction ring.

Facemasks, I noticed, were still occasionally in evidence. Presumably to protect against dust as well as infection. By Jove, it was hot. The temperature was well into the 30s. Umbrellas came in handy.

At one stall, we met a trader called Osman. Dandan explained: 'The dealers here can negotiate and conclude a deal without ever having to name a price out loud. Osman will show you the trick.'

Osman duly obliged. Max, grasping the essentials, summarized them for my benefit.

'It's a kind of secret sign language,' he explained. 'Say you're the buyer and you don't want anyone except the seller to know the price you're offering. What do you do? You hold out your hand with your fingers curled in such a way as to denote a particular price. Maybe one curled finger means you're offering 10,000 yuan. The seller grasps your hand, and he uses his own fingers to make a counter-offer. Long sleeves help to conceal the hands.'

'You mean if he wants 20,000 yuan, he might secretly signal that with two curled fingers.'

'Yes, that kind of thing. I didn't follow all the details.'

'And if they both agree?'

'The deal is sealed with a slap on the palm. Only the buyer and the seller know the price actually paid.'

Osman, Max and I spent a bit of time then slapping each other's palms. Just to get the hang of it.

'A bit like the freemasons, isn't it?' I commented.

Osman told us that on a good day he could sell 25 bulls at £2000 each. A ram could go for £500.

By half-eleven we were ready for lunch. Max and I headed for one of the little food-stalls that offered refreshments to hungry traders. We felt we had earned it.

In the afternoon, we headed for Huangdi Township Central Primary School on the outskirts of town.

In the car, I sank into a kind of torpor. The noise, the heat, the dust, the sheer mass of people and animals may have had something to do with it. Or maybe the proximate cause was the huge plateful of rice and mutton we had consumed in the market.

Nadia, riding shotgun in the front seat, always had our best interests at heart. For example, she would sometimes very politely remind Max and me to buckle our seatbelts, if we had failed to do so. On this occasion, she wanted to be sure we knew where we were going and why.

'Just to brief you guys' she said, turning in her seat to make sure we were listening, 'China's goal is to win the Women's World Football Cup in 2031, and it's running a pilot scheme in primary schools across Xinjiang to train the stars of the future. We're about to visit one of those schools.'

Her words caught my attention. I was wide awake now. If I had learned one thing over the years, it was that when China sets a national goal, there is more than a sporting chance that they will achieve that goal.

I said to Max: 'Makes sense to pick Xinjiang for a pilot training scheme, doesn't it. High altitude, like Kenya. Kenyan runners often get the gold'.'

The kids were already on the field, practising, when we arrived. Eight boys. Four girls. The coach was waiting for us.

Max introduced himself. 'I'm Max and this is my dad, Stanley.' Surveying the busy scene, he continued: 'Wow, they look so good! Tell me about this football programme that they have going on?'

The coach – a fit-looking young man in his twenties wearing black shorts and a green sweat-shirt – in turn introduced himself and answered Max's question.

'I'm Alimujiang Aimati. What you are seeing here is one of our usual training sessions. We train for 90 minutes every afternoon after class, practising skills like dribbling, passing, ball control and scoring.'

'I know that China won the Asia Football Cup' Max said. 'They beat Korea – do you think some of your players one day might play for the China national team?

'Yes!' Ali replied 'We were very excited and happy about that, and now more and more girls are playing football at the school.

'Who's better here, the girls or the boys?' asked Max.

'Girls play better.'

Max rolled up his sleeves and, looking very professional, positioned himself in goal. The children, looking even more professional, lined up, one behind the other, waiting their turn to take the penalty.

Max was superb, hurling himself right and left, jumping like a stag to nudge the ball over the bar, or round the post. But the kids – boys and girls alike – didn't pull their punches. The score, when all twelve players had had their shot at goal, was evenly balanced. Six shots saved, but six goals scored.

I was standing on the touchline, feeling faintly frustrated. Why did Max get all the action stuff? I suspected that Dandan, concerned as ever that I might trip and break a leg, was keeping me as far as possible out of harm's way.

Well, if that was Dandan's plan, I had something else in mind.

'Coach Ali' I began 'I've got an idea. In this great match – China versus the UK – the score at this moment is a dead heat, a tie. Your team has scored six goals, but our team has saved six goals. Why don't I take the last penalty, the decider? If I score a goal, you win. If Max blocks it, we win. I promise I'll give it everything I've got.'

I placed the ball on the spot, stepped back a few paces, called out to Max 'I'm going for the top left corner. Better watch out!'

Max may have thought I was bluffing. As I kicked the ball, he threw himself to his right. Meanwhile, thrown off balance by the effort I had put into the kick, I fell flat on my face,

From the ground I could see that my shot went high, over the bar, and on towards Tibet.

'China wins!' I shouted, getting back on my feet. The girls were over the moon, given their ambition to be part of China's 2031 World Beating Women's Football Team. They threw their arms in the air and cheered.

In the car on the way back into town, I said to Max: 'Judging by what we've seen today, I'd put money on China winning the Women's World Football Cup in 2031. Wouldn't you?'

'How much money are we talking about?' Max asked.

I remembered the lessons we had learned in the livestock market that morning about how to strike a deal using a secret handshake.

I held out my hand with the fist clenched. Max checked out my bid.

'I'll double that' he sounded confident.

When the deal was done, we slapped palms.

'You guys having fun?' Nadia asked.

On the way back to town, we stopped in front of a huge statue of Chairman Mao Zedong. Mao, I noticed peering up at the giant figure, was wearing a greatcoat. I remembered, back in the summer of 1975, when I first came to China with that EEC group and Mao was still in charge, I had bought not a greatcoat but a blue Mao suit. I took it back to Brussels with me and wore it on several occasions at meetings of the Environment Council, causing a few eyebrows to be raised. I don't know what happened to the suit, but I still have the Little Red Book they gave us.

On our last evening in Kashgar we had a drink at the top of Kashgar's Telecommunications or Kun Lun Tower. Max and I stood side by side by the railing on the Observation Deck. We could look down at the Great Gate, and at the city wall which encloses the Old City. We could see Id Kah Mosque and the great central square.

During the four or five days we had in Kashgar, when we weren't filming, we had time to wander around and explore what Marco Polo, coming from the mediaeval city of Venice, might have called its 'passaggios' and 'sottoporticos.' He certainly must have felt quite at home in Kashgar with its narrow twisting streets and secret alleyways.

Kashgar was, of course, an ancient city even in Marco Polo's time. Its history goes back 2000 years. A restoration programme, which began in 2010, has aimed – to quote the official guidance – at 'improving living conditions, and earthquake protection, while maintaining Kashgar's unique cultural and historic aspects.'

I'm as ready as the next man to be sceptical about official 'blurbs.' But in this case, I think scepticism would be misplaced. Kashi Old Town has the only C5 rating for being an 'historic and humane' site in the whole of Xinjiang. I'd go further. I'd say that, in addition to this top national rating, Old Kashgar deserves to be put forward as a candidate-site for UNESCO's World Heritage list.

21

Muqam Music

Under the Mongols, the Silk Road reached its zenith. Genghis Khan and his successors had conquered all the small states, unified China and promoted trade in a huge empire that stretched across Eurasia. The Silk Road played a crucial part in all this.

A merchant like Marco Polo coming into what is now China from the West towards the end of the 13th Century had a choice to make once he reached Kashgar. If he planned to head further east, to Beijing for example as Polo did, he had – immediately on leaving Kashgar – to negotiate the Taklamakan desert, the world's sixteenth largest desert, and the second largest shifting sand desert, extending 1000 klm to the east, and more than 500 klm north and south.

Marco Polo may not have known these precise geographical statistics but one thing he would certainly have understood. There was no question of going straight across the middle of the Taklamakan desert – not unless you wanted to end as a bleached pile of bones by the wayside. The only sensible course of action was to skirt round the edge.

He would also have known that there were two alternative Silk Road routes round the edge of the Taklamakan, a northern route via Hami, or a southern route via Yarkant. Both routes started from Kashgar (if you were going – as Marco Polo was – in an easterly direction). They joined up again at Dunhuang to continue through the Hexi Corridor to Xian and other Points East.

Back in 1961, as we planned that first expedition, Tim Severin and I knew that Marco Polo had opted for the southern route via Yarkant. We had Polo's book and had noted his precise calculation: '*The province of Yarkant is five days' journey in extent.*'

Sixty-two years later, confident that we were following in Marco Polo's footsteps, we took the G3012 highway out of Kashgar. Another beginning, I thought. There was really no turning-back now.

In his book, Marco Polo mentions the 'skilled craftsmen' of the region. We had indeed seen plenty of skilled craftsmen in Kashgar, not least my friend Zuli, the potter, whose professionalism I had so signally failed to emulate and whose hat I had temporarily purloined. We had seen farmers and the herdsmen in Kashgar's livestock market, as well as carpenters and bricklayers painstakingly restoring and renovating mediaeval dwellings in the Old City for present-day purposes.

Marco Polo also refers in his book to '*many musical instruments and the people who make and play those instruments.*' Basically, he was travelling from oasis to oasis. Once the camels and the cameldrivers had been fed and watered, there might have been time for music. I imagined him strumming out a remembered melody from one of Venice's famous Trecento composers. Or maybe the locals put on an impromptu concert to cheer up way-worn travellers.

As we approached the outskirts of Yarkant, we turned off the highway. Disembarking, Max and I were directed down a short track, then round the corner of an old stone building into a large, covered area which was obviously a workshop.

In the middle of the working area, a man was sitting there on a wooden stool with a large wooden musical instrument resting in his lap. He looked about thirty years old, bald and wearing a T-shirt. Another younger man, presumably his assistant, sat nearby.

Dandan introduced Max and me. 'This is Zakar Maimaiti,' she said, 'a local craftsman who specialises in making traditional Uyhgur musical instruments.'

Zakar returned our greetings. Then he held up the instrument for our inspection.

'This is a traditional Uyghur musical instrument, the Dutar. We play it when we are happy.'

I asked him whether the instrument he was holding was made to a traditional design.

He replied: 'Each pattern carved on the dutar has its own meaning. Nowadays, we use plastic plates to make the patterns for our instruments. But in the past, we used animal bones and horns. For example, we used the ribs of a cow or a camel to design the white pattern like this.' He pointed to a half-finished dutar on a bench beside him.

'And for the black pattern, we used goat and cow horns. These materials were combined to create different patterns. Each pattern is interesting. This is a vase, and this is an ear of wheat. That one is a knife, and that is a flower. These patterns make each dutar more charming.'

We spent an hour with Zakar in his workshop. Dutars are not the only musical instruments he fashions there. Other traditional Uyghur instruments – some or all of which he also makes – are Tämbür, Rawap, Khushtar, and Ghijäk.

The most prestigious genre of Uyghur music is the Muqam, the large-scale suites of sung, instrumental and dance music. In November 2005 the Art of Uyghur Muqam was named a Masterpiece of the Oral and Intangible Heritage of Humanity by UNESCO.

Next morning, in a hall far from the workshop we had just visited, Max and I were privileged to witness a full-dress Muqam rehearsal by the local Uyghur choir.

There are 12 main muqams, each one lasting about two hours. All 12 start with a rhythmic introduction, followed by characteristic patterns that gradually increase in speed. But it's not just musical skill on show here. Men and women portray folk stories, often about love and lust through dance and some incredible headwear. The lyrics not only contain folk ballads but also poems written by Uyghur masters.

Our guide that morning was Wang Jiangjiang who had studied music in Italy before returning to Xinjiang to pursue his passion for muqam music.

He explained to us the underlying theme of much Muqam music: 'In Muqam, the lyrics and the music, a major part is about the love … *amore*. In Uyghur language we call it *Mohabbat* but maybe it's not a happy love. As you saw, two people, they dance together, it's about the love.'

Max asked: 'There was no conductor, so how do they all stay in rhythm with each other?'

Wang replied: 'Because the musicians, every day they play the music. Everyday sing the muqam, play the muqam, this is their life.'

Max: 'And is muqam music finding its way into modern pop music or rock music in China?'

Wang: 'Yes, in Xingjian, in Urumqi and the other places we have many young musicians.'

At the end, they all posed for a group photo. I look at those faces as I write these words. These are proud people. And they have much to be proud of. Max and I were so lucky to have been able to spend time with them that day.

In the car, as we drove on eastwards to Hotan along the desert highway, I couldn't get the sound of the muqam music out of my mind. And it remains, even now, an enduring memory.

22

Hotan Jade and Carpets

Marco Polo describes the province of Khotan as 'lying towards the east north-east' from Yarkant and being 'eight days journey in extent. He says *'it is subject to the great Khan. The people all worship Muhammad and there are plenty of cities and towns.'*

We left Yarkant heading, as Marco Polo did, east north-east for Khotan, now called Hotan. Marco Polo followed the camel tracks of the Silk Road, and he says he took eight days. We had advantage of the tarmac surface of G3012, so we managed the journey in less than five hours, including a stop for lunch.

Polo describes Hotan, the capital of the province of that name, as 'the finest city.' He says *'it is well provided with all things and cotton growers plentifully along with flax, hemp and grain. There are many vineyards, farms and orchards. The people live by trade and crafts and are not at all warlike.'*

You must make quite a leap of the imagination to re-create, in the mind's eye, the oasis town which Marco Polo had visited. You don't get much sense of the oasis when you are in Hotan – no camels in evidence at watering holes, for example.

But what we did see, as Marco Polo had observed, was an amazing trading centre with people coming together from all over the province, and indeed from much farther afield, to buy and sell.

That first morning in Hotan we headed for the Jade Market, for it is this extraordinary mineral – jade – which more than any other feature accounts for Hotan's elevated status in the league table of Chinese cities.

Jade has been a part of Chinese civilization from the earliest days. In the sixth century BCE, for example, Confucius wrote: 'When I think of a wise man, his merits appear to be like jade.' Jade stands for beauty, grace, and purity. It symbolises nobility, affection, constancy, and immortality.

Hetian jade, i.e. jade coming from Hotan, is also known as nephrite. Throughout the centuries, it has been valued for its rarity, durability, and beauty. It remains today highly sought after by collectors and artists. It is used in a wide range of art and decorative objects, including sculptures, jewellery and household objects.

Hetian is, in fact, considered one of the four Greatest Jades of China. It is mainly produced in areas along the Yurung-kash River and the Kara-kash River in the (relatively) nearby Kunlun Mountains, and includes white jade, yellow jade, green jade, jasper, black jade, and so-called 'mutton-fat' jade.

Mutton-fat Jade is in fact ranked at the top of the white jade category, though the intense translucent green jade known as 'Imperial Jade' must come a close second.

Hotan's jade market is vast. We walked down endless rows of traders, with jade stones of every size and shape displayed on tables in front of them. From time to time, the traders – both men and women – sprayed jets of water on the stones. Whether this was purely cosmetic, to keep them looking nice and gleaming and able to catch the eye of a potential purchaser, or whether there was some chemical reason for making sure the jade stayed moist, I didn't discover. Possibly both.

Max and I spent an hour that morning passing from one table to another. Many of the stones on the tables were massive, weighing several kilos; others could be held in the palm of the hand.

Some of the carving, sculpting, polishing, and engraving was being done in the market itself. We stopped to talk to one of the craftsmen. Introduced as Long Jihua, he had just finished a pendant depicting an ancient Chinese mythological dragon.

He told us it took three years to learn the basics, but to become a professional jade carver took much longer.

'Hetian jade' he told us 'is famous all over the world and is the national stone of China. Jade is good for livelihood and is handed down from generation to generation, as well as the inheritance of jade carving techniques.'

Long explained how much jade means to them in everyday life. Apart from its cultural and economic qualities, there was a health aspect too. 'We wear jade, and it works through contact and friction. It releases elements that will benefit our body.'

'A must-have product in every way' Max commented as we left. 'No wonder it was traded all over Asia and Europe. Maybe we should be talking about the Jade Road not the Silk Road.'

In that summer of 1961, when we were gunning our motorcycles through Turkey, Iran, Pakistan and Afghanistan, carpets were a constant feature of our lives. If we crossed a bridge over the river and looked down to the drought-shrunken riverbed, we would see women beating the dust and dirt out of their carpets at the water's edge. Come nightfall, we would pitch up at whatever caravanserai we could find to see other parched travellers arrive with a rolled-up carpet on their shoulders. They would have their tea – their 'chai' – first but before long they would spread their carpet out on an unoccupied 'charpoy' if they found one, or on the ground if they didn't.

Or again, if we were invited into the homes of the villagers, as we sometimes were, we might find a loom in that home. Like as not, the women of the family – including the children – would be working at the loom, weaving a garment or rug or carpet of some kind.

One day on that first Marco Polo trip I even bought a carpet from a peasant woman in eastern Turkey. She had been working at her loom in her clay and wattle dwelling and had put in the last stitches. I pulled out a crumpled handful of notes and she seemed only too pleased to accept them. It wasn't an enormous carpet. More like a prayer mat. I packed it in a camel-hide bag on the motorcycle and, amazingly, I managed to hang on to it until finally we caught the SS *Stratheden* in Bombay, heading for England. I still have that carpet today.

Carpets may not be as important as jade in the economic and cultural life of Hotan, but they certainly come a close second. Carpet making in Hotan has a very long history. They have been making them here for over 2000 years. Apparently, Hotan today has 157 carpet factories providing 120,000 jobs.

One of the reasons for this is the quality of the wool they use. Hetian sheep wool is tough. It must be if the carpet is to withstand the pressure of everyday use. But it also flexible. And this is just as important as toughness. Quality carpets need a lot of knots for each square centimetre of fabric. The 'knottability' factor is vital.

That afternoon we visited a carpet making enterprise owned by a young Uyghur entrepreneur called Maiwulan Muhetaer.

As his employees – all young women, I noted – worked at the looms, Maiwulan explained: 'Local weavers here have been hand-making carpets the traditional Hotan way for thousands of years. Although Persia is often considered to be the birthplace of the carpet, archaeological records point to this city, right here in China, dating back over two thousand years.'

He stepped closer to the one of the looms where the carpet was nearly finished.

'See the pomegranate flower pattern? This is one of our traditional patterns in Hotan. Our Hotan design has many geometric patterns. And this pomegranate flower is a traditional pattern handed down the generations. This is because the Hotan area has been planting pomegranate flowers since ancient times. People love pomegranates.

'A handmade carpet's quality is shown on the back' Maiwulan continued, 'because you can see the density of the carpet when you look at the back. It is said that the closer the stitches are, the more valuable the carpet is.'

'So can we examine the carpet's backside?' I asked.

I think our interpreter had some fun with this, because Maiwulan laughed uproariously anyway.

Max, joining in the merriment, asked one of the weavers to budge up and took his place at the loom. He picked up the technique quickly, shooting the shuttle back and forth much to the delight of his young co-workers.

'How do I know which pattern to follow?' Max said, without missing a beat. 'How do I know where to put the wool?'

'Behind the carpet there is a pattern that shows you what to do' Maiwulan replied. 'You just follow the pattern.'

'How many hours does it take for the weavers to finish one carpet?' Max asked. Was he flagging already, I wondered.

'It takes two to two and a half months to finish one carpet,' Maiwulan said.

Well, we didn't have two and a half months to see that particular carpet in a finished state, so we went into the display room next door to look at some already completed items. The finished carpets are sold to local customers, but they are also exported across the world.

There were carpets on the floor. Carpets on the walls. I expected to see carpets on the ceiling too. Most of them were based on traditional Uyghur designs: flowers, fruits, branches and so forth, as well as animals and geometrical features of various kinds.

One large carpet, hung high up on the wall, took my fancy. It depicted a herd of yaks in the foreground, the snow-covered steppe in the middle ground and, in the background, the high mountains of the Pamir.

'What wouldn't I give to have that carpet hanging on my wall at home?' I exclaimed.

It was a rhetorical question. At least I thought it was. As it turned out, I hadn't seen the last of that carpet.

23

Heruo Desert Railway

In 2022, less than a year before we arrived in China, the Heruo Desert Railway was officially opened for operation. It runs for a total length of 825 klm between Hotan and Ruoqiang. Together with the existing Geku Railway and the Southern Xinjiang Railway, it forms a 2,712-kilometre circular railway, around the perimeter of the Taklamakan Desert.

It is clear from his own account that Marco Polo, heading east, took the southern Silk Road route round the southern edge of the Taklamakan Desert, moving from oasis to oasis. He spent seven weeks on that journey. Even in our splendid Prado, we would have needed two full days. As it was, using the new train, it took us a little over 11 hours.

Senior Train manager Liang Fenfen joined Max and me in our carriage at around the half-way mark. We had been on the train all morning. We had had a makeshift lunch of hot noodles, tea, and crackers. We had spent hours watching the desert out of the window ('deserts of vast eternity', as Andrew Marvell put it) without seeing a single camel, so we welcomed her company.

She was glad to see us too. Realistically, since the railway had opened in the middle of a Covid lockdown, not many foreigners had travelled this way.

These moments when we got to talk with real people in real life settings were also, as far as I was concerned, one of the highlights of our trip. I did not get any sense that the person, male or female, we were talking to had been told what to say and what not to say. Liang Fenfen seemed quite happy in her job and ready to talk about it.

'What is so special about this railway?' I asked.

'This is the first one that passes through the Taklamakan Desert' she answered, 'and it is also the only train in the world that is built on a desert road'.

Max chipped in: 'We are having such an enjoyable time on this train ride.' he began diplomatically. 'Could you tell us more about the railway and how important it is for this region?'

'Well,' Liang Fenfen replied, 'We can take the train directly from our doorstep. We go to Urumqi to visit relatives, friends, seek medical treatment, study, tourism. So, it is very convenient for everyone.'

'Are there cargo trains here as well?' I asked.

Liang explained: 'Local agricultural and food products, such as walnuts, dates, silk and some other local materials are all transported along this railway.'

My mind wandered back several centuries. 'So this is really the modern version of the Silk Route, but with another special factor? This railway has people like you to look after the passengers.'

Liang accepted the compliment gracefully. 'Thank you, it's what we do.'

The Taklamakan is the second biggest shifting sand desert in the world. Acted upon by the force of the wind, or by gravity, huge mountains of sand move from place to place across the desert. The dunes themselves have a distinctive shape, one side being a gentle gradient, the other a precipitous drop.

Building this desert railway must have been a nightmare. Max and I were keen to find out more.

Obviously, we couldn't jump off the train while it was moving but the next morning we drove back into the desert from Ruoqiang, where we had finally arrived after that 11-hour train journey, to examine one of the elevated sections of the railway close up and to learn a bit more about it.

I do a piece to camera. I say: 'We've hopped off the train to visit an area of the desert called the 'sea of death.' This part of the desert struck fear into the hearts of Marco Polo and all travellers along the Silk Road.'

It was hot in the sun, really hot. I kept my bush-hat on.

'I am immediately humbled by the power of the sun' I continued. 'It's 40 degrees centigrade out here, like walking in an oven.

'The 'sea of death' was so named because of its enormous and constantly shifting sand dunes that have taken the lives of so many travellers over the centuries. This also proved to be particularly challenging for the engineers who constructed the railway line.'

With the camera running, I point to the bridge. 'This bridge, named the Yimlakut bridge, had to be built to go over this notorious section of the desert. It is over 50 kilometres long!'

Dandan as always has worked her magic. Yang Baorong, the lead engineer tasked with building the bridge, is here to talk to us.

Stanley: 'What were the big problems you had building the railway here?'

Yang: 'The biggest hazard is a sandstorm because after the railway is built, if the sandstorm hazard cannot be prevented it could easily bury the railway tracks, causing traffic interruption and endangering safety. We raise the tracks to let the wind and sand pass under the bridge.'

Max: 'And what about where it's not elevated? How do you stop the sand blowing onto the railway?'

Yang: 'For other places where damage is caused by wind, where the sand is not particularly serious, we build grass grids of different widths on both sides of the railway embankment. On the inside of this grass grid, there are some hardy plants that can survive in this desert and are resistant to the wind and sand.'

I knew exactly what Yang was talking about. Driving back into the desert that morning, we could not help noticing the grass grids which he described.

This is indeed a multipurpose venture. The railway is not only a convenient way for locals to travel across the Taklamakan and to convey their goods from one part of the country to another. It also as a defence against desertification, part of China's strategy to halt and even reverse the spread of deserts in the country.

Has it worked, I wondered?

At the great UN environmental summit ('the Earth Summit') which I attended in Rio de Janeiro, Brazil, in June 1992, the UN adopted two important treaties: on climate change and biodiversity. Both treaties have entered into force and their regular Conferences of the Parties (COPs) attract considerable publicity. The 1992 Rio environment summit adopted a third, less well-known global treaty too, having to do with the fight against desertification.

That treaty is known as the UN Convention to Combat Desertification (UNCCD). UN experts estimate that 2 billion tonnes of sand and dust equal to the volume of 350 Great Pyramids of Giza are ejected into the atmosphere every year and at least a quarter of that is due to human activities.

As it happened, a major meeting on the topic of desertification took place in Samarkand (November 2023) soon after we returned to England. UN Secretary General António Guterres, addressing the meeting, which was organised by UNCCD, pointed out that more than 80% of central Asia is covered by deserts and steppes which, coupled with climate change, represent a major natural source of sand and dust storms.

In a report released during the meeting, UNCCD said at least a quarter of the storms could be attributed to human activities, including over mining and overgrazing. Topsoil losses were not only having a material impact on food supplies in some of the world's most vulnerable countries, but were also driving migration, impeding navigation and creating security risks.

According to Reuters, UNCCD's Executive Director Ibrahim Thiaw identified China as one of the success stories in combating desertification and controlling dust, with a long-term land restoration and reforestation program helping to reduce sandstorms.

One of China's pioneering efforts in this field is surely Xinjiang's 'multi-tasking' Heruo Desert Railway.

It is probably too early to assess the extent to which the Heruo Desert Railway has been successful in preventing or reversing desertification. What I am sure about is that the desertification issue is soon going to rise to the top of the international agenda, particularly as the link between increasing desertification and south-to-north migration pressures becomes ever more obvious.

24

Miran: Lost City of the Desert

In 1961, when we were planning that first Marco Polo trip, Tim Severin and I had noted that the great Venetian explorer had gone from one vast desert, the Taklamakan, straight into another one, even more dangerous, namely the Desert of Lop, or the Gobi Desert. Talk about jumping from the frying pan into the fire!

Dictating his memoir years later to his fellow prisoner, Rustichello, in a Genoese jail, Marco Polo said: *'Lop is a large city to the east-northeast that stands at the entry point to the great desert, which is known as the Desert of Lop. This city belongs to the great Khan and its people worship Muhammad. And I can tell you that travellers who intend to cross the desert stay in this city for a week to refresh themselves and their animals. At the end of the week, they stock up with a month's worth of food for themselves and their beasts. Then they set out from the city and enter the desert.'*

This was a pretty daunting description just by itself, but Marco Polo went on to rub his point home: *'And I can tell you that this desert is said to be so long that it would take a year to cross it from end to end, and at its narrowest point you would be hard-pressed to cross it in a month.'*

Marco Polo had camels and progressed from one oasis to another. Two-humped Bactrian camels, as we would see later, are brilliantly adapted to desert conditions and can walk for days without refuelling with food and water. But camels don't need petrol at regular intervals. We did. The key problem, as Tim and I saw it, was whether we would be able to find it as we crossed the desert. If we couldn't find petrol at the watering holes or oasis settlements along the way, we would have to lash cans of fuel to our already heavily laden machines.

There was another problem. At the time we were planning that first Marco Polo trip, Lop Nur – a dried-up lake in the heart of the Desert of Lop – was the site of China's nuclear testing efforts. In the days of the Cold War, that dried-up lake in the middle of nowhere was a prime surveillance target. The US Air Force purportedly flew U2 planes at heights over 70,000 feet above Central Asia. We weren't naïve. We realized that if the authorities let us into China at all they might insist on us missing out the Desert of Lop altogether even though that would mean straying from Marco Polo's route.

In the event, of course, we didn't get to China on that first trip, so the issue of how to avoid Lop Nur, and yet still follow Marco Polo's route to Beijing, didn't arise.

Between then (June 1961) and our expedition's departure for China (May 2023) the international situation had changed. Over the intervening years, various international treaties relating to both underground and overground nuclear tests, including a Comprehensive Test Ban Treaty, had been signed. Unless something drastic happened on the international scene, I doubted that we would suddenly find ourselves in the middle of a nuclear test as we crossed the Gobi Desert.

Proof of that, if any were needed, came as we headed up the G315 into the Desert of Lop and saw a road-sign: 'Lop Nur 180 kilometres.'

'Would you really advertise a still top-secret destination?' I asked Max.

'Could be a double bluff' he replied.

For me, the real excitement that morning lay not in seeing a sign to a place where the Chinese once tested their nuclear weapons, but in the fact that we were about to visit one of the most important, yet possibly least visited, sites of Central Asia: the desert city of Miran, buried for centuries beneath the sands.

In Kashgar, a week or two earlier, we had visited the site of the former British Consulate-General. We had deciphered the marble plaque which had been set up in the shadow of a huge and ancient elm tree – *ulmus densa*. We had seen the special reference on that plaque to the early 20th century explorers: Sven Hedin, Aurel Stein, and Paul Pelliot.

The plaque also said that these men were trying to 'follow their dream.' And what was that dream? In a nutshell, it was to discover the lost cities of central Asia, cities which had flourished – and then disappeared beneath the desert sand – long before Marco Polo's time. Marco Polo would have gone right past them; indeed, he might have walked right over them, without ever realising they had existed at all.

For me, arriving at the spot where the city of Miran had once flourished, this was an 'Ozymandias moment'. Like Percy Bysshe Shelley's 'traveller from an antique land' I was looking at a vast evocative monument, namely Miran Fort, a structure whose heyday had been during the Tibetan Empire in the eighth and ninth centuries A.D. but which today is a huge crumbling mound of hard-baked clay. Beyond it, as Shelley might have said, 'the lone and level sands stretch far away.'

Aurel Stein was the first to study the ruins at Miran. In 1906, he had made a trial excavation of the fort, uncovering eight rooms and over a hundred Tibetan documents on wood and paper. He returned in January 1907 to excavate 44 rooms, while discovering many more official Tibetan documents and military information dating from the 8th and 9th centuries. These are some of the earliest examples of the Tibetan script.

I said to Max as we got out of the air-conditioned car to face the searing heat of the Desert of Lop: we are not just following in the steps of Marco Polo; we are following in the steps of Sir Aurel Stein too!'

I rattled off a piece to camera as I stood in front of Miran Fort.

'Today I am at one of the most important archaeological sites in the world ... Miran, where the Taklamakan and Gobi Deserts meet. Just as they did when they excavated the Valley of the Kings in Egypt, archaeologists here in Miran – like Sir Aurel Stein – have uncovered countless artifacts that give us an extraordinary understanding of the ancient civilization that once flourished here.'

We walked round the Fort and over to some still standing stupas. We had a wonderful guide, Feng Fing, who worked at the Chinese Institute of archaeology.

We learned that a river used to run through this once lush region. Some of the best-preserved mummies in the world have been unearthed in the Ruoqiang area. Most notably of all: the Beauty of Loulan, the body of a local woman who lived here 4000 years ago.

This was the place where Aurel Stein discovered in a ruined Buddhist temple a series of magnificent murals, one of which, a painting of winged angels, could be dated all the way back to the Western Han dynasty (202 BC to 9 AD). Archaeologists around the world were sent into a frenzy of excitement, suspecting that the artwork was of Roman influence, indicating that cultural exchanges with Europe could date back 2000 years.

Max: 'What would this place have looked like? Would it have been full of people and full of life?'

Feng: 'Absolutely. Firstly, because it is relatively close to the water melted from the Altun mountain and the second reason is that the land was fertile and suitable for farming, so this place is perfect to start farming during this period. Later, the Silk Road became very popular, making Miran a meeting point for cultural and economic exchange. It would have been visited mainly by Monks and businessmen. The city became prosperous, and the population reached more than 40,000.'

Max: 'What types of artifacts have you found here?'

Feng: 'We found the earliest inscribed pieces of wood. One we found that dates to the Han Dynasty shows evidence of farming. Some others are translations of Buddhist texts. At the Miran ruins, we unearthed more than three hundred of these wooden documents.'

Having Feng Jing's perspective that day was very valuable. Men like Aurel Stein, Sven Hedin and Paul Pelliot were indeed the giants of their time. But they were still colonial giants. Yes, they could be first rate scholars, but they were also ready to grab some of the greatest treasures, before packing them in cases to be shipped back to national capitals.

But the world has moved on. In my view at least some of the treasures of Central Asia which found their way to London, Paris, Berlin, or Tokyo in the first decades of the last century should be returned to their country of origin, and best of all to the very site where they were plundered if they can be properly displayed and visited there. Western museums which hold these objects should make a proper inventory of their collections. What objects have they got? Where do they come from? Are they being properly displayed? Is there a case for returning these items to their place or country of origin?

At the end of a long day, we left the Taklamakan Desert and the Tarim Basin to continue to our next destination, the Mogao Caves at Dunhuang, 800 kilometres away. As it happens, Dunhuang was precisely where Aural Stein headed when he left Miran.

The little red light on the camera in the car was glowing as we buckled our seat belts.

'I can't help feeling' I said, 'that Aurel Stein might have overstepped the mark. He carted off loads of stuff. I wonder what they think about him in Dunhuang,'

Dale's voice came over the intercom. 'You can turn the camera off, chaps. We're done for the day.'

25

The Mogao Caves at Dunhuang

After Marco Polo left the city of Lop, now known as Luobupozhen, he headed east to a city called Shazhou, now known as Dunhuang.

At the end of the 13th century, the Yuan Dynasty was in its heyday. International trade between Europe and China flourished thanks to the transcontinental peace and prosperity achieved under the rule of the Mongol emperors: *the Pax Mongolica.*

Geographically and politically, Dunhuang occupied a crucial place in the world at that time since the Northern and the Southern Silk Routes converged there. Anyone travelling east through the Taklamakan Desert, whether on the Northen Route via Hami and Turfan or, as we did, on the Southern Route via Yarkant and Hotan, had to pass through Dunhuang on the way out of the desert. The city not only guarded the entrance to Gansu's Hexi Corridor, leading on to Zhangye and Lanzhou. It also straddled the north-south trading route from Tibet to Mongolia.

When Tim Severin and I were planning our 1961 Marco Polo expedition, Dunhuang was high on the list of our priorities. Of all the places we hoped to visit on our journey, Dunhuang's Mogao Caves (25 klm south-east of the town itself) seemed likely to be among the most fascinating and important.

These sacred caves were also known as the Caves of the Thousand Buddhas. They contained some of the finest examples of Buddhist art, spanning a period of 1000 years. The caves had been dug out of the cliff as early as the 4th Century AD as places of Buddhist meditation and worship. This is where travellers broke their journeys east or west, north, or south. They replenished their supplies, regained their energy and – most important –offered up their thanks for the fact that they had survived the rigours of the desert through which they have just passed, while praying that they might survive hardships still to come.

Tim and I learnt that 469 of these temples had still survived. We hoped we would have a chance to visit some of them.

Doing our Marco Polo homework assiduously (about the only homework we did that year at Oxford), we had also read how the Aurel Stein had heard from an Urumqi trader an extraordinary story about a Taoist priest called Wang Yuan-Lu who had accidentally stumbled upon a vast hoard of ancient manuscripts walled up in one of the caves at Dunhuang. Stein had interrupted his research at Miran (he believed he had found a westward extension to the Han Wall there) to make a 380-mile dash through the desert to Dunhuang.

On May 21, 1907, Wang Yuan-Lu took him into the one of the caves. Stein subsequently described the scene as the wall blocking the entrance into a small secret chamber was taken down: 'the sight the small room disclosed was one to make my eyes open. Heaped up in layers, but, without any order, there appeared in the dim light of the priest's little lamp a solid mass of manuscript bundles rising to a height of ten feet, and filling, as subsequent measurement showed, close on five hundred cubic feet.'

116 years after Stein's first visit to the Mogao Caves, I got out of the car to look at the great wall of rock which confronted us. The surface of that wall was pitted with hundreds of caves and grottos.

I said to Max: 'I can't believe we're here. I've been thinking about this place for so long.'

A group of Chinese tourists had arrived before us. Pete, the Camera, waited until he had a clear shot of Max and me standing in front of the huge pagoda that carved out of the rock face.

Then it was time for my commentary.

'The Mogao caves are home to a priceless collection of Buddhist artworks, culturally important writings and over half a million square feet of murals.

'This was a place of worship for travellers who came together at this crossroads on the silk route and today it is one of the most important historical Buddhist sites.

'The first caves were dug out in 366 AD as places of Buddhist meditation and worship. Caves continued to be dug out at the site all the way up until the 14th century, reaching a total of 735 caves, painstakingly carved by hand.

'Impressive from the outside, but just wait until you see the inside' I half-turned and waved at great cliff behind me, then continued. 'The Mogao caves contain some of the greatest examples of Buddhist artwork spanning a period of 1,000 years.

'These caves became a crucible of cultural exchange. For travellers from the West, like Polo, this would have been their first significant encounter with Buddhism. Buddhism was first introduced from India via Central Asia and spread East by travellers on the Silk Road.

'To preserve these magnificent caves, a team of technicians are hard at work digitally mapping every square inch of them to make replicas in order to preserve the originals as well as giving people chance to take a virtual tour of them online.'

'Today we are lucky to be meeting Zhang Yuanlin who has been working here for more than 30 years. He's taking us to an original cave where a treasure trove of Buddhist artefacts was discovered … but it's a bit dark.

Stanley: 'Incredible … I'm assuming there's no light in here because you're protecting the artifacts?'

Zhang: 'Yes. Using lights harms the murals, it will cause the murals to fade and change color. So we are not allowed to use lights in the cave. We see there is a Fangnan in the center of this Cave, and the center of the image. But what attracts the most attention in this cave is not the Buddha statue just mentioned, but a small cave, which was opened on the north wall of the cave corridor which we call the Sutra Cave … It's over here'.

Zhang Yuanlin explained that when the entrance to this small cave had been unblocked 'a large number of ancient documents were discovered.'

What an extraordinary moment that was! There we were, clustered round the entrance to Cave 17 or the Library Cave as the 'small cave' was now called. I could imagine how Aurel Stein must have felt when, 116 years earlier, the entrance to that 'small cave' was finally opened and its treasures, bundle after bundle of manuscripts of incalculable interest and value, revealed for the first time.

Max: 'How many documents did you find?'

Zhang: 'Around 60,000 pieces: These documents have high historical and academic value. It includes Buddhism from the fourth century AD to the eleventh century AD. It also included some important social documents as well as some Buddhist documents and some other religious documents like traditional Chinese Taoism, Persian Manichaeism and Christianity.

'These documents are of great importance for us to study the exchanges between different cultures on the ancient Silk Road and understand the history of religious transmission.'

Max: 'Where are these documents now?'

Zhang: 'They can be seen in more than 30 countries and regions around the world. They are in museums in England, France, Russia and Japan. Even as far as the United States and South America.'

Stanley: 'Well, I believe we have a lot in Britain too.'

I mentioned the British Library which has a collection of manuscripts which Aural Stein brought back from Dunhuang, including the Diamond Sutra, printed in the year 868, and described as the world's earliest printed book.

The evening Max and I had dinner in the night market. It was a lively crowded place. A band was playing catchy tunes and people were dancing. It was a moment to relax.

Max said: 'Today we've seen one of the wonders of the ancient world, haven't we?'

'Yes. One of Chinese World Heritage Sites too. And rightly so. What surprised me was that our guide was very restrained in what he said. He talked about the paintings and manuscripts which they found in the cave being distributed to museums and collections around the world. He didn't really tell us about how bitter the Chinese still feel about the way Stein behaved. Basically, Stein stole those treasures. That's all you can say.'

'Maybe Britain should offer to give them back' Max said.

Chapter 26

Singing Sands and Crescent Moon Lake

Next morning, May 26, we set off a few kilometres to the south to visit Dunhuang's other major tourist attraction: The Singing Sand Dunes and The Crescent Moon Lake.

In Marco Polo's time, Dunhuang was known as Shazhou, the Town of Sand. And for good reason. The Mingsha 'sand mountain' range stretches from the cliff where the Mogao Caves are located to the Danghe Dam in the west. Known as the Singing Sand Dunes of Dunhuang, they are the most impressive sand-dune scenery in China. The dunes extend about 40km in length, 20km in width, and average some 100m in height, with the highest peak being a mind-boggling 1,715m.

They are called Singing Sand Dunes, because they literally sing in windy weather. Marco Polo ascribed the phenomenon to the presence of evil spirits. He wrote: *'sometimes they call him by name; often they entice him to follow their voices and stray from the path, and he is never seen or heard of again.'*

There are other more technical explanations. Apparently, the valley that is formed between the peaks of the sand mountains can act as a resonance box. When the sand moves or falls, the sound is amplified through the resonance box. In the event, the sands didn't sing when Max and I were there. Not enough wind, perhaps. But we had a long and glorious ride on two Bactrian camels, spending an hour or more in full Lawrence of Arabia mode.

The slope of the 'sand mountains' on the windward side slope is relatively gentle. You can sit quite comfortably on your camel's back as the animal zigzags its way up to the top. But on the leeward side of the dune, it is a different picture entirely. Poke your head over the edge and you see that you are on a cliff edge, peering down at the desert floor, hundreds of feet below.

Dozens of camel trains, each containing twenty or thirty camels and riders, were out on the slopes that morning.

Pete the Camera, never to be deterred, grabbed at a passing camel and hoisted himself on board.

'Follow me' he shouted. Amazingly he managed to position himself so that, while the animal was facing forwards, he was facing backwards, his camera tracking our every movement.

His eye glued to the viewfinder, Pete shouted 'what's the collective noun for a crowd of camels?'

'Camelot!' I shouted back.

On the way back down, I found myself singing a song I first learned as a child from my half-French mother who grew up speaking French before she spoke English.

The desert sands may not have been singing that day, but I certainly was!

Perdu dans le désert immen-ense
L'infortuné Bedouin douin-douin-douin-douin
N'irait pas loin loin-loin-loin-loin
Si la divine providen-ence
N'allégeait son fardeau deau-deau-deau-deau
Par un cadeau deau-deau-deau-deau.
Ce cadeau précieux,
Ce précieux cadeau,
De la bonté des cieux,
C'est le chameau! Ali, Alo!

I remembered the refrain, so I belted that out too, twisting round in my saddle to encourage Max to join in.

Ali, Alo, et vive le chameau,
Voyez comme il trotte

Ali, Alo, et vive le chameau,
Voyez comme il est beau!
Himalaya, Java, Calcutta,
Sidi Borina
Allez, allez, allez allez oh!

Marco Polo spent week after week on the back of a camel crossing the Gobi Desert. I was quite happy to get down from my mount after a couple of hours. I wanted to leap off without more ado but well-trained camels sink gracefully to the floor, front feet first, to enable their riders to dismount in a dignified way.

Max went off to test out the latest electric dune buggy in a high-speed excursion which nearly ended in disaster when the vehicle almost overturned on one of the vertiginous peaks of sand.

Par contre, I kept my two feet firmly on the ground and went off with Mimi (Hermione Templar-Gay) to visit the Crescent Moon Lake.

The earliest Western record about the Crescent Moon Lake is the book *The Gobi Desert* written by Mildred Cable & Francesca French who stayed in in the region in the nineteen twenties and thirties. They visited the Crescent Lake and recorded their impressions: 'All around us we saw tier on tier of lofty sand-hills, giving the lie to our quest, yet when, with a final desperate effort, we hoisted ourselves over the last ridge and looked down on what lay beyond, we saw the lake below, and its beauty was entrancing.'

The lake, which Mildred Cable and Francesca French were so pleased to discover, is in fact nearly 100 meters long from south to north; it is 25 metres wide and five metres deep. It appears to be fed by an underground stream because even in the driest weather it retains water.

During the Tang Dynasty (AD 618–907), there used to be a large complex of halls and towers by the side of lake, but many of them were ruined in the later eras.

For me one of the most intriguing aspects of my visit was to see old framed photographs on the wall, recording that the redoubtable Dr Joseph Needham himself had stayed here at the Crescent Lake in the 1940s when he was working on his amazing multi-volume work '*Science and Civilisation in China.*'

Even today, wherever you go in China, Dr Needham's is a name to conjure with. That afternoon, spending time in one of the places in China where the great scientist had lived and worked, I couldn't help remembering my one and only encounter with him back in his lab in Cambridge in the early summer of 1961.

What if I haven't lost that vital letter? Would we have got our Chinese visas? Maybe so. Back then, Needham's name carried a lot of weight. It still does today.

27

Shouhang Power Plant, Gansu

As we left our hotel in Dunhuang to head into the Gobi. I couldn't help thinking of my school chaplain who one Sunday in chapel chose as the text for his sermon the famous line from the Gospel according to Saint Matthew: 'But what went ye out into the wilderness for to see? A reed shaken in the wind?'

The answer, according to our programme, was the Shouhang Power Plant, Gansu.

An hour or so after leaving Dunhuang, we turned off the highway to drive towards an array of what looked like solar panels, only massively bigger. These huge structures were arranged in circles around an immensely tall tower (almost as high as the Eiffel Tower in Paris), the upper half of which was literally white-hot.

We parked half a mile away from the tower. For good measure, we were handed protective jackets and helmets. While we were waiting for the camera crew to set up, I read the information panel, mounted at the base of one of the super-panels. I learned that 'the Shouhang Resources Saving 100-megawatt molten salt solar thermal power plant in Dunhuang is the first molten salt solar thermal power plant in Asia that can generate power continuously over 24 hours.'

I studied the fine print. 'The station covers an area of 7.8 sq km and is designed to generate 390 million kWh of power annually, reducing carbon dioxide emissions by 350,000 tons per year. There are 12,000 reflective panels here, known as 'multi-sided heliostats' Each small mirror is 3.3 square meters. There are 35 large mirrors in total for each large mirror (115.5 square meters)'.

This was mind-boggling territory but Dandan, as always, had turned up trumps. She had arranged for Huang Wenbo, who had been working at the plant since it started operating in 2018, to brief us.

We found a place in the shade, beneath one of the giant solar panels. I wouldn't say it was cool but at least it reduced the temperature by a couple of degrees. Max took the lead. On the whole Max was much better at this kind of thing than I was. He has an MBA from Tsinghua, one of China's top universities. He tends to get straight to the point.

'What is the difference between these panels that we are looking at and traditional panels in another solar panel plant?' Max asked.

'This kind of power station uses ultra-clear glass.' Huang Wenbo replied. 'But a photovoltaic plant uses a solar panel made of silicon. The two materials are different, and the working principle is also different. One is used to reflect light, and the other is used to absorb light.

'This power station is close to 100% clean,' Huang Wenbo continued 'because it uses very conventional glass for reflection, so it does not produce such high energy consumption. So it is basically a clean, green, low-carbon, and sustainable project. Some large bases are being built in China that complement each other with wind and solar energy. They form a whole, with wind power, photovoltaic power, and solar heat power. Then, after integrating electricity, it is balanced. After that, it will be sent to the grid, so that the entire unstable wind power and photovoltaic power can be turned into a stable power source, that is sent to the grid. This way, it is guaranteed that its electricity is stable and controllable.'

Max: 'You must be proud of the achievement? Was it complex building in the desert in these conditions?'

Huang Wenbo: 'It took us 10 years to build such a power station, and then we used more than 500 million yuan (~£55 million) of funds to carry out from research and development to commercialization, so this process is still relatively difficult. Coming here, it is a desert, and now it has become a place that can provide energy, and it can provide stable and controllable energy. So our whole team is very proud of this project.'

I didn't understand all this, but I tried to wing it anyway. Pete, the Camera, was looking expectant. Mimi Templar-Gay, Director, shouted 'Action!'

'This is the Shouhang Power Plant.' I begin. 'A solar farm with a difference ... and it is something that wouldn't look out of place in a sci-fi blockbuster. As the sun moves across the sky, each panel rotates to as to optimize its own reflective capabilities. The rays from the panels are bounced towards a 260m high tower which you can see behind me. That tower uses the energy radiating from the panels to heat up salt until it turns molten. The energy stored within the molten salt is used to heat water, the steam from the water turns turbines which then creates electricity which is diverted to the grid. So Bob's your uncle!'

28

Jiayuguan Pass and Great Wall of China

The next morning, May 27, we headed for the Jiayuguan Pass at the entrance to the Hexi Corridor.

The Hexi Corridor itself runs between the Gobi Desert and the Qilian Mountains, at the southern edge of the Tibetan plateau, called nowadays the Qinghai-Xizang Plateau. The Corridor was part of the Northern Silk Road and the most important trade route in Northwest China.

Known also as the 'Impregnable Defile Under Heaven,' it is one of the main passes of the Great Wall. With one 'li' equalling 500 metres, the Great Wall fortification system had one beacon for every 5 li, one beacon tower for every 10 li, one fortress for every 30 li, and one Pass for every 100 li.' Jiayuguan Pass has been regarded as an 'Impregnable Pass' since ancient times.

It is also the most magnificent and best-preserved Pass among the Great Wall's fifteen Passes.

Construction of the Jiayugan Fort began at the end of the 14th century and was not finished until halfway through the 16th century so it is not surprising that it does not feature in Polo's account. But it is certain that Marco Polo would have been there. Whether you are travelling East to West, or West to East (as Marco Polo did) there was no way of avoiding the Hexi Corridor.

Max and I spent the morning walking around what can only be described as an immense military complex. There is an inner city, an outer city and an outer moat, as well as three large towers, several watchtowers and defensive structures including artificial walls, trenches and natural hazards. We learned that 17m-high towers with upturned flying eaves and double gates would have been used to trap invading armies.

The installations here were not used for defensive purposes only. The stronghold doubled up as a control point for anybody crossing the border into what was then Ming dynasty China. This was the place where travellers were checked, and passes issued.

At one point, Max and I walked round the corner of a watch-tower to be confronted by a fearsome-looking official, covered head to foot in tattoos and medallions.

'Your papers' he shouted, 'Do you have to have permission from the Great Khan to pass this way? Illegal immigrants not allowed!'

Max had pocketed one of the little bottles of shampoo from the previous night's hotel and he produced it.

'This is a flask of sacred oil which His Holiness the Pope has given us as a present to the Great Khan. Please do not impede our journey.'

'I thought the Great Khan was 'transitioning' away from oil' I whispered to Max.

The fearsome-looking official played his part well. He sat down at a table and spent some time writing and stamping an impressive document. When he finished, he put it in a yellow pouch and handed it to us with a flourish.

As we took a break in the shade of one of the watchtowers, Max scrutinised the document. He can read scripts up to a point, but this was really challenging.

He handed it back to me. 'For all I know, it might say 'please put the bearer on the first available camel, mule or yak, and send him to Rwanda!"

Every time I visit China, I find that seeing the Great Wall of China somewhere along its 21,000 km route is a highlight – if not *the* highlight – of the trip. The sight never ceases to amaze and inspire.

We never got to China in 1961 on that undergraduate 'in the steps of Marco Polo trip'. But I vividly remember the time, fourteen years later, I first saw the Great Wall – at Badaling – one of the restored sections, not far from Beijing. It was the summer of 1975, about the time of the UK's (first) European Referendum. As I have already mentioned, I was travelling with a group of officials from the European Commission in Brussels, the first such group to visit China since that country had 'opened up' to the West, following the historic Nixon-Kissinger overtures of the early 1970s.

Seeing the Wall then was a mind-blowing experience, for any number of reasons. There was the element of personal satisfaction. At last, I had made it to China. But there was a political aspect too.

President Nixon, a year or two earlier, had climbed the very same steps that I was climbing. When we reached the watchtower at the top, he had seen the Great Wall snaking over the hills and summits into the far distance, and then he had solemnly opined: 'You would have to say that this is a Great Wall, and it was built by a great people.' Whatever you want to say about President Nixon – and people often want to say quite a lot about him – his achievement in building a bridge between the US and China, was surely one of the most remarkable achievements of any 20th-century statesman.

And I was green with envy when, in the mid-1980s, the author and explorer, Robin Hanbury-Tenison, and his wife, Louella, rode along more than 1000 miles of the Great Wall as it cut and curled its way across the country from Shanhaiguan on the Yellow Sea to Jiayuguan in the Far West.

Hanbury-Tenison's Robin's brilliant book, *A Ride along the Great Wall'*, was published in 1987. Robin's sturdy and long-suffering mount was called Marco and Louella's was called Polo!

Years later, when Max was studying for his MBA at Tsinghua University in Beijing, I visited a different section of the Wall. On that occasion, as I remember, Max and I descended helter-skelter from the wall onto the plain below, being funnelled down a chute on tin trays, as though we were bobsledding on the Cresta run in St Moritz.

If I suffer even today from what I might call Great Wall 'mania,' I am certainly not alone. Chinese President Mao Zedong wrote a famous poem which includes a line which can be roughly translated as 'Not reach Great Wall, not good man' or 'He who doesn't reach the Great Wall is no hero'.

And the Chinese national anthem in its very second line includes the stirring exhortation: 'With our flesh and blood, let's build our newest Great Wall!

For the record, the full verse reads:

'Stand up! Those who refuse to be slaves!

With our flesh and blood, let's build our newest Great Wall!

The Chinese Nation is at its greatest peril,

Each one is forced to let out one last roar.

Stand up! Stand up! Stand up!

We are billions of one heart,

Braving the enemies' fire, March on!

Braving the enemies' fire, March on!

March on! March on! On!'

I lay no claim to heroism of any kind – and I'm sure Max doesn't either – but even in this era of mass travel I would argue there is something special about being able to say you have seen the Great Wall of China 'up close and personal', truly one of the Wonders of the World.

Of course, there is not just one Wall. There are many walls, built at different times and in different places. The Wall at Jiayuguan, like other parts, has its own story.

In the spring of 1372, for example, the Ming Emperor sent 150,000 soldiers on an expedition against the Northern Yuan. This massive battle wiped out the Yuan forces in Gansu and brought Gansu and the vast area around Gansu under the jurisdiction of the Ming Dynasty.

The Ming war against the Yuan dynasty was basically over, but the military power of the Yuan dynasty was not completely destroyed, and a part of the Yuan army that had retreated to the north of the Gobi Desert was a potential threat to the Ming dynasty. To prevent this, the Ming dynasty poured material and financial resources into the construction of the Jiayu Pass.

Dandan had arranged for the Curator of the Jiayuguan Great Wall, Zhang Xiao Dong, to brief us in person that day.

'The Great Wall was built in different forms in different areas' Zhang told us. 'In the East it is made from bricks but in the West, it's made from mud and rocks. They would use materials from the local area. If there is soil, they use soil but if they can fire bricks, they use bricks. In some places they would adapt the natural landscape by making the mountains steeper instead of building a wall, to form a natural defence. This is the wisdom of the ancient Chinese.'

That phrase, the 'wisdom of the ancient Chinese,' as evoked that day by Zhang Xiao Dong, Curator of the Jiayuguan Great Wall, has stayed with me. Not just the words. The way of seeing things too. Something for the 'lessons learned' file.

29

Zhangye – The Sleeping Buddha Temple

Zhangye (Marco Polo's Ganzhou) is about 600 kilometers west of Gansu's capital, Lanzhou, and about the same distance from Dunhuang to the east so it is roughly half-way along the Hexi Corridor.

The Polos stayed in Ganzhou for about a year. In his book Marco Polo devotes several long paragraphs to the town. *'The inhabitants'* Polo says *'have a very great number of idols, and I tell you that there are some that are 10 paces long: some made of wood, some of earth and some of stone – all of them covered with gold and very well wrought. The large idol is lying down, and several other small idols are around the large one and seem to be showing him humility and reverence.'*

During his lifetime Marco Polo was sometimes accused of exaggeration. They called him *'Il milione'* – a man who talks about a million things, not all of them necessarily true. This was a charge which Polo vigorously refuted. Indeed, on his deathbed he is reported to have said, as his parting message: 'I never told the half of it.'

For me this was an intriguing moment. Were we about to see with our very own eyes the 'large idol' which Marco Polo himself had seen and described?

As always, Dandan had done her best to ensure that we did not lack scholarly advice. Guozeng Tang, a local historian, was on hand to brief us as we gathered outside the temple.

'In 1098', he told us, 'During the Western Xia Dynasty, a monk called Sineng Weimie saw numinous lights and heard heavenly sounds coming from a nearby hill at the foot of a mountain.

Investigating the area, Sineng unearthed a hoard of treasure. That hoard included a reclining Buddha statue. So Sineng Weimie set out to build a great temple in honour of the image, which he believed had been revealed by divine favour.

'The Giant Buddha Temple – Dafo Temple' he continued 'is named after the statue worshiped there. It is also known as 'Wofo Temple – Sleeping Buddha Temple. It is very famous because it contains the biggest indoor Sleeping Buddha in all of China.'

We spent the next hour inside the temple. I looked at the briefing note our Chinese hosts had kindly supplied. 'The Sleeping Temple Buddha in Zhangye is 34.5 metres long and its shoulder spans a width of 7.5 metres. The ear is 4m long and the feet 5.2m long.

The note included the helpful observation 'Up to 8 people can stand on the ear of the reclining Buddha and his finger would allow one person to lie down upon.'

We gazed in awe at the gigantic recumbent figure in front of us.

'What is the Buddha made of?' Max asked.

'This lying Buddha structure is unique' Mr Tang replied. 'It is hollow and made from wood and clay. Inside there are five large chambers like rooms in a big house. Inside the head there are books, which represent that the Buddha is very wise. Near his heart there is a mirror, which represents purity. In his stomach there is a copper pot with grain, which represents having a good harvest.

'He is lying on his right side, his head resting on a cushion or relying on his right elbow, supporting his head with his hand. This indicates that he is looking forward to death, having attained nirvana.'

We spent a few more minutes looking at the Reclining Buddha in close-up, then walked on round the hall to see the murals and other paintings.

Mr Tang explained: 'Qing dynasty murals tell the story of Xuanzang and his followers, showing Xuanzang riding on a horse and the monkey king Sun Wukong kneeling on the ground.'

Outside, Mr Tang had a few more minutes for us. It was time to ask the 64,000-renminbi question.

'Mr Tang' I said 'we have so much enjoyed and profited from your insights and knowledge today. Marco Polo writes in his book about being here for a year and seeing huge recumbent images. Do you think the Buddha we have just seen this could have been one of them?'

Guozeng Tang paused before replying with scholarly precision. 'This monastery fits well with Marco Polo's description.' Then he continued with the words I was hoping to hear. 'Marco Polo must have been here.'

Back in the hotel that evening, finding that the wifi was working well, I googled 'reclining Buddha' This is what I found:

'A reclining Buddha is an image that represents Buddha lying down and is a major iconographic theme in Buddhist art. It represents the historical Buddha during his last illness, about to enter the *parinirvana* used to refer to nirvana-after-death, which occurs upon the death of someone who has attained nirvana during their lifetime. It implies a release from Samsara, karma and rebirth, well as the dissolution of the skandhas.'

I sent the quotation to Max with a comment of my own. 'Hi, Max. Great day today. Did you know that once you've attained *nirvana*, you don't have to be born again, not in any form, up or down the ladder of life. It's game over. You don't have to come back onto the pitch at all.'

30

Zhangye's Rainbow Mountains

Max and I were on the observation platform in Zhangye's GeoPark before dawn the following morning to watch the sun to rise on one of the world's most extraordinary sights. Think America's Grand Canyon, think Australia's Uluru-Ayers Rock, think France's Massif de Bauges! China's Rainbow Mountains in Zhangye, Gansu Province, must be right up there with the world leaders as far as scenic panoramas are concerned.

I shall never forget the sight which greeted us as the sun's rays caught the mountain peaks. This was a technicolour wonderland. And I'm not just talking about the visual impact. In geological terms, too, Zhangye's Danxia or Rainbow Mountains are in a class of their own. The vast array of technicoloured peaks which Max and I were looking at that morning has been produced as a result of millions of years of tectonic shifts, climate changes and erosion. The Rainbow Mountains have even been included by UNESCO in its list of Global Geoparks.

Now that the sun was up, I lowered my binoculars to study the notice which had been erected on the observation platform where we were standing. The mountains, so the notice said, had been formed between 137 and 96 million years ago. About thirty-six million years ago, an 'uplift made the strata to be exposed which were shaped into low and gentle hills due to weathering, flowing water, and wind erosion and gravitational collapse.'

I read the last line aloud.: 'The different mineral-bearing strata display variegated belts, just like coloured glaze.'

'I'm not sure I really understand all that' I said to Max. 'I barely got maths O-level.'

Happily, help was at hand. I turned away from the explanatory notice to realise that, standing beside me, was a young woman dressed in Yugu costume with a conical Yugu hat on her head. Her dress was as colourful as the mountaintops which I had been contemplating seconds before.

'My name is Wang Jie. I will be your guide.'

We shook hands. With her hat on, Wang Gie was as tall as Max.

The term 'Danxia' she told us 'was originally defined by Chinese geologists to describe landscapes looking like rosy, red clouds. Millions of years ago, this area would have been a lake. The different colours are because the land was formed over many years, each colour coming from different minerals. Affected by climate and environmental factors, the minerals inside present the colourful colours of red, purple, yellow-green, grey-green, and grey-black that we see now.'

Geology wasn't the whole story. There were cultural and anthropological aspects to be considered too.

'The original story,' Wang Jie continued, 'as told in ancient Chinese myth, features the goddess of nature, and mother of humankind: Nuwa. The colourful stones were left behind when Nuwa smelted stones to mend the cracks in the sky. They were left at the foot of Qilian Mountain, and they covered the landscape with thousands of colours. So, she sent a multi-coloured deer to protect the Danxia mountains and the colourful deer, who then turned into a girl, worked together with the colourful local tribes to fight against the demons and protect the homeland. This is the origin of colourful Danxia from the perspective of mythology.'

'Wow!' I said to Max, 'That's pure gold, isn't it? Golden Bough stuff. Someone ought to write that down.'

'You will, Oscar' Max said. 'You will.'

We learned a lot more from Wang Lie and others that day.

For example, in 2002, a journalist was introduced to the colourful hills by a local shepherd called Lei Xingyi. The rumour spread and attracted many photographers and film crews.

From 2004 shepherd Lei started building roads near the Danxia mountains by selling his sheep. In 2010 he opened his own hotel and was currently a local guide. He had been on French and Japanese TV.

In 2005 the region was named as one of the seven most beautiful Danxia in China by Chinese National Geography.

Blockbusters were filmed here including The Sun Also Rises (2007) and A Simple Noodle 24 Story (2009). The shepherd, Lei Xingyi, even acted briefly in A Simple Noodle Story.

In 2011 the region was listed as one of the Top 10 Geological Wonders by (the US) National Geographic. In 2013 it became a 4A national scenic attraction.

To better promote tourism, Zhangye held China's first hot-air balloon festival on July 19, 2019. About one hundred balloons lifted off during the two-day event, which was attended by about 50,000 tourists. It was also held in 2020.

Cultural tourism has become the strongest support for the city's economic growth. As of December 2020, there are two sightseeing helicopters, ten powered hang gliders and 30 hot air balloons here.

Talking of balloons, I was not sure how keen Dandan was on letting Max and me go for a balloon ride.

'We wouldn't want to see a headline in the press: 'Former father of UK Prime Minister lost in balloon over Chinese mountains!' She was only half-joking.

'Some people might be quite pleased!' I said. 'Anyway, I'm not the former father of the Prime Minister. I am the former Prime Minister's father!'

She agreed to let us have a go in the end, so Max, Pete the Camera, and I all clambered into the balloon's tiny gondola (think Marco Polo in Venice!) and we took off with a whoosh and a roar as the blowtorches blasted hot air into the balloon above us. The horizon expanded as we rose. Zhangye's Rainbow Mountains seemed to go on forever, north and south, east and west.

I had imagined that our pilot would steer us here and there, taking advantage of gusts of wind to move us in the right direction. Clever balloonists, I had heard, also managed to change direction by spilling wind, like clever yachtsmen.

But I was wrong about this. As we rose, I could see that the balloon was connected by a long rope by a rope to the ground. That meant we could go up and down, but we couldn't go off-piste altogether.

But still we had a good time. An amazing time. One of the high points of the whole trip, you might say.

Strictly speaking, we shouldn't have stayed aloft more than 10 minutes. But I'm sure our capable balloonist overstayed his allotted time. He kept on blasting hot air into the canopy to maintain altitude.

Far below, I could see Dandan waving her 'In the footsteps of Marco Polo' hat at us, telling us to come down.

'I guess we've reached the end of our tether,' Pete the Camera said.

Did Marco Polo ever see the Zhangye's Rainbow Mountains? Given that he stayed in the city over a year, it would be nice to think if he did. But one thing is sure. Even if Marco Polo missed the mountains, you can't miss Marco Polo.

On the way back from our ballooning adventure, Max and I jumped out of the Prado to weave our way perilously through the traffic to pay our respects to the huge 'Marco Polo' statue which stands at the junction of two big boulevards. The year 2024 would see the 700th anniversary of his death. We were sure tributes would be coming in to Zhangye from all over the world.

In the Footsteps of Marco Polo

Taking the train

Yimlakut bridge

In the Footsteps of Marco Polo

Miran Fort

The pagoda at the Mogao Caves

In the Footsteps of Marco Polo

Mogao Caves

Max and I followed the Deputy Director, Zhang Yuanlin, into Cave 16.

In the Footsteps of Marco Polo

Crescent Moon Lake, near Dunhuang

Shouhang Power Plant, Gansu

In the Footsteps of Marco Polo

Jiayugan Fort

'Your papers!' he shouted, 'Do you have to have permission from the Great Khan to pass this way? Illegal immigrants not allowed!'

In the Footsteps of Marco Polo

The reclining Buddha, Zhangye

In the Footsteps of Marco Polo

'My name is Wang Jie. I will be your guide.'

Talking of balloons, I was not sure how keen Dandan was on letting Max and me go for a balloon ride.

Author and Max in front of the Marco Polo statue in Zhangye.

In the Footsteps of Marco Polo

Lanzhou Beef Noodles Vocational Training School

Max and I stood there at the counter in our white gowns and tall white chef's hats while the top man, Zhou Xing-guo, who had been teaching at the school for the past ten years, gave us a quick briefing.

Crossing the Yellow River on inflated goat skins.

In the Footsteps of Marco Polo

Two Venetian travellers from the Marco Polo era!

In the Footsteps of Marco Polo

With the Darkhads at the Genghis Khan Mausoleum, Ordos, Inner Mongolia.

Statue of Genghis Khan on his horse.

In the Footsteps of Marco Polo

You don't have to kickstart these modern motorbikes, not like my old BSA Shooting Star. Nowadays, you just turn the key.

Max and Yuandeng, wearing the zodog, before the wrestling match.

In the Footsteps of Marco Polo

Remains of Kubla Khan's
'Pleasure Dome' at Xanadu.

Dr Rana makes a surprise visit
to the Great Wall at Juyong Pass.

Journey's end. At last, we reach the Forbidden City, Beijing.

In the Footsteps of Marco Polo

Forbidden City roofs

There they were, gleaming monsters. Drivers already kitted out and in the saddle.
Engines ticking over, ready to go.

In the Footsteps of Marco Polo

Team photo, Beijing, June 21, 2023.

One-Tribe TV's film 'In the Footsteps of Marco Polo' was premiered at the Curzon Cinema, London, on July 3, 2024.

31

Lanzhou – Pizza Parlour Encounter and Zhongshan Bridge

We finally completed our passage through the Hexi Corridor and checked into a hotel in Lanzhou, capital of China's Gansu Province, around 8 pm on the evening of Tuesday, May 30.

Max felt in serious need of a pizza. 'I just don't think I want any more rice and mutton tonight.'

He consulted his phone. Mini-seconds later the screen started buzzing. There were five places within a 2 km radius where we could find pizzas, one of them only 400 m away, down a side street off the main road.

'Piece of cake,' Max was delighted.

'Piece of pizza, you mean.'

We snuck out of the hotel. Ten minutes later we pushed through a hanging curtain to find ourselves in a tiny 'pizza parlour'. The only other customers were a middle-aged Chinese woman and another much younger woman, whose head was bent over a textbook of some kind.

Max ordered our pizzas and then struck up a conversation with the older of the two women. He gave me the gist.

'Tomorrow nationwide civil service exams are being held. The girl's mother has brought her daughter so she can study in peace. Probably too much noise at home. She says her daughter dreams of becoming a civil servant and of going to live and work in Beijing. Being a civil servant is a very great honour and achievement, but first her daughter must pass the test.'

Max obviously knew what he, and the young woman's mother, were talking about. He had lived and worked in China for more than a decade. The Chinese civil service had survived and flourished for more than 2000 years. Social mobility was much more than a slogan. Your parents could be scratching a living from some tiny, parched plot of land somewhere upcountry while their children, if they were smart enough, could sit the famous civil service exam and end up one day as fully-fledged mandarins in Beijing.

After a while the mother whisked her daughter away. The young woman put her textbook in her bag, looked at the camera and raised her hand in the traditional Chinese 'good luck' gesture.

Next morning, we headed for the river. I had Marco Polo's book in my hand. He uses the Mongolian name – Qara-Muren – for the Yellow River and describes it as being 'so big it cannot be spanned by a bridge, for it is very wide and deep.'

Marco Polo's observation was well-founded. It wasn't until 1909 that the first permanent bridge – Zhongshan Bridge, named after Sun Yat-Sen, the first Provisional President of the Republic of China – was constructed across the Yellow River with steel truss components, cement and other equipment and materials being brought in from Germany.

Nowadays, traffic on the bridge is limited to pedestrians, cyclists and rickshaws. It is a big tourist attraction. Max and I joined the morning crowd for a gentle stroll.

Back in the 80s, as I mentioned in an earlier chapter, I wrote a novel called *Dragon River* which featured, inter alia, the Sino-Japanese conflict of the 1930s and 1940s. Remembering this, I said to Max: 'Lanzhou, by the way, was the terminus of the China-Soviet Highway. This is where Soviet supplies arrived to help China resist the Japanese invasion. Losing Lanzhou could have been disastrous. But the Japanese never captured the place. There were aerial dogfights in the skies right above the city, but the Chinese held on.'

Later that morning, we visited the Gansu Provincial Museum

in Lanzhou to find ourselves surrounded by a multitude of schoolchildren who were obviously on an organised visit. They all wanted a 'selfie' with Max!

Gansu Provincial Museum may be spelt with a capital P but there is nothing 'provincial' about this museum otherwise. Our guidebook told us: 'It has amazing ceramics from the Neolithic age as well as a huge collection of wooden tablets and carvings from the Han Dynasty.'

Max and I took our turn to gaze at the Flying Horse of Wuwei. Some workmen dug up this astonishing sculpture by accident back in the sixties when they were building an air-raid shelter in nearby Wuwei case of a Soviet attack. (The wartime alliance between Russia and China had long since disintegrated).

Max and I were dumbfounded. Gobsmacked.

Had Marco Polo seen the Flying Horse of Wuwei on his journey through the Hexi Corridor? He might well have done. In Marco Polo's Day Wuwei was called Erguiul or Liangzhou. It was a key stopping point on the Northern Silk Road on the border with Inner Mongolia

'We went past Wuwei yesterday, on the road from Zhangye to Lanzhou. I saw the turnoff' I said to Max. 'Marco Polo went there too. He might have seen the Flying Horse. I would like to believe that he saw the Flying Horse. It might have given him that extra impetus he needed to finish the journey!' I'm sorry we didn't make the detour.'

I meant it. I really was sorry. When Tim Severin and I, in our undergraduate days at Oxford, first had the idea of following Marco Polo's route to China, we treated Marco Polo in a rather cavalier way, basically as a peg to hang an amazing adventure on. But now I felt differently. Older and wiser, maybe. I didn't want to let Marco Polo down by missing some obvious historical clue or link. To quote Wordsworth, for me by then Marco Polo had indeed become: 'A presence which is not to be put by.'

If we ever got to Xanadu, I was looking forward to quoting Coleridge too!

We had lunch by the river, and in the afternoon took the chairlift up to the top of the western hills.

10 or 20 years ago, visibility in a large city like Lanzhou would have been poor, to say the least. Motorcycles, cars, trucks and buses had replaced bicycles as the main means of transportation, The resulting pollution was truly atrocious. You had to wrap a handkerchief round your face to breathe.

But all that has changed. Industries have been moved out of town, and the arrival of huge numbers of electric cars has made a colossal difference to pollution levels.

Max and I stood in front of the pagoda which has been constructed on the summit of the hill and gazed out across the river to the city in the foreground and, beyond that, the distant shape of the Mongolian plateau,

'That's just amazing', I said to Max. 'I remember being in Tian'anmen square in Beijing a few years back and you could barely see from one side of the square to the other. Almost as bad as London in the fifties'

That evening, we took an Uber (electric, of course) to an upmarket bar we had heard about on the other side of town.

Halfway through the second glass of Johnny Walker Blue Label (they served top quality Japanese whiskey too), my phone rang. It was Dandan, solicitous as ever.

'Where are you?' she asked. 'Shall I come and get you?'

'We're fine' I said 'Absolutely fine. I'm sure we can find our own way back.'

Dandan was hovering in the lobby when we returned. She seemed relieved to see us.

'We've got a busy day tomorrow. We are visiting the Noodle School! You need to be fighting fit!'

32

Oodles of Noodles

Street food merchants from as early as 1915 have been selling beef noodles in Lanzhou. Since then, it has become became a staple diet. There are 35,000 beef noodle restaurants across China, and 2000 of them are found here in Lanzhou.

Why Lanzhou? The answer to that question seems lie in the fact that south of Lanzhou you have the grassland where you can source the high-quality Tibetan yak beef. North and west of Lanzhou is the Hexi Corridor, famous for its crop production. In Lanzhou itself you can find Heshang Tou wheat to make the best noodles. And, of course, Lanzhou is on the Yellow River, an area rich in vegetables.

Add to this the special culinary skills developed here over more than a century, and it is not surprising that Lanzhou has been called the beef noodle capital of the world.

We arrived early and parked outside. The huge red and gold sign said in English as well as Mandarin: Lanzhou Beef Noodles Vocational Training School.

As we stand on the pavement, I do a 'piece to camera:' 'Lanzhou is famous for its noodles and today Max and I have enrolled in the Lanzhou Beef Noodles Training School.'

I glance back over my shoulder to point at the sign behind me before continuing: 'This place has been training chefs about how to make noodles for over 16 years with up to a hundred chefs at the time coming from all around China and even the world to learn the Lanzhou way. The course lasts one month and predominantly focuses on hand-stretching of the noodles with immense precision, with noodle thickness ranging from super-wide to super-thin.

'Before we go any further, I need to debunk a myth. There is a common misconception that Marco Polo took the noodle back from here to Italy to make what we know today as pasta. I can tell you pasta existed in Italy way before Marco Polo even left Venice …'

I subscribe to the motto: If you can't stand the heat stay out of the kitchen. But that morning I realised there was no chance of staying out of the kitchen. They had the kit ready and waiting for us. Even the hat-size was correct.

Max and I stood there at the counter in our white gowns and tall white chef's hats while the top man, Zhou Xing-guo, who had been teaching at the school for the past ten years, gave us a quick briefing.

'Creating the noodles is an art form' he said. 'You start with a dough and after a few pulls you have very thin noodles. It's like a magic performance which appears entertaining, and people like it because the soup tastes nice and the texture of the noodles is good.'

I looked over Mr Zhou's shoulder as he spoke. Behind him, in the kitchen, I could see 20 or 30 chefs all busy pulling and slapping and pummelling as though their lives depended on it.

I'm never going to forget that morning. The trainees who come here spend three weeks learning the essentials of making doodles before they go out into the wide noodle-hungry world. Max and I were expected to produce recognisable noodles in the space of a few minutes with some very elementary basic training.

As far as I can understand the principle, you start off with a thick piece of dough, you stretch it as far as you can, then you twist and shake and – lo and behold – that thick piece of the dough has divided itself into two thinner pieces of dough and then you do the same thing again until finally you end up with some absolutely wafer thin pieces of dough – the super thin noodles Mr Zhou has been talking about.

I didn't really enjoy myself. I couldn't get the hang of it. Just when you thought you had a nice firm but pliable string of dough, already to be divided, and then subdivided, the chain would collapse, and you would be left facing the void.

There came a moment when, totally frustrated, I grasped whatever strands of dough I could find and draped them round my neck!

'I'm off, I'm outta here' I said, or words to that effect.

We have lunch that day at a nearby noodle restaurant. Dandan says it is one of the best noodle restaurants in Lanzhou. You take your turn in the queue. In due course you are given a large bowl of soup but down in the depths of that soup, hidden from view, the succulent hand-pulled super thin noodles are lurking. I sense more noodle trouble ahead. There are no knives, forks or spoons to be seen. It is chopsticks or nothing.

To this day I don't understand how you can fish noodles out from the bottom of the bowl in a manageable way just using chopsticks. That lunchtime in Lanzhou, I tried once, I tried twice, but to no avail.

Max could see the trouble I was in.

'Give it another go' he advised.

This time I used both hands with my elbows on the table to get better leverage. Bingo! I realised I had got a solid grasp. Now, I simply had to get the noodles to the surface.

There was a sudden 'whoosh' as the whole coagulated ball of noodles emerged like a nuclear submarine from the surface of the soup. The soup lapped over the edge of the bowl. Random strands of pasta flew into the air, but the bulk of the noodles was still, miraculously, attached to the chopsticks.

'Gotcha!' I exclaimed.

33

How did Marco Polo cross the Yellow River?

We were keen to know how Marco Polo had crossed the Yellow River. As I have already noted, it would be centuries before the first bridge across the Yellow River would be constructed. Given the sheer volume of water coming off the Tibetan or Qinghai-Xizang plateau to be funnelled through the gorges, fording the river would have been out of the question. What other possibilities were there, way back in the 1270s?

After our noodle lunch, we piled into our vehicles and headed some 30 miles downstream from Lanzhou. This is where, over the period 1958 to 1975, China's first hydroelectric dam was constructed.

We boarded a small riverboat at a landing-station above the dam and chugged serenely upstream, wondering what Dandan had in store for us.

We soon found out. After 20 minutes in the boat, we put into shore and disembarked.

Seconds later a man appeared out of nowhere driving a battered old Suzuki 4x4 with a trailer in tow.

'What on earth is that?' I asked Dandan, as I looked at the trailer's cargo: several strange bulbous objects, lashed together with rope.

'I'll leave that to the experts' Dandan replied. And with that she introduced a young man whom she appeared to have magicked up out of nowhere.

'This is Li Cong', she said.

I must hand it to Dandan. She never let us down. If she didn't know the answer herself, she almost always managed to find someone who did.

Li Cong could not have been more eloquent. 'This is a goat skin raft' he pointed to the strange object on the trailer.

Max: 'I can see this is a raft. How is it made?'

I am not sure if Max needed all the gory details, but he got them anyway.

'The goat skins' Li Cong said, 'must come from goats that are more than three years old. We slaughter them and make a cut through the buttocks. Then we remove the internal organs, and then turn it inside out, similar to the way you would take off your clothes. After turning it inside out, we put sesame oil and salt water inside and wait for it to ferment. We then tie it up with string. It is very easy to make.

'To inflate it, we have to inflate it through the goat's mouth. If we need to inflate many pieces of skin, we will use an air pump. If there are just a few we will blow it up with our mouths.'

As he was speaking, willing hands lifted the goatskin raft from the trailer and carried it to the riverbank.

'12 goats were used to make this raft' Li Cong explained. 'The goat skin rafts of my father's generation were usually tied up as two or three rafts together. One raft can support the weight of 1000kg, so at that time they tied a maximum of three rafts, so that would be 3000kg'.

By now the goatskin raft was bobbing on the water. Dandan, solicitous as ever, insisted that Max and I should put on life jackets.

'I'm sure Marco Polo wouldn't have had a life jacket,' I complained half-heartedly. 'I bet he didn't put a lifejacket on every time he jumped in a gondola in Venice.'

Though we would have liked to emulate the great Venetian explorer, Max and I didn't go all the way across the Yellow River on that raft made of 12 inflated goat skins. By the time we got halfway across the current was running quite swiftly. I won't say we were being tossed around, but it was worth hanging on to something if you could find something to hang on to. We turned back to hug the bank.

The raft had no motor any kind. You had to steer it with a paddle. We drifted downstream quite fast until we found a landing point about half a mile downstream.

In the event, I was glad we had worn our lifejackets.

34

Ningxia Vineyards

After leaving Lanzhou, Marco Polo headed north-east in the direction of Inner Mongolia with a view to reaching Xanadu, the Summer Palace of Kublai Khan, before going on to Beijing.

Crossing the Yellow River in Lanzhou, just as Marco Polo did, Max and I headed into the Province of Ningxia on our way to the great Mongolian plateau. This northern swing provided us with a splendid opportunity for another culinary adventure. Not noodles, this time. Wine!

In Marco Polo's time the region we were now entering was already famous for its vineyards. Marco Polo writes: *'There grow here many excellent vines, supplying great plenty of wine; and in all Cathay this is the only place where wine is produced. It is carried hence all over the country.'*

But even Marco Polo could not have foreseen the astonishing developments as far as viticulture is concerned which have taken place in this region in recent years. Ningxia could soon come to rival the world's great wine producing districts such as France's Bordeaux, California's Napa Valley, Western Australia's Margaret River, or New Zealand's Central Otago Wine Region.

As Marco Polo himself noted, from the wine producing point of view, the geophysical characteristics of the region are ideal. This is frontier land, surrounded by deserts. There is little or no rain, and no humid air. Instead, there is lots and lots of sunshine.

A few miles west of the Yellow River as it runs north past Ningxia's capital, Yinchuan, lie the Helan Shan mountains. Running north to south, the Helan mountains block the cold from Siberia, as well as stopping an invasion of the sand from the Tengger desert, the fourth largest desert in China.

The sheer scale of the winemaking venture here is amazing. The Helan Mountain east foothill area, where we were heading, is home to 33,000 hectares of vineyards and over 100 wineries by 2020, covering over 500 km² of land. Today this area of Ningxia produces nearly 40% of all of China's wine.

On our first day in Ningxia, Dandan arranged a visit to the Xige Wine estate, the oldest and biggest vineyard in the Helan Mountain area. She also arranged for Zhang Yanzhi, chief vintner, to brief us before taking us on a tour.

We gathered in the splendid atrium of the estate office.

Zhang Yanzhi who had himself studied in Bordeaux, told us how this extraordinary story of how Ningxia's 'wine explosion' began.

Though Ningxia's winemaking culture – viticulture – goes back thousands of years, Ningxia's wine 'explosion' is of recent date. In the 1990s, he told us, a group of Ningxia businessmen, realising the region's potential, went to Europe to study winemaking there. They noted carefully what they saw. They returned to China not only with enhanced knowledge and skills, also with some of the key grape varietals.

That first generation of Chinese vintners thought long term, he continued. They sent their children to study winemaking in Europe too. 'Now many of these wineries are run by these second-generation vintners. I am one of them' he added proudly.

'And what brought you to this particular region?' I asked.

Zhang replied: 'To produce wine, you need to find a suitable terroir which is in the right place. If we look at this region at the Eastern foot of the Helan mountains, there are more than 3000 hours of sunshine per year. The soil conditions are especially suitable for producing high end wines. 5 years ago, when deciding on a place for the winery, we chose here.'

'So, what are we talking about in terms of volumes here?' I asked.

Zhang said: 'Our vineyard covers an area of 2000 hectares and produces 10 million bottles of high-end wine every year. This is a large-scale production in China and even around the world.'

Max asked: 'And how many different types of grapes do you have here?'

'There are about 20 varieties of grape here.' Zhang replied. 'The one that best represents this region, and China as a whole, is known as a Cabernet Gernischt which came from Europe originally. It thrived here in China even after wine disease wiped it out in Europe'.

I knew what he was referring to. Cabernet Gernischt was not the only variety of grape wiped out by the phylloxera outbreak in Europe at the end of the 19th century.

The Xige Estate uses state of the art equipment to produce 7.5million litres of wine per year. But they still use traditional methods to age their wine in oak barrels.

Max asked: 'How big a business is wine consumption in China?'

Zhang replied: 'Since 2010 the consumption of imported wine, as well as wine produced in China, has annually grown at a rate of more than 20% every year. China has a huge population and consumer market. I believe that in the future, the wine market in China, will be much larger than it is now.'

'How about the education process' Max asked, 'educating people how to drink wine, how to really appreciate wine?'

Zhang said: 'Many young people are becoming more and more interested in wine. Some educational institutions teach young people how to taste wine. In addition, many young people here are willing to learn wine because wine tasting is a new lifestyle. Chinese young people are more willing to accept new things.'

We spent the best part of two hours at the Xige Wine Estate. I was astonished by the sheer scale of the operation. Outside, the planted area extended as far as the eye could see. Inside, one vast hall contained stainless steel vats full of wine. In another vast hall oak barrels were stacked to the ceiling.

When we finished the tour, we gathered for the tasting.

Max and I stood, glasses in hand, in front of a row of bottles containing different wines and different vintages while another one of Xige Estates wine experts, a young woman called Dong Chunjuan, explained what was on offer.

She served us a Chardonnay first.

My experience of wine tastings over the years is that the best technique is to swell the swirl the wine in your mouth a bit, then spit it out. Otherwise, you soon get drunk. But that first Chardonnay was altogether too good to 'swirl and spit'. Besides we weren't driving.

We held out our glasses for a second helping.

'Is this your first Chinese Chardonnay?' Ms Dong asked. 'I hope it is good for you.'

'Very good' Max said.

'I agree' I said.

Ms Dong could have been a sommelier at the Savoy. 'This Chardonnay was aged in oak barrels' she explained 'which gives it a strong aroma of tropical fruits such as bananas. When you first taste it there is a creamy texture. This is typical of a good Chardonnay.'

Next up was a Cabernet Gernischt, the famous varietal which Mr Zhang had referred to earlier that day.

Max and I swirled and swallowed and once again held out our glasses for more.

'What do you think of it?' Ms Dong asked.

I channelled my inner Jancis Robinson. 'Endearingly presumptuous' I ventured.

Joking aside and judging by what we saw and tasted at the Xige estate that morning in Ningxia, I would argue that Chinese wines – if they aren't already in that category – will soon be rated among the world's best.

35

Helan Mountain Rock Paintings

In the distant past the Helan Mountains, about 60 klms from Yinchuan, were home to northern Chinese peoples, including Qiang, Tiele, Huns, Xianbei, Tujue, Uyghur, Tibetans, and others. They carved the scenes of their daily lives on the stones of the mountain 3,000 to 10,000 years ago. Today, they are the site of one of the most important displays of rock art in the world. It was listed by UNESCO's International Committee of Rock Painting in 1997.

Dandan's advance team had, as was so often the case, managed to line up the top expert to brief us.

Zhang Jianguo, Director of Archaeology, Helan Mountains, who greeted Max and me as we got out of the car around 9 am, had spent more than two decades studying this vast array of cave carvings. He told us that this part of the Helan mountains, leading up to the Helan Pass, had the densest displays of rock art in the whole region.

'At present,' he said 'we have counted about 2,319 group carvings and 5,685 individual petroglyphs, ranging from 3,000 to 10,000 years old. Before the year 2000, the local Aboriginals still lived here. In 1969 they then began to promote the petroglyphs here to the world and this place became open to the public.'

Stanley: 'We know that Marco polo came to Ningxia at the end of the 13th century, what would he have found had he come here, where we are now?'

Zhang: 'When Marco Polo arrived in Yinchuan, we have some documents that show there were people living here.'

Well, that was something, I thought. Marco Polo doesn't

mention specifically encountering nomads in the Helan mountains. But it seemed that even when Marco Polo came the caves were still occupied.

We walked on. Zhang pointed out carvings of special interest.

Zhang: 'This petroglyph on this side of the stone is depicting a group of hunters, In this picture, we can see that on the far left is a hunter drawing a bow and shooting arrows, and on the right are twelve animals, which are relatively large. Its composition is very simple, using a single line method.

'But what is very interesting is that the ratio of the hunter to the prey is out of proportion. In fact, this shows us that people in that period had begun to express themselves in a realistic way. With things which are nearer appearing bigger than things which are far away which appear smaller. This kind of realistic expression at the time is a technique that we now call three dimensional.'

Stanley: 'So, these were hunting scenes, are there many different pictures, lot of different scenes?'

Zhang: 'In fact, there are many topics that the petroglyphs depict. The one we are looking at is a hunting scene and we can also see some petroglyphs which reflect the spiritual world. The Sun God rock painting is a masterpiece among the rock paintings in the Helan mountains. It is carved on the stone wall more than 40 m above the ground.'

Zang led the way up the narrow stone path. Max and I followed. We couldn't get right up close because the carving was on the opposite wall of the cliff. But through the long-distance lens of my Canon, I could see the radial lines on the Sun God's head, the round face, the double ringed eyes, the long eyelashes, and that bright and energetic look which even across the divide which separated us – in time as well as space – I found totally inspirational.

I don't know how often Zhang had seen the Sun God the way we saw the Sun God that morning. But familiarity certainly had not bred contempt.

Zhang: 'This is known as the Sun God because of the circle around the face, as well as the strokes showing the beams of light coming from it. It is common to see depictions of the sun all around the world but in different regions and in different cultures, there are a variety of expressions of it. This image of the Sun God is a humanized portrayal of the Sun. In the carving, they give it eyes, a nose, and a mouth. Giving it five senses makes people feel closer to the gods.'

When Henrik Schliemann, the famous German archaeologist, unearthed a magnificent gold mask at Mycenae in 1876, he famously exclaimed 'I have gazed on the face of Agamemnon.'

As we climbed back down. I said to Max, 'I think we just gazed on the face of the Sun God.'

36

Mimi's Magic Carpet and Zhenbeibu China West Film Studio

We spent much of our last day in Ningxia at a desert 'pretend' fort near Zhenbeibu at the foot of Helan Mountain. There was once a real Ming dynasty (1368–1644) fort here, functioning as a frontier stronghold to protect China's borders from nomadic invasion, but that fort was destroyed by an earthquake. The renowned Chinese writer Zhang Xianliang took the crumbling site over and transformed it into a film studio. Featuring both original and ancient castles, primitive and desolate landscapes, Zhenbeibu China West Film Studio is now one of the three largest film studios in China, and the most famous in western China. The studio has produced many world-famous films, including Zhang Yimou's Red Sorghum, which won the first Golden Bear for China in 1988.

The studio is also very popular with tourists. You can dress up as your favorite character, posing in various movie sets, and even starring in short video clips.

Mimi, OneTribeTV's director, had a brilliant idea. 'Why don't Max and Stanley dress up as two Venetian travellers from the Marco Polo era?' she suggested. 'We can film them too.'

Overnight she magicked up a script. Max and I rode our horses into town, like gunfighters in a Western, and hitched our reins to the post outside the 'Yuan Dynasty saloon'.

Max had once starred in an acclaimed BBC production of the Prince and the Pauper, directed by Julian Fellowes, and has appeared in several TV and film productions since. He knew exactly what to do, and how to do it.

I noticed that I didn't seem to have any part to play in the script at all except right at the end when I say 'well, gentlemen, what about a drink?'

I tried to raise the point with Mimi, but she didn't seem interested. 'Let's leave this one to Max,' she said.

We enter the 'saloon bar' or its 13th Century equivalent to find a group of men playing a form of Chinese poker around the table. While I sit and watch, Max joins in. He grasps the principle of the game immediately and suggests a wager. If he loses, he will forfeit his stake. If he wins, he will carry off the prize. And what will the prize be? They consult the young woman who is serving the drinks and generally looking after the card-playing party.

The young woman has been well briefed by Mimi. She is word perfect. I think maybe she is studying for a doctorate, and this is just a summer job. 'If Max wins the wager', the young woman says, 'you will be able to return to Venice tomorrow on a magical flying carpet!'

'I quite like the idea of an aperitif at Florian's in the Piazza San Marco' I whisper to Max.

But he is made of sterner stuff. He negotiates in fluent Mandarin. 'We don't want to go back to Venice at this point,' he says, 'tempting though that might be. We want to press on to Inner Mongolia, to visit the tomb of Genghis Khan, get on our motorcycles or whatever.'

More discussion ensues. I get quite bored sitting there. There are several retakes.

Eventually everything is agreed. If Max wins the wager, we will not only get our magic carpet trip, but we will be able to choose our next destination!

I don't want to give too much away. Suffice it to say that Max won the wager with a convincing demonstration of prestidigitation.

I hadn't said much during this whole performance. Indeed, I hadn't said anything at all. I felt I needed to contribute something, pull my weight.

'I once met Paul Daniels, the magician, once at a dinner at David and Penny Mellor's in London' I said. 'There were several ladies there with low-cut dresses. As a magician, Paul Daniels was delighted. He liked to look for missing objects in ladies' bosoms.'

'Let's not go there," Mimi said firmly.

That night at dinner Dandan informed us: 'We're thinking of flying from here to Ordos in Inner Mongolia rather than go by road. Everyone happy with that?'

Ordos, in the middle of the Yellow River's great inverted U, is over 400 klm from Yinchuan. It would be a long tiring drive at the best of times.

Max and I knew the back seat of our Toyota Land Cruiser very well by then. We weren't going to quibble about taking the plane to Ordos.

'Magic carpets can come in all shapes and sizes,' I said. 'Thank you, Dandan And thank you, Mimi!'

37

Genghis Khan Mausoleum

With a window seat on our 'magic carpet' flight from Yinchuan to Ordos, I had a clear view of the Yellow River as it began its great northward sweep to create the huge loop of territory, the ∩-shaped expanse, which Marco Polo crossed on his way to Xanadu. I felt totally exhilarated.

And there was a special extra reason for my high spirits that day. This at last was Genghis Khan country, the land and the people – the Tartars – Marco Polo talks so much about in his book. And how real it must have been to him then! When Marco Polo first set foot in what is now Inner Mongolia, barely half century had elapsed since the death of the first Mongol Emperor, Genghis Khan.

That sense of exhilaration stayed with me. Next morning, with the two gigantic wings of the Genghis Khan mausoleum stretched out on either side behind me, like a majestic eagle in flight, I faced the camera to deliver my first PTC on Mongolian soil.

'I'm standing in front of the Mausoleum of the most famous Mongolian of all: Genghis Khan. A man whose legacy is revered by some and loathed by others, but whatever your opinion on his methods there is no arguing with his success.

'This was a man who managed to unite the tribes of Mongolia with the people of China to create the seeds of the largest contiguous empire ever known to mankind, both before and since.'

Moments later, Max and I were formally welcomed to the Mausoleum by Haschiluu, Deputy Director, and his colleagues.

Through an interpreter, Haschiluu explains that he is part of a subgroup of Mongol people who believe they are the direct descendants of Genghis Khan's generals. They are called the Darkhad. The tribe has passed down stories of the Great Khan for generations. They mainly work at the Mausoleum. He tells us that his people have now safeguarded Genghis's soul for 40 generations — 795 years.

One of their crucial tasks is to keep an oil lamp alight which is said to have been burning since the Great Khan's death in 1227.

During Genghis Khan's time, Shamanism was the main religion among Mongolians. They believed that spirits continue to exist after people die. The mausoleum was built as a place to worship his spirit rather than his body.

When Max asks where Genghis Khan's body is buried, Haschiluu tells us that after Genghis Khan died in or around Gansu on 18th August 1227, his remains were supposedly carried back to central Mongolia and buried secretly and without markings, in accordance with his personal directions. His actual burial site remains unknown, but it is certainly not here in Ejin Horo, where we were at the time, since this territory was only recently conquered from the Tangut Empire when Genghis Khan died.

Haschiluu explains that, not having Genghis Khan's body, the Mongols honour the Khan's memory and spirit through his personal effects. When I asked Haschiluu why he and the Darkhads think it is important for the rituals to Genghis Khan to be upheld, he replies:

'Genghis Khan's influence on China and the rest of the world cannot be underestimated.

'Most people think of Genghis as just a warrior' Haschiluu continues. 'They forget that under his reign there was religious tolerance, meritocracy and the use of one-writing system.' And he adds: 'He created one cohesive political system along most of the Silk Road which led to a huge boost in global commerce and improved communication between the East and the West.'

In the PTC I had just delivered, I had decided to say rather positive things about Genghis Khan, notwithstanding the fact that history – or at least some historians – seemed to link him with pillage and carnage on an industrial scale. Listening now to Haschiluu, I was glad to know that in his estimation at least I was not entirely *off piste*.

I tried to pin it down. 'If it hadn't been for Genghis Khan,' I asked, 'would Marco Polo ever I have gone on his amazing journey?'

'Marco Polo's journey would have been less likely as there were fewer merchants traveling the Silk Road before Genghis Khan united the regions.' Haschiluu replied.

Pillars carved with golden dragons support the roof of the Main Palace which itself resembles a golden Palace-Yurt. In the centre stands a 5-metre-high white marble statue of Genghis Khan. As a backcloth there is a 13th century territorial map of Eurasia, while a notice advises visitors that 'Genghis Khan and his descendants unified the Eurasian continent and have promoted the process of world civilisation.'

We followed our guide into the Ceremonial Hall.

At the far end of the room three large white yurts have been mounted on the stage. In front of the middle yurt, a golden statue of Genghis Khan presides over an altar decorated with flowers and offerings of various kinds, including – I noticed – a large drinking vessel.

When the ceremony begins, Haschiluu and his team of Darkhads stand in front of the altar, facing the congregation. There are 40 or 50 people present. Max and I squat cross-legged towards the back. We don't wish to appear conspicuous. Who knew what strange tasks the Darkhads might suddenly call on us to perform?

I soon found out. The Sheep Offering Ceremony was about to begin.

Moments later the Sacrificial Sheep is carried in and laid on the altar. The ensuing religious service involves a lot of deep-throated repetitive chanting. I don't understand any of the words, but the intent is clear. This is a ceremony to honour the memory – and indeed the actual spiritual presence – of the great Genghis Khan.

About half an hour in, while the chanting and intoning continues, it is time for the large cup – shaped like a Greek amphora – to come into play. The shaman lifts the cup from the altar and holds it and aloft. Then he lowers it to chest height and approaches members of the congregation nearest to him.

The scene I am witnessing reminds me of being back at Sherborne School, Dorset, in the summer of 1956. Some twenty of us, in our early teens, are being confirmed that day. We are kneeling at the altar rail in the School Chapel, while the Bishop of Exeter, clad in his episcopal robes, moves along the row intoning 'Bless, Oh Lord, this Thy child and this Thy Child with Thy heavenly grace that he may daily continue more and more, until he come to Thy everlasting kingdom,'

I groaned inwardly. Am I really going to swear allegiance to the great Khan? Wasn't I committed elsewhere?

When it was my turn, I took the cup from the shaman with both hands. That's the good thing about amphoras. They have two nice handles either side of the neck. Easy to grab. I looked deep into the cup. Raised it. Sniffed. Fermented rice wine, eh? Better than sheep's blood, surely. To drink or not to drink. That was the question.

I raised the cup to my lips, then I handed it back.

I don't think the shaman was fooled. I had taken the cup, but I had not drunk from it. He knew that. He had eyes to see, and ears to hear. He was disappointed for sure, but he was not going to make trouble. Not then anyway. Mongolia's Darkhads have been fighting for Genghis Khan for almost 800 years. They'll fight again if they need to.

The crowd dispersed after the Sheep Offering Ceremony was over. Pete the Camera said he had found a perfect spot for me to do another PTC.

'Why don't you stand near that amazing statue of Genghis Khan on his horse, looking at the Triumphal arch in front of you and the distant Tibetan plateau?'

We followed him out of the Main Palace down the wide stone path – the Sacred Way – towards a circular enclosure in the middle of which stood the largest plinth I have ever seen. On top of that plinth, an equestrian statue of Genghis Khan has been placed. It was, literally, gargantuan. The horse is rearing with his left front hoof high off the ground. Champing at the bit. Genghis himself wears a look of fierce determination. There are still worlds out there, waiting to be conquered.

While Pete sets up the camera, Nadia holds an umbrella up to give us a bit of shade.

'What the hell am I going to say?' I ask her. 'I already said what I wanted to say about Genghis Khan. PTCs are meant to be special, aren't they? You can't just waffle on.'

'I'm sure **you** can' Nadia says. I think she means it as a compliment.

Max has gone off for lunch with the Darkhads. Mutton on the menu, no doubt. Home-killed, home-cooked.

'I'm sorry Max isn't here to do this one' I say. 'He was brilliant when we were on that film set. Rattling away in Chinese.'

'Mandarin' Nadia corrects me.

'Whatever. I'm glad he's doing some of the PTCs now. He's much better at this than I am.'

Nadia is unfailingly polite. 'Yes, he is' she agrees.

Pete the Camera signals that he is ready. Nadia puts the umbrella away and we walk over. I have an idea.

'Look at that, Nadia' I say.

'Look at what?'

I point at the statue. 'See the way Genghis has his foot in that stirrup. Did you know the Mongols invented the stirrup? That's how the Golden Horde conquered Eurasia. Marco Polo describes it brilliantly, how the Mongols pretend to flee, encouraging the enemy to pursue them. But the enemy only has axes and lances whereas the Mongols have bows and arrows. Using the stirrups to control their mounts, the Mongols are able to swing 180 degrees around, and actually fire backwards at the enemy while they are galloping in the opposite direction. That's how they won battle after battle. Of course, they were supreme horsemen anyway, with amazing horses, too but having the stirrup was crucial.'

'Are guys ready' Pete asked. 'You know what you want to talk about?'

'How to change the course of history' I replied.

Pete grinned. I could see a joke coming.

'How many steppes did Genghis Khan conquer?' he asked.

I didn't want to let him down. 'Well, thirty-nine, I guess. According to John Buchan anyway.'

38

Mongolian Steppe Cowboys

Tianjin Airlines 'magic carpet' services came in handy one last time, whisking us painlessly between Baotou Donghe Airport and Xilingol. Google maps told us that it would take 10 hours 41 minutes to cover the 850 km to Xilingol by road.

At dinner in the hotel in Xilingol League that evening, Dandan explained that next day we would be out on the steppe meeting a young Mongolian farming couple.

'Their names are Saratoga and Chogbadrhe. They took over the farm from Saratoga's parents a few years back and they've made some important changes, while preserving the traditional elements of Mongolian rural life.'

Breakfast was already waiting for us when we arrived at the farm next morning.

'It's going to take us all day to get through this,' Max contemplated the groaning board.

We made a good start, anyway.

While we ate, Sarutougga told us her story. She said she had left the family farm to go to university, where she met her husband Chogbadrhe. But the desire to return home proved irresistible.

'We Mongolians' Saratoga said 'have been herding animals for generations. So no matter where we go, we always want to return to our roots to be near our animals. It's a deeply rooted desire. We all want to go back home to graze our herds, like our ancestors have done for centuries. I lived here when I was very young so I'm very close to the livestock.

'My family owns more than 300 hectares of pasture, and we lease another 300. So we have now 600 hectares in total. We have 53 cows, more than 200 sheep and more than 60 horses.'

After breakfast, Saratoga took us out and showed the dairy, proudly demonstrating new cheesemaking technology. It all looked super clean and efficient. A far cry from our early days on Exmoor when my mother would try to make clotted cream by scalding pans of milk on the Rayburn.

'Blessed are the cheesemakers' I murmured.

After that, they show us round the outbuildings. Pete lines up the camera. Time for a PTC. I stand there with half of Mongolia, dotted with horses and cows, stretched out behind me.

I've been totally impressed by this splendid Mongolian couple: who they are, what they're doing. 'They have brought ingenuity and enterprise here in a big way,' I begin. 'Now they're even using drones to monitor the sheep and cattle, find lost horses. They're using modern technology to prepare and sell their products. Try tasting the cheese they make! This has been a revelation in so many ways.'

I turned to Saratoga and Chogbadrhe when I finished the PTC. 'Please can Max and I have a go on your motorbikes?'

You don't have to kickstart these modern motorbikes, not like my old BSA Shooting Star. Nowadays, you just turn the key.

Moments later, before anyone could raise some footling objection (helmets, insurance, driving licences?) Max and I roared off on the bikes into the vastness of the Mongolian steppe. One of the farm dogs ran after us but otherwise we were on our own. Short of jumping on a horse, no one could catch us up anyway. We had commandeered all the available transport! Total bliss. Brought back so many memories.

39

Mongolian Wrestling

Monday, June 12, 2023. We are 20 miles or so from Xilingol in Inner Mongolia. It is a clear sunny morning. A few weeks earlier the summits of the distant hills might have been capped with snow but now, in early June, the snow has disappeared.

Inside the yurt or 'ger' which is what the Mongolians call their traditional felt tents, it is still quite chilly. I am half-sitting, half-lying sitting on a pile of embroidered cushions, with a blanket over my legs.

Gazing out through the open doorway, I can see a herd of white horses in the middle distance, a hundred or more of them. They gallop full tilt in one direction, then they wheel right-handed to gallop up the hill before turning again and yet again to get back to their starting point.

As far as I can see, nobody has asked them to gallop around like this as though their lives depended on it. These are wild horses – there are hundreds of thousands of them in Mongolia. Galloping is what they do whenever the mood takes them. With horses like these, no wonder the Mongols conquered the world.

If horsemanship is a national obsession, so is wrestling. This is the morning when Max is scheduled to meet one of the local champions on his home pitch.

I knew Max had done a bit of karate or taekwondo during his time in Asia. But, as I understood it, Mongolian wrestling was a different kettle of fish. There is only one round, and it lasts as long as it takes for one man to win, and the other man to lose. You aren't allowed to touch the ground with anything except your foot. If your opponent throws you, or if you trip and fall, that's it. You've lost.

There's another important rule. You can't touch your opponent's legs with your hands.

When we arrived at the appointed RV, I was whisked off to one yurt or 'ger' to use the Mongolian term, while Max was taken to another. I felt strangely conflicted. I have never doubted Max's ability to escape unscathed from tricky situations, but this one had me worried.

I hoped Max's opponent had been fully briefed. This was not going to be a proper bout of Mongolian wrestling. Not a 'practice bout' either. Not even a training session. It was just meant to be a quick run-through of some of the key moves.

Dandan popped her head inside the yurt. 'Everything okay?' she asked. 'Max is just getting ready.'

'I hope the other fellow, whoever he is, doesn't give Max a hard time.'

'The other fellow, Yuandeng, is the local wrestling champion' Dandan laughed. 'But don't worry, he will have been fully briefed.'

She didn't have time to say more, since I could see Max – tall and handsome – emerge from the open doorway of his own yurt, like Achilles emerging from his tent outside the walls of Troy. He was bare-chested, but an embroidered cape covered his back and shoulders. This was the zodog. The reason the front is cut away leaving the wrestler's chest exposed is that – according to legend – on one occasion a wrestler defeated all other combatants, then ripped open the chest-covering to reveal her breasts, showing to all that she was a woman. From that day, the zodog had to reveal the wrestler's chest.

At that moment, Yuandeng emerged from a nearby yurt. He too had stripped to the waist and wore the zodog leaving the chest exposed, He also wore some brilliantly coloured pantaloons.

My sense of unease grew. Yuandeng looked like a seriously tough nut. He started flexing his muscles as though he was looking to win.

I went outside too, waiting for the umpire to start the bout. I did a bit of boxing myself, years ago, at prep school. There's always that dreaded moment when the referee shouts 'Seconds out! Time!' And the bell pings.

But it wasn't like that. There wasn't a proper ring, like they have in boxing matches. Max and Yuandeng simply walked away from the yurts to an area of open grass, where they stood facing each other, about two metres apart. The spectators spread themselves around in a wide circle.

While we waited, I had a nagging sense of unease. Had the message got through? Did tough-looking Yuandeng, who now confronted Max across the grass circle, realize that this was just meant to be a gentle tutorial not an actual contest?

Since the film team still wasn't ready, I dashed back into my yurt to get my own camera.

I shall always regret that decision. I thought I was quick as a flash but, by the time I returned camera in hand, Max was picking himself off the floor and the match was over.

I had missed the key moment.

Max was massaging his left hand with his right. He was clearly in some pain.

'The chap threw me to the ground three times in about 30 seconds.' Max snorted. 'The first time I dislocated my finger, but I snapped it back into place there and then. Then he threw me again. A couple of times. I don't think he quite got the message about this not being the real thing.'

Max was whisked off to the local hospital and returned with a splint on his left hand. It turned out that he had fractured not one but two fingers.

He had to keep that splint on for the rest of our trip. I still don't understand how he managed with the chopsticks.

40

Mongolian Bows and Arrows

If our last morning in Inner Mongolia had been devoted to wrestling, our last afternoon was devoted to archery.

Dandan has lined up a top-quality instructor, a young woman called Nangsil. She wears an embroidered apron, with gloves and a blue tunic top. Her hair is in a bun.

'This is Nangsil, an archery teacher.' Dandan says 'I am sure she will be happy to answer your questions.'

'We are following Marco Polo route across China.' I began 'Marco Polo gives a wonderful description of how the Mongol horsemen could turn completely round while they're galloping away from the enemy, then fire backwards at the pursuing enemy. Apparently, they could shoot an arrow two hundred metres or more and still hit the target.'

Max chipped in with a question: 'Can *you* do that too? Can you use your bow when you're riding a horse.'

Nangsil replied: 'Of course I can shoot while riding a horse. Lots of us can. Unlike archery when you're standing, when you're on horseback you need to tense your entire body. You must be agile and controlled at the same time.'

She has brought her bow with her.

Nangsil's assistants set up a target on the steppe, then and there. I didn't measure the distance precisely, but I'm sure it was over hundred metres.

Effortlessly drawing back the bow, Nangsil aimed and fired. Bullseye! She fired again. Another bullseye!

One of her assistants scooted ran off to pluck the arrows from the target, then ran back to hand them to Nangsil.

She turned to Max. 'Do you want to have a go?'

Max shook his head. He had a splint on his hand. This wasn't the moment. Thanks, but no thanks.

Nangsil put her bow back in its case. Pete replaced the lens cap on the camera. Dandan wandered off. Stumps were about to be drawn on this one.

I was a bit put out.

'Hold on a moment' I said. 'I wouldn't mind having a go myself.'

As I spoke, my mind flipped back to Sports Days at my Devon prep school. Apart from the long jump and the high jump, the relay races and the sprints which everyone took part in, there had also been an archery competition. I'd enjoyed that.

'Are you right-handed or left-handed?' Nangsil asked, handing me her bow.

'Right-handed'

'Stand up, stand straight' Nangsil instructed. 'Point your left shoulder at the target.'

Nangsil made it look simple. But it wasn't. Not for me anyway.

The English longbow is made from the wood of a yew-tree. (That's why they always planted yews in English churchyards, to be sure there was a good supply of yew for their longbows, even if the trees were cut down elsewhere). But the Mongolian bow – shorter than the English longbow – is a composite, made from wood, sinew and bone, and fixed with a super-adhesive. It's not as supple as yew. You've got to put real muscle – back and shoulder – into it. As with any bow, if you want to get maximum power, you must draw the string right back, till the tip of the arrow is almost level with the front of the bow. That takes some effort, and all the while you are trying to keep the arrow pointing in the right direction.

'Remember the wind' Nangsil instructed. 'Aim off for the wind.'

Max called the shots.

'Nine o'clock left and wide!', he shouted, as I fired the first arrow. 'High and wide!' on the second. 'Twelve o'clock high!' for the third.

My last effort fell feebly to the ground well short of the target. Max didn't need to call that one.

In Marco Polo's Day, your typical Mongolian archer could fire 12 arrows a minute. It had taken me two minutes to fire six arrows. And I was feeling the strain.

A posse set off to look for the missing arrows in the thick grass. I handed the bow back to Nangsil.

'Six shots' I apologized 'and every one of them missed the target.'

Ellen, Dandan's deputy, who had been acting brilliantly as an interpreter throughout the session, passed on my apologies to Nangsil. I couldn't help feeling I'd let the side down.

Nangsil said something, smiled and shook my hand. Ellen explained.

'She says it is not easy to pull the bow. You did well.'

It was a nice compliment, but still all my shots had missed.

In the car, as we drove back to base, Owen came through on the RT.

'You guys want to offer a quick comment for the tape?' Owen asked.

I looked at Max. He had his eyes shut. His hand was giving him trouble.

'I'll take this one, Owen' I said.

I thought for a moment. The search party had come back from the steppe with five, not six arrows. Henry Wadsworth Longfellow's famous lines seemed quite appropriate.

"*I shot an arrow in the air*" I said, "*it fell to earth I know not where*".

'That will do splendidly' Owen said.

41

Xanadu I – 'In Xanadu did Kubla Khan'

We all got up early on the morning of June 14, 2023. It would take 30 minutes to drive from our hotel to Shangdu, the Summer Capital of the Yuan Dynasty.

The title of Leonard Woolf's autobiography is 'The journey, not the arrival, matters.' I'm not so sure. For me, the arrival, i.e. actually reaching Xanadu, was a defining moment, as indeed it had been for Marco Polo.

I had my battered copy of Marco Polo's *'The Travels'* with me in the car. The on-board cameras were primed and ready to go. Feeling like a Detective Inspector interviewing a suspect in one of those TV dramas, I looked at the camera and said: 'Recording now. It is 0800 hours on Wednesday, June 14, 2023. After travelling almost 5000 km from our starting point in the Himalayas, we are finally approaching Xanadu.

'In 1275 Marco Polo, his uncle Niccolò, and father Matteo, were themselves nearing Xanadu at the end of a four-year journey from Venice in Italy. This is how Marco Polo described their approach to the city of Great Khan.'

I had put a yellow sticker to mark the page, so now I turned quickly to Marco Polo's book and read aloud from it.

'When the traveller sets out from the city I have just told you about and journeys for the three days, he comes to a city called Shangdu that was built by the Great Khan who now reigns, whose name is Khubilai Khan … When the great Khan heard that Messer Niccolò and Messer Maffeo were approaching, he sent his couriers no less than the distance of

a 40 day journey to meet them.'

I put the book down and gazed out of the car window. We were still in Inner Mongolia. The endless grass steppes stretched out on all sides. How happy the Polos must have been, I thought, to have met those couriers and to know that they were within striking distance of their destination.

Mimi, on duty as director, came through on the RT.

'Can Max perhaps read out the bit about the Polos' actual arrival in Shangdu or Xanadu?'

Max needed no urging. Marco Polo's account of their arrival is vivid and full of action. Max did it justice.

"When Messer Niccolò, Messer Matteo and Marco arrived at this great city they went to the chief palace, where they found the Great Khan and a tremendous assembly of barons. They knelt before him and made obeisance with the utmost humility. The Great Khan told them to rise and received them courteously, with great celebrations and festivities in their honour. And he asked many questions about their circumstances and how they had fared since their departure. The two brothers replied that things had turned out very well, seeing that they found him healthy and flourishing. Then they presented the privileges and letters that the Pope had sent, which greatly pleased him. Next, they handed him the holy oil, which he received with joy and prized very highly."

'Marvellous. Totally marvellous.' I said, listening with my eyes shut. 'How does it go on?'

Max continued: *'When the Great Khan saw Marco, who was a mere stripling, he asked who he was.*

'Sire' said Messer Niccolò 'he is my son, and your servant, I have brought at great risk and trouble upon those faraway lands, to present him to you as your slave.'

'He is welcome' said the Great Khan and he held him in great favour and had his name inscribed alongside those of the other honoured members of his household, because of which he was greatly esteemed and valued by everyone at court.

"But why make a long story of it? You may depend upon it that the Great Khan and his whole court welcomed the envoys with tremendous revelry and festivities. And they were very well served and attended in every regard. They stayed at court and had a place of honour above the other barons."

Fifteen minutes later we had arrived at our destination. We pulled into the parking area on the south side of the palace grounds. I looked at my watch. It was 8.10 a.m.

As requested, the Polos had brought oil from the Holy Sepulchre in Jerusalem, though they hadn't managed to corral the 'one hundred Christian priests' the Great Khan had asked for. I had long ago decided that, if we ever did get to Xanadu, I would pay my own a special tribute. And I knew precisely what I wanted to do.

We were scheduled to interview one of China's top archaeologists at 8.30 a.m. The timing would be tight, but I reckoned I could do it.

We climbed up to the stone cairn which marked the very centre of the area where the Imperial Palace had once stood.

I said to Mimi. 'I need a few moments to do a Piece to Camera.'

'Please keep it short,' Mimi said. 'We've not got a lot of time.'

At precisely 8.20 that morning, as the camera rolled, I launched on an unscripted but heart-felt oration.

'We are here today,' I began, 'in one of the world's most celebrated places. Kubla Khan's Palace in Xanadu, where we now stand, is as famous as Delphi in Greece or Machu Picchu in Peru. It is as famous as the Table Mountain in Cape Town, South Africa, or Uluru – once known as Ayers Rock – in Australia.

'And why is it so famous?' I went on. 'One reason is that over two hundred years ago, a man wrote and published one of the greatest poems in the English language. That man was Samuel Taylor Coleridge. And the poem was called Kubla Khan.'

I knew the poem by heart. I had learnt it at prep-school and could still remember it word for word 70 years later. So, I began to recite it then and there.

'In Xanadu did Kubla Khan
A stately pleasure-dome decree:
Where Alph, the sacred river, ran.
Through caverns measureless to man
Down to a sunless sea.'

I paused. I couldn't help noticing that Dandan, off to one side, was checking her watch. I'll give it one more verse anyway, I thought.

'So twice five miles of fertile ground
With walls and towers were girdled round;
And there were gardens bright with sinuous rills,
Where blossomed many an incense-bearing tree;
And here were forests ancient as the hills,
Enfolding sunny spots of greenery …'

I would have gone on. I could have gone on. The 'deep romantic chasm' still lay ahead of me. The 'damsel with a dulcimer' had not yet manifested herself. But Dandan was now making 'please wrap it up signs' quite urgently.

So, I wrapped it up then and there. 'Sunny spots of greenery' seemed like a good note to end on.

Although I had not recited the whole poem, I was pleased to have been able to pay a fulsome tribute that morning in Xanadu to Samuel Taylor Coleridge. I hoped I had made clear that the world owes a great deal to Coleridge and his brilliant, amazing poem about Xanadu and Kubla Khan.

But just how much I wondered did Coleridge himself owe to Marco Polo?

Coleridge famously claimed that he had dreamt the entirety of the poem, not just the 'fragment' he published. In his own notes he explains that he had been staying in a farmhouse on Exmoor, close to where I live. He had gone for a long walk and then fallen into a deep sleep.

He goes on to say that, as soon as he woke up from that deep sleep, he started writing down the 'vision' which had come to him in his dreams.

Referring to himself in the third person, he describes in detail what happened:

'At this moment he was unfortunately called out by a person on business from Porlock, and detained by him above an hour, and on his return to his room, found, to his no small surprise and mortification, that though he still retained some vague and dim recollection of the general purport of the vision, yet, with the exception of some eight or ten scattered lines and images, all the rest had passed away like the images on the surface of a stream into which a stone has been cast, but, alas! without the after restoration of the latter!'

Coleridge, as can be seen from the above quotation, begins to write down the images that have come to him in his dream or 'vision,' but he is interrupted by 'a person on business from Porlock.' On returning to his desk, he finds that he cannot complete the task of recapturing the 'vision' on which he had embarked before being disturbed.

How convenient it would be if Coleridge had added to his own account of this strange event an admission that he had, for example, gone to bed that night with the 'Travels of Marco Polo' in hand and that he had still been reading that book, as he fell into a drug-induced sleep. Alas, we have no such record.

Did Coleridge ever read Marco Polo's *Travels*? There is no hard evidence one way or another. Coleridge was a voracious reader and Marco Polo's book in various translations was widely available at the time. But there is no evidence that Coleridge read or possessed the book.

My farm is on Exmoor. Living as I do just a few miles from the place where Coleridge was staying when he wrote Kubla Khan, I have often wondered who this 'person from Porlock' was. Did he or she ever learn what an important part they played in the history of English literature? Do that 'person's' descendants, if any, still live in the area?

If they do, I would like to meet them.

42

Xanadu II – The Summer Palace

Wherever Max and I went in China, Dandan and her team aimed to make sure that we were properly briefed. Archery, wrestling, noodle-making, winemaking, Buddhist caves, how to cross fast-flowing rivers – Dandan and our wonderful Chinese colleagues managed to produce experts on all these subjects and more.

These experts were usually men and women at the top of their profession. In Xanadu that morning, for example, Dandan had arranged for us to meet one of China's top archaeologists: Wei Jian, Director of the Institute of Frontier Archaeology, Central University for Nationalities.

Wei Jan had arrived while I was still orating about Coleridge and Xanadu.

'I apologize profusely for keeping you waiting' I said.

'I enjoyed the poem' Wei Jan replied. 'You were right. It has echoed around the world.'

Max and I introduced ourselves properly. 'This was a big moment for Marco Polo' I said. 'It is for us too.

We Jian bowed. 'Delighted to welcome you.'

We walked over to the viewing platform.

Max and I stand beside Director Wei, looking out at the sweep of Mongolian grasslands and the grass-covered legacy of one of the most powerful dynasties the world has ever known.

Wei Jian's arm swings in a great arc across the steppe. 'From here Kubla Khan's conquering warriors extended the reach of the Yuan Dynasty right across northern Asia.' he tells us.

I can almost hear the thunder of Mongol hooves as he speaks. I can almost see the gates of the Imperial City swinging open as fearsome Mongol warriors burst forth on their mounts to conquer new worlds.

Wei Jan has been working at Shangdu for more than 30 years. He knows the place like the back of his hand. As we stand there, he points out the precise north-south orientation of the city. Xihua Gate to the West. Donghua Gate to the East. Mingde Gate to the South with the Muging Pavilion to the North.

'The site of the city' Wei Jan tells us 'was carefully chosen by Kubla Khan's most powerful adviser, Liu Bingzhong. He was familiar with Confucianism, Taoism and Buddhism. He chose this beautiful location. It was a rich grassland with a river flowing through it so when Ministers and Kings from distant lands came to visit, there was good quality grazing and water for the animals.'

Max and I listen enthralled.

'Beijing was built later', Wei Jan explains.

Once again, so we learn, the Great Khan's advisor, Liu Bingzhong, was the key figure. Having a Southern Capital in Beijing as well as a Northern capital in Shangdu, Wei Jian told us, helped unify the vast Yuan empire under one man's leadership.

'Kubla Khan visited every summer' Wei Jan continued. 'People from the Mongolian grasslands, foreign envoys, government officials all travelled here. There would have been yurts stretching as far as the eye could see. It would have been a vibrant and bustling place.'

Max asked: 'How many people would have lived here in Shangdu?'

'The total population of Shangdu and the surrounding area was around 120,000,' Wei Jian replied.

120,000! During the 13th century London had a population of around 80,000, so Shangdu was half as large again.

'This is a place which had a short but very exciting history' Wei Jian says. 'It was built and destroyed in little more than a century.'

I still have Marco Polo's book in my hand. While Wei is talking, I skim through some of the key passages. I know this is a crucial interview. There are still people out there who don't believe Marco Polo came to Xanadu or saw the great Khan and the Imperial Palace. There are people who don't believe Marco Polo ever came to China to all! You could call them 'Marco Polo deniers' like 'climate-change deniers!

This was a good time, I thought, to get a truly authoritative view.

'As I see it, Director Wei' I said, 'the issue which confronts us is quite simple. Is Marco Polo telling the truth? Does he describe what he has seen or is he just inventing it?

'I don't want to waste time today' I continue, 'I think it's important to look at Marco Polo's exact words. Let's look at this first passage in his book.'

I read out, slowly and clearly, the passages where Marco Polo's describes the Great Khan's Palace, what Coleridge called the 'stately pleasure dome':

"And in this city Khubilai Khan had a vast palace built of marble and other ornamental stones. Its halls and rooms are covered with gilded images of birds and animals, trees and flowers and many other things, so skilfully and ingeniously worked that it is the light and wonder to see. The whole building is richly decorated and quite astonishingly beautiful. It extends from the centre of the city to the city wall, round to join the other side, enclosing a good sixteen miles of land replete with springs, rivers and lawns. Here, facing the palace, another wall runs out from one side of the palace abutting the city walls and goes such a way that the park can only be entered by going through the palace."

Dandan's tireless deputy, Ellen, acted as 'interpreter' as I read. It must have been challenging work, but she did it brilliantly. I could see Wei Jian nodding from time to time. He was obviously familiar with Marco Polo's work.

'Is that all?' Ellen asked me, when she had finished.

'Just one bit more' I replied. 'There's a wonderful description of the Cane Palace too.'

I read out that one last paragraph. *'You should also know in the middle of this walled park, where there is a beautiful grove, the Great Khan has built another large palace, instructed entirely of canes but all gilt inside and decorated with exquisitely worked images of beasts and birds ... The great Khan stays here but three months of the year, in June, July and August. He stays here during this season to escape from the heat and to enjoy its delights. During these three months the Great Khan keeps the Palace of Canes standing; the rest of the year it is dismantled and stored. And he had it designed so that he could erect and dismantle it at pleasure.'*

I put the book down.

'Honourable Director' I continued. 'As you can see, we are extremely interested in Marco Polo's own description of the Imperial Palace. Take the passages I have just read. Do you think Marco Polo is a good historical source? Can we believe what he says? Are there other contemporary sources which might confirm what he says?'

Wei Jian is a scholar of international renown. I don't expect him to rush to judgement.

He points out that only major events, truly important events, were recorded in China's historical documents. As an example, he cites the last Mongol Emperor Toghun Temur's 'Lament' which chronicled the end of the Mongol Empire.

'Minor and trivial events' he says, 'were rarely recorded.'

I felt a bit disappointed. If there are no contemporary descriptions of the Imperial Palace it might be hard to corroborate Marco Polo's observations. Without such evidence, how could we be sure that Marco Polo wasn't just giving full rein to his imagination, rather than recounting something he had witnessed at first hand?

It was Max who pulled the chestnuts out of the fire. Max realized that it was not just written historical evidence, like contemporary chronicles, we had to look at. The archaeological evidence could be crucial too. And if anyone was qualified to talk on that subject, that person was the Director of Archaeology, Wei Xian.

Max asked the key question in clear straightforward terms.

'Director Wei, please can you tell us' he said, 'whether you have found any direct archaeological evidence which might corroborate Marco Polo's account of the Imperial Palace?'

I can remember now how tense we felt waiting for Professor Wei Xian's reply. This could be the decisive moment.

Ellen asked Max to repeat his question. She wanted to be sure she got it right.

Wei Jian took his time replying but his answer, when it came, was unambiguous.

'I had to study Marco Polo's travel notes in order to solve many of Xanadu's archaeological mysteries.'

He goes on to say that he has been leading a team of archaeologists investigating the ruins near Zhenglan (which is where we are) in Inner Mongolia since 1992. He has absolutely no doubt that Marco Polo came to Shangdu/Xanadu.

And then comes the clincher. 'Everything Marco Polo described, we have found.'

I have been listening closely to the conversation. I want to be sure about what I think I heard.

I ask Ellen. Did the director just say, *'everything Marco Polo described, we have found.'*

'That is what he said', Ellen confirmed.

I turned to Max and said: *'You shot an arrow through the air./I think you scored a bull's-eye there!'*

Back in my hotel-room that evening, while Max and the crew went off for a meal, I fired up my laptop.

People say you can't use Google in China. I'm not sure whether I was using Google or some other search engine, but I never had any difficulty looking things up on the Internet, all the time we were there. I suppose it depends on what you're looking for.

There was one line of thought I wanted to pursue. I remembered Director Wei had mentioned Mongol Emperor Toghun Temur's 'Lament' about the end of the Mongol Empire: viz when the Mings took over in 1368. So that would have been written only a few years after Marco Polo himself left China. In other words, it was a contemporary account, give or take a decade or two. Worth looking at, surely.

That evening, with a couple of bottles of Yuan beer to keep me going, I embarked on a little 'quest within a quest.'

I 'googled' Toghun Temur to discover that his 'Lament' refers not only to the capture of his 'cool and pleasant' Kaiping/Xanadu but also to the loss of his 'dear' Dadu/Bejing as well. The Southern Capital, as well as the Northern Capital. A Tale of Two Cities, indeed.

I delved further and found the full text of Toghun Temur's poem.

I was stunned by the quality of the poetry. It was poignant, evocative, lyrical. Samuel Taylor Coleridge: Eat your heart out!

Toghum Temur begins by referring to all the bad things that have happened in the year of the Bald Red Rabbit, the year when the Mongol or Yuan dynasty lost out to the Mings or, as he puts it, 'China.'

'My Daidu, straight and wonderfully made of various jewels of different kinds

My Yellow Steppe of Xanadu, the summer residence of ancient Khans.
My cool and pleasant Kaiping Xanadu
My dear Daidu that I've lost on the year of the bald red rabbit.'

At that moment I got a message on my i-phone from Max: 'How are you getting on? Do you want to join us?'

I sent a message back. 'I think I am onto something. May join you later.'

I read the rest of The Lament. In literary terms, it was superb. But I was not looking for poetry at that moment but rather for some solid nugget of evidence that might prove that Marco Polo had 'been there, seen that!'

It wasn't until I reached the last lines of Toghun Temur's Lament that I found what I was looking for.

The Cane Palace had been established in sanctity
Kublai the Wise Khan spent his summers there!
I have lost Kaiping Xanadu entirely – to China.
An impure bad name has come upon the Sage Khan.
They besieged and took precious Daidu
I have lost the whole of it – to China.
A conflicting bad name has come upon the Sage Khan.
Jewel Daidu was built with many an adornment
In Kaiping Xanadu, I spent the summers in peaceful relaxation
By a hapless error they have been lost – to China.

What caught my eye was not the repeated reference to 'China' which was obviously a shorthand for 'Mings and things', but the specific mention of the 'Cane Palace.'

Only that morning, I had read out loud to Wei Jian Marco Polo's own description of the Cane Palace. I checked the text. There it was: *'You should also know in the middle of this walled park, where there is a beautiful grove, the Great Khan has built another large palace, instructed entirely of canes but all gilt inside and decorated with exquisitely worked images of beasts and birds …'*

Marco Polio in fact goes on to say much more about the Cane Palace than I had read out that morning. He talks about how during the construction the canes were sliced, and made into tiles, and how the Great Khan would spend just three months – June, July and August – in the summer Capital and then the Cane Palace would be dismantled and stored until the next season.

As far as I was concerned, it was a slam-dunk! Given this reference in The Lament (c. 1369), it was perfectly obvious to me at least that the Cane Palace was not just one figment among many of Marco Polo's fertile imagination. Add that to Director's Wei's clear statement that morning about the archaeological evidence – *'I had to study Marco Polo's travel notes in order to solve many of Xanadu's archaeological mysteries'* – we were surely home and dry. Marco Polo *did* come to China, and he *did* see the Palace of the great Khan. Case closed.

I sent Max another message. '*I fired an arrow after you/I think I scored a Bullseye too!*'

43

Highway 66 and the Grass Skyline Drive

In his book Marco Polo says: 'Every year, on the twenty-eighth of August, the Great Khan leaves this city and this palace' to return to Beijing (or Dadu as Beijing was then known.)

Marco Polo also explains why this particular day was chosen. 'In the past', he says, the 'Horiat people helped the Great Khan win a great victory'. To commemorate that victory, the Great Khan had to head for the steppes every year to 'douse the air and the ground with the milk of 10,000 white mares … And so the Great Khan departs with this place in order to perform the sacrifice of milk with his own hands.'

Most historians believe that the Polos, having acquired 'a place of honour above the other barons,' would have been reluctant to jeopardize that status. So far from lingering in Xanadu, they would have continued their epic journey that very year in the company of the Emperor, leaving Xanadu for Dadu when the Great Khan himself left at the end of August to return to the 'other' capital.

That said, Marco Polo does not clarify this point in his text, one way or another. Nor does he indicate the precise route they took from Xanadu to Beijing.

There were four well-trodden routes Beijing and Xanadu during the Yuan Dynasty: two post roads and two Royal Chariot roads. Communications between the two capitals were impressively quick. Marco Polo says that runners could cover a journey which would normally take ten days in just a day and a night.

Dandan briefed us on our last evening in Inner Mongolia.

'You guys are in luck she said. 'Tomorrow, we're going to take the Royal Route to the Juyong Pass. That means we'll be travelling on Highway 66. You'll enjoy that. It's like Route 66 in the United States. A destination in its own right.'

The next day, for once, we didn't have an early start, so I brought the laptop down to breakfast. Max, being far more adept at these things that I am, hit the keys.

The Beijing Tourism office website in splendidly purple prose described Highway 66: as 'one of the ten most beautiful highways in Chinese Mainland … Along the Road, wild poppies, alfalfa, potato flowers, sunflowers and rape flowers, all kinds of colour flowers dot on the grassland all over the mountains, swaying with the wind, as if in a fairy tale.

'Wind turbines, commonly known as windmills, stand tall and scatter along the sky, occupying the entire line of sight. White windmills, blue sky and white clouds, as well as green grassland complement each other, forming one of the most classic sceneries of Highway 66.'

Highway 66 certainly lived up to its billing. Our route that day wound through lush forests and skirted rich wetlands. This is where the Khans hunted wildfowl and imperial families escaped the stifling summer heat of Dadu.

Mid-afternoon, we stopped at a vantage point. The grasslands stretched in every direction as far as the eye could see.

'Funny thing, isn't it? I said to Max. 'Every open space, every hilltop, every mountain, seems to have a wind turbine on it. Nowadays, if I see a hill without a wind turbine on top of it, I'm beginning to feel something's missing.'

'We could put a couple of wind turbines on the farm down on Exmoor' Max suggested.

'That's a thought' I said.

The Grass Skyline Drive, forming part of Highway 66, ends at the Chongli Ski Area, site of the 2022 Winter Olympics.

'God knows how they managed to host the games,' I said, 'given that Covid was still raging.'

'God knows how they managed without real snow' Max said.

We drove on through the mountains, hemmed in by rocks and cliffs on both sides of the road. There was only one way Marco Polo could have reached Beijing and that was precisely the way we were going now – through the fearsome Juyong Pass.

44

The Great Wall: Juyong Pass

In the hierarchy of Great Wall structures, the Pass comes at the very top. Passes were major strongholds along the Wall. They were usually located at key positions such as the intersections with trade routes.

There are only thirteen Passes along the Great Wall of China. Max and I had already visited one of the most important: the Jiahu Pass which guards the entrance the Hexi Corridor. Another key Pass is Juyong Pass, 50 klm from central Beijing, which enjoys the title of 'The Toughest Impregnable Pass under Heaven.'

Juyong Pass is the last Pass through the mountains which Marco Polo would have taken before he reached Beijing. The Great Wall jinks from crest to crest, from watchtower to watchtower, from beacon to beacon. The Wall served not only as a barrier against invading tribes; it was also a brilliant means of communication, with messages being flashed from height to height almost instantaneously.

Passes always had gateways. Juyong Pass's gateway, known as the Cloud Platform, is one of the most impressive gateways of the Great Wall.

Prof Zhang Fan from the Department of History at Peking University welcomed Max and me mid-morning in front of the Cloud Platform on June 16.

The marble edifice, edged with intricate Buddhist and other religious carvings, was – he explained – once topped by three pagodas. Though the bulk of the Great Wall as we see it today was built under the Ming Dynasty, which succeeded the Yuan dynasty, the Cloud Platform itself dates from the Yuan or Mongol era. Marco Polo, travelling in Central Asia when the Mongol era was at its peak, would certainly have passed through it on its way on his way to Beijing-Dadu.

Professor Zhang pointed to the carvings on the wall. 'The various scripts we see here were used by Buddhists. But there are also symbols relating to other religions like Islam and Christianity. The Yuan Dynasty was a very culturally open and inclusive.'

Others on the Silk Road with their mix of cultures, religions and ethnicities contributed to this open mindset. Under Mongolian rule, the region became much more accessible to the world although some links with the outside world already existed.

The inner roof of the arch is covered with mandala patterns and Buddha images surrounded by flowers, all fine examples of Yuan Dynasty craftsmanship, the Professor added.

'The Mongolians defeated many other regimes' he said, 'which made travelling between China and Europe easier. That's the time when Marco Polo came to China from Europe.

'Later on, more Europeans travelled here, and Chinese people went to Europe. Before the Yuan Dynasty, there is no evidence of Chinese people travelling to Europe, so this shows the Yuan Dynasty's influence.'

Not for the first time during this trip, Max and I were struck by the readiness of the experts who briefed us to credit the Yuan Dynasty – and Mongol rule – as one of the key unifying forces which had made travel, like Marco Polo's, possible.

Having put on end to the Yuan Dynasty in 1368, the succeeding Ming Dynasty emperors, understandably enough, were anxious to strengthen their defences against any possible further invasions, whether from the still powerful Mongols or other northern races.

Professor Zhang Fan led Max and me through the central arch of the Cloud Platform. We began to climb the Great Wall. In the distance, high above us on the mountain, I could see the first watchtower. How long would it take us to get up there, I wondered? Half an hour? An hour? Did we have time? I knew we had a tight schedule.

I asked Max what he thought. 'Shall we go for it?'

"Not reach Great Wall, not good man" Matt said, quoting Chairman Mao's famous dictum.

In recent years I have climbed to the summit of Mount Kilimanjaro twice and that's at almost 20,000 ft. I refused to be daunted.

'Let's do it then, Max' I insisted. *'The longest journey begins with a single step!'*

Pete the Camera was not so thrilled by our decision to press on regardless. He knew he would have to walk backwards up the steep steps while filming us.

'Why don't I use the long-focus lens and just film you guys walking back down.' he suggested. 'Makes sense in narrative terms too. Marco Polo is coming down to the gateway, the Cloud Platform, at this point, not climbing uphill away from it.'.

Max and I knew the drill by then. Even on these long-distance shots, you never look at the camera. Even if you don't quite know where the camera is, you have to try not to look at it.

We were, I would say, still two hundred yards from wherever Pete was filming, when I saw the man, walking quickly up the Wall towards us wearing slacks, a lilac-coloured short-sleeved sports-shirt and a peaked cap. His gaze seemed to be fixed on the watchtower, high up on the hill behind us since we were on our way down.

Still concentrating on the view, the man walked past without even looking at us.

'Good grief!' I muttered to Max. 'Do you know who that was?'

Max and I, of course, were the only ones who weren't in on the joke.

'Caught the overnight plane from Dubai. Drove out from Beijing this morning.' Dr Rana said, ten minutes later when we were having a wrap-up photo session on the battlements. 'Arrived this morning. Thought I ought to stop by and see how you all are getting on. Would have said 'hi' when I passed you on the Wall up there, but I could see you are being filmed at that point.'

It was very good to see him. If ever a man made this trip possible, that man was Dr Vishwajeet Rana and GEDU's affiliate:English Path.

I couldn't help remembering that evening – so long ago now ago – when Dr Rana, his wife, Tatiana, and I had been having dinner in the desert under the stars. He had offered his support then. And he had come through with that support. In spades.

Pete, the Camera, came over while I was talking to Dr Rana. 'Shame you and Dr Rana didn't actually talk to each other up there on the Wall. You were miked. We would have picked it up. You could have shaken hands and said something memorable, like when Stanley met Dr Livingstone."

"*Dr Rana, I presume?*" I suggested.

'That would have done nicely' Pete the Camera said.

45

The Marco Polo Bridge

In the course of our long journey, we had come across statues, public squares, plazas, and even teahouses which bore Marco Polo's name. The most famous architectural tribute to Marco Polo in the whole of China is the Marco Polo Bridge on the outskirts of Beijing.

That bridge is famous in its own right, regardless of any connection with Marco Polo. The armed clash between Chinese and Japanese soldiers (known as the Marco Polo Bridge Incident) which took place here in 1937 marked the beginning of the second Sino-Japanese War in 1937 and is now often regarded as the beginning of World War II in Asia.

Marco Polo could not have anticipated or foretold the future. But for him the present was real enough.

Crossing that bridge made an indelible impression on him. He wrote in The Travels: *'ten miles outside the city of Khanbalik, the traveller comes to a large river called the Pulisanghin that flows into the Ocean Sea. Many merchants sail it, carrying large cargoes. This river is spanned by a magnificent stone bridge. In fact, you should know that there are few bridges in the world that compare to it or match it in beauty.'*

Khanbaliq is the Mongol name for Beijing which Marco Polo uses interchangeably with Daidu. The river is the Sanggan, known near Beijing as the Yongding.

Marco Polo goes on to say: *'I assure you that it is no less than 300 paces long and eight wides, for ten horsemen can easily right across it abreast. It has twenty-four arches and piers in the water and is constructed entirely of grey marble, finely worked and well-seated.'*

Marco Polo estimates the bridges the bridge's length as quote 'more than 300 paces long.' This is remarkably accurate given that the measured length of the bridge today is 266 m.

He devotes several paragraphs to the bridge, writing: *'Running along each side is a parapet of marble slabs and columns … The space between the two columns is closed off by a grey marble slab, decorated all over with different sculptures and inset into the columns, to prevent people from falling into the water.'*

When Marco Polo came this way, in early September 1275 (assuming he had left Xanadu with the Great Khan at the end of August that year), the bridge was a relatively new construction. It was built in 1192 at the end of the Song Dynasty, to link Dadu (Beijing) to the Imperial Highway which ran through Xian, Lanzhou, and Xinjiang towards Europe.

And when Marco Polo wrote about 'different sculptures' he was probably referring to the extraordinary collection of carvings which graced the parapets on both sides of the bridge. There were at least 500 of them and most, if not all, represent lions.

Qiao Yajun Deputy Director, Marco Polo Bridge Development Research Centre, was on hand to tell us more.

'Can you tell us a bit about these stone carvings, the lions?' I asked.

'They're all from different eras and have different characteristics' Director Qiao replied. 'For example, the stone lions from the Jin Dynasty are smaller and thinner. In the Ming Dynasty lots of small lions appear. Since then, all the lions' mouths are open, and their tongues are sticking out. The Qing Dynasty lions are not as ferocious-looking, and the carving is more delicate. Their eyes are elongated.'

Traffic on the bridge was banned in 1985 but the tell-tale signs of centuries of use remain. As we walked with us across the bridge, Director Qiao said: 'Look at the ruts in the flagstones. See how they have been grooved by the carts on the bridge.'

Halfway across the bridge, we paused, leaned our arms on the marble balustrade and surveyed the scene on the river.

Our visit had coincided with the annual rowing races. The Marco Polo Bridge was the starting point. Some way downriver, a line of boats marked the finish.

It was all action. Coxes were shouting at crews. Coaches were bellowing instructions through megaphones. It could have been Eights Week in Oxford. A veritable regatta. Marco Polo could have brought his gondola.

Max, who had taken an MBA in Beijing and had afterwards spent several years living and working in the nation's capital, recognized the pennant of his own Alma Mater on one of the boats.

'Come on, Tsinghua!' he shouted.

I'm not sure Tsinghua heard. The crews were already under starter's orders.

The umpire, standing at the stern of official boat, lowered his flag. They were off!

A flotilla of small boats followed the crews. The sound of banging drums, whistling and shouting, faded as the boats, catching the current, moved quickly downstream.

We couldn't stay. We simply didn't have time. That was just the first heat, and the races would go on all morning.

In the car, as we drove into the city, Max said: 'Some years Tsinghua is up against Peking University in the final. That's like Oxford v. Cambridge in the Boat Race. Whoever wins, will be celebrating tonight. That's for sure.'

I looked out of the window. We had passed already crossed the Second Ring-Road. We would be at Tian'anmen Square within minutes. We were within a stone's throw of the Great Khan's Palace.

'We could do some celebrating too' I said. 'We've made it to Beijing at last!'

46

The Forbidden City

In 1215, Genghis Khan sacked the old Jin capital, Zhongdu, which had occupied what is now Beijing's Xicheng District. His grandson, Kubla Khan, founded a new city, next to the old one, called Dadu. When the Polos finally arrived in Beijing, they would have been entering a city which to them must have seemed modern, even futuristic, in contrast to the higgledy-piggledy densely packed mediaeval cities they would have been known in Europe.

Marco Polo wrote: *'the whole city is laid out on a grid; for the main streets are so straight and broad from one end to the other that if anyone climbs on the wall at one gate and looks straight ahead, he can see all the way through to the gate on the opposite side … The whole city inside the walls is laid out in squares, just like a chessboard, and it is so beautiful and so skilfully planned that no description can do it justice.'*

He continues: *'Everyone should know that this Great Khan is the mightiest man, whether in respect of subjects or of territory or of treasure, who is in the world today or who has ever been.'*

I first visited China, as I have mentioned earlier, in the summer of 1975, when Mao Zedong was still President.

Beijing airport was not very busy in those days. The road into town went through largely untouched countryside where local farmers spread their sheafs on the surface of the road and relied on the wheels of bullock carts or passing cars to help separate the wheat from the chaff.

We stayed at the old Peking hotel on Tian'anmen Square (now much upgraded), ate rice and dumplings with chopsticks, studied the Little Red Book and were taken out in the evening night to watch mind-improving operas.

I was travelling at that time with a dozen colleagues from the European Commission in Brussels on a semi-official visit. We wandered around – often on foot – through the alleys, poking our heads into the then still plentiful hutongs, and sometimes managing to evade our watchful guides.

We must have spent three or four days in Beijing on that first trip, before we left for a wider sweep around the country which included both industrial and rural centres.

In that summer of 1975, the UK had just held a referendum on Europe, enthusiastically endorsing our membership of what was then called the European Economic Community (EEC). I wasn't even 35 years old, and I was doing a job I loved – working out how environmental policy would be delivered throughout Europe in a way which made a difference. President Nixon had visited China just three years earlier and the Vietnam war was finally over.

Bliss was it in that dawn to be alive! I couldn't help feeling back then that I was in the right place at the right time.

So how did I feel, almost fifty years after that first visit to China, when Max and I, on June 19, 2023, entered the Forbidden city, once the Palace of the Great Khan?

Surprised by joy, impatient as the wind. That's how I felt.

We arrived at Wumen, the Meridian Gate, around 10 a.m. that day. Wumen is the largest and grandest of the Forbidden City gates. It was reserved for the emperor's sole use. This is the famous gate, overlooking Tian'anmen Square, where on October 1, 1949, Chairman Mao proclaimed the founding of the People's Republic of China. His gigantic portrait still hangs there today.

It was a greyish morning. Max and I walked in slowly. Solemnly. This was a moment to be savoured.

'I can't believe this' I said to Max, when we saw the first great vista of the Forbidden City on the north side of the Meridian Gate.

'What can't you believe?'

'I can't believe there's no one here apart from us' I replied. 'Where are all the visitors? The tourists?'

The fact that the place was empty, apart from us, made it seem even more enormous than it is.

Dandan was standing nearby. 'Where is everyone?' I asked. 'I thought the Forbidden City had 16 million tourists a year.'

Dandan's smile said it all. Yes, June 19, the day of our visit to the Forbidden City, was a Monday. And yes, the museums were shut on Monday but still …

Leaving the Meridian Gate behind us, we crossed across a vast paved courtyard. There was another Gate ahead of us, its entrance guarded by a magisterial pair of lions.

'That's Taihemen,' Dandan said. 'The Gate of supreme Harmony.'

'The Gate of Supreme Harmony' I repeated. 'Just saying it sounds good.'

Today's Beijing maintains the north-south axis that characterized Kubla Khan's Dadu. Due north of the Gate of Supreme Harmony, there is another even vaster courtyard. This is where the principal Imperial audiences were held and where the emperor's entire court, up to 100,000 people, could be accommodated.

We progressed, as the Polos themselves might have progressed on the day of their arrival, from the Gate of Central Harmony to the Hall of Supreme Harmony (Taihe Dian). The tallest and most spectacular of the three main ceremonial halls, Taihe Dian was used for the most important state occasions, such as the emperor's coronation or the nomination of generals at the outset of the campaign.

'One down, two to go' I said to Max.

I sounded flippant, but actually I was overwhelmed. I found it hard to believe that we were where we were and seeing what we were seeing – in this vast imperial citadel which had been home for more than 500 years to 24 Chinese emperors. If Beijing is the centre of the universe, as generations of Chinese believed (and maybe still do), then – when you stand in the Great Khan's Palace – you are standing in the very centre of the centre of the universe. The centre's epicentre, as it were.

We moved on to the Hall of Central Harmony (Zhonghe Dian). This is where the emperor would have greeted foreigners. This is where he would have addressed the Imperial offspring, including the offspring – according to Marco Polo – of numerous concubines. This is where the emperor examined the seed for each year's crop.

Finally, we visited the Hall of Preserving Harmony, the Baohe Dian, used for state banquets and imperial examinations.

I took out my faithful companion: The Travels of Marco Polo. I waved the book in the air.

'Listen to this Max,' I said. 'This is how Marco Polo describes this place. He says it's *'the largest palace ever seen … The walls of the rooms and chambers are completely covered with gold and silver and decorated in relief with pictures of dragons, birds, knights, scenes of battle and various kinds of beasts. The ceiling is likewise fashioned in such a way that nothing but golden and pictures can be seen anywhere. The hall is so vast and so wide that more than 6000 men could easily eat there. The number of rooms is quite bewildering. The whole building is at once so immense and so finely wrought that there is not a man on earth who could imagine improving on its design or construction even if he had the power to do so.'*

We were doubly lucky that day. Not only did we have the Forbidden City to ourselves, but we also had the chance to see parts of it that are normally off-limits to visitors, sites where crucial archaeological work is still being carried out.

I did a Piece to Camera.

'For three or four months of the year,' I said, quoting Marco Polo himself, *'the Great Khan stays in the capital city … In this city he has his great palace … It is the largest palace ever seen … The walls of the rooms and chambers are completely covered with gold and silver … The number of rooms is quite bewildering.'*

I put the book aside and continued in my own words. 'The actual palace which so overwhelmed Marco Polo is long gone. In its place the Mings built this, the world's largest palace complex, covering 72 hectares. The city was surrounded by 10-metre-high walls and a 52-metre-wide moat. We've been given exclusive access to a part of the Forbidden City which is currently closed to the public.

'Secrets of the Yuan Dynasty past are being discovered at this excavation site enabling us to see and touch what Polo saw. Buildings which Marco Polo described so vividly are now being uncovered beneath layers of history.'

Actually, we were not just doubly lucky that morning. We were trebly lucky. We would have a top expert to guide us from now on.

As we left the Baohe Dian, the Hall of Preserving Harmony, Wang Guangyao, Researcher at the Palace Museum Research Institute, was waiting for us.

'The Yuan Dynasty capital city was on this site' Wang said. 'The Yuan Dynasty palace was also here. Archaeologists have found Yuan Dynasty foundations in several places here. Later the Ming Dynasty built their palace on top of Yuan foundations. That continued for centuries. So that Yuan, Ming, and Qing Dynasty palaces were partially built on top of each other.'

Wang Guangyao took us to the site of his current excavation, somewhere in the north-east corner of the Forbidden City, not far from the Palace of Longevity and Health. Like many archaeological sites, it all looked a bit of a muddle.

'Watch out as you go' Wang advised.

We took his point. If you slipped off a plank, or tripped on rough ground, you could end in a pit.

At one point, Wang himself clambered down into the excavation site to come up with a handful of glazed shards or tile fragments. He passed them over to me.

'Would Marco Polo have seen tiles like these?' I asked, looking at the bright glazing and varied colouring.

Wang replied: 'Marco Polo had been to the Yuan Dynasty palace and met Emperor Kublai Khan. He and Kublai Khan were very close so Polo would have had access to the palace. So, he must have been here, he must have seen the Yuan Dynasty buildings with their glazed tiles and bricks. Marco Polo probably saw the very same glazed tiles and bricks we have excavated today.'

Wow, I said to myself, another bull's-eye! Just like Xanadu's Cane Palace. Wang, as an archaeologist, clearly believed these fabulous green glazed roof tiles, buried for centuries, were from the Yuan Dynasty. Proof once again that Polo's account is still the authority experts consult when looking for a detailed credible record of life under Kublai Khan's rule.

I took out my Bible, yet again, to double-check. Yes, there it was! Marco Polo writes:

'The roofs are a place of scarlet and green and blue and yellow and every other colour; they are so splendidly and skilfully varnished that they shimmer like crystal and their gleam can be seen all around the palace from far away. And let me tell you that the roof is so strong and so sturdily built that it lasts for many years.'

We walk back the way we have come, past the three great Ceremonial Halls – Baohe Dian, Zhonge Dian and Taihe Dian, past Taihemen, the Gate of Supreme Harmony into the great square, bisected by the Golden Water Stream with its five marble bridges, which lies to the north of Wumen, the Meridian Gate.

The camera crew weren't allowed to fly drones in the Forbidden City, but two of them climbed right up inside the Meridian Gate so as to be able to gain a panoramic view.

Time for another PTC.

Owen was in charge that morning. 'Say what you like' he instructed. 'Talk up to the chaps with the camera up there on the Gate as though you want to be sure they can hear you.'

I turned the volume up. 'This visit to the palace in Beijing marks the end of Marco Polo's journey' I boomed. 'But it wasn't the end of his time in China because he was so taken by his life here in the service to the Great Khan that he stayed on another 17 years as envoy and confidante of the Khan himself …'

A couple of pigeons, perched on the head of a carved lion, took off in fright as the sound of my voice disturbed the silence, but they soon came back.

47

Departure

After the climax, the coda.

We hadn't had much time on motorcycles during our trip, certainly not as much as we would have wished. As a surprise, Max hired two huge motorcycles, complete with drivers and sidecars attached.

'They are parked in a side street round the corner' Max told me. 'Walk straight out of the lobby and turn right. Don't talk to anyone. Don't stop. I've got a quick phone call to make. I'll join you.'

I walked swiftly out to the street, then swung right. There they were, gleaming monsters. Drivers already kitted out and in the saddle. Engines ticking over, ready to go.

Seconds later, Max emerged. As he put his helmet and goggles on, he gave me a thumbs up. He had obviously sorted out whatever it was he had to sort out.

The helmets were wired for sound. Our drivers-cum-guides took us wherever we wanted to go. We circled the Temple of Heaven, squeezed through the narrow streets of the old hutong districts, visited the Bell and Drum Towers and stopped for lunch at the Peking Duck Restaurant.

We even had time to visit the site of the old summer Palace, once nicknamed China's Versailles, but – in 1860 – entirely destroyed by French and British troops in the Opium Wars.

As we rode away, I talked to Max on the intercom: 'I'm surprised the Chinese want to deal with us at all after the way we treated them back then, when we were trying to ram opium down their throats.'

'Up their noses, actually' Max observed.

Owen Gay, Max and I, together with Dandan and Dr Rana (who was still in town) were invited to dinner that same evening by Mr Tang Shiding, the then President of China International Television Corporation, the national broadcaster which had commissioned the film and TV series 'In the Footsteps of Marco Polo.'

When it was my turn to speak, I expressed both gratitude and amazement. Gratitude, because of the sheer effort the Chinese side had put into this venture, in terms of manpower and resources. Amazement, at the imagination and inventiveness shown by Chinese colleagues at every point.

'And I must, Mr President,' I said 'pay a special tribute here to all the CCTV team who worked with us on this project. 'Your team were just superb. We had transport, we had lodging, hotels, we had food – sometimes more food than we could eat, especially noodles!'

As I spoke, I remembered the complete ass I had made of myself in that noodle school in Lanzhou. 'But it was not just the practical side, Mr President' I continued. 'It was the intellectual and imaginative side as well. Your team found the experts to talk to us wherever we went. So thank you.'

I turned to CCTV's Dandan. Even felt a bit of a lump in my throat as I spoke. 'We're all going to miss you, Dandan' I said.

The next evening was our last evening in Beijing. Dr Rana had had to leave town already, but apart from him the whole team gathered for dinner in a nearby restaurant.

There were 25 of us altogether. Max, with his usual inventiveness, had kitted us all out with black motorcycle jackets. Each jacket bore a large photographic image – a technicolour photo of Max and me on the Mongolian steppe, riding the motorcycles which we had 'borrowed' when their owners were looking the other way!

And Max had one last trick up his sleeve. Way back in Hotan, when we were visiting the carpet factory, I had been specially taken by a big woven yak wool rug. At the time, it was hanging on the wall, among other exhibits. It was a tremendously evocative object, showing distant mountains, grass plains, and – in the middle of those plains – a herd of yaks.

I had said to Max at the time something like: 'what would I give to have that carpet, that yak carpet, hanging on my wall at home?'

As we finished dinner that evening, there was a roll of drums, and two flunkies, dressed in white and wearing tall chef's hats, walked into the room carrying a long, obviously heavy roll of something on their shoulders.

They cleared a space on the floor. A large space. Took off the wrapping. Unrolled the long heavy parcel then and there.

'I can't believe this!' I exclaimed.

I felt a bit like Lord Byron must have felt when Lady Caroline Lamb popped out of the silver soup terrine at his dinner party. But I wasn't looking at a naked lady. I was looking at that wonderful carpet which had caught my eye the day we visited the carpet weaving factory in Hotan, way back in Xinjiang Province.

How on earth had Max managed to track that carpet down and get it to Beijing before we left China? I've no idea.

I have had that carpet mounted. Today it hangs on the wall in the living-room of our London house.

I don't have to imagine those mountains, that herd of yaks, nor the thick green grass of the Pamir plateau in summer. Those things are already there, before my very eyes. In the morning, when Nick Robinson is holding forth on the BBC's Today Programme, or Nick Ferrari on LBC, I lift up my eyes unto the hills, from whence cometh my help.

In 1291, after 17 years at Kubla's court Marco, Niccolò and Matthew Polo sailed from the South China Sea to the Persian Gulf on the first step of their journey home to Venice. They reached Venice in 1295, 24 years after they left.

Much as we would have liked to emulate the Polos by taking a long sea voyage back to the UK, Max and I didn't have the time. We headed instead for Daxing International Airport and there, in front of the ultra-busy Departures Board (where else?) I delivered my positively last Piece to Camera.

'This is it, isn't it, Pete?. '*Urbi et orbi?*'

'Go for it', Pete said.

In real life, you don't always say what you mean or mean what you say. That's the way it is. But I know that I meant what I said that morning, before our plane took off for London, and I don't think I can improve upon it now.

'We're leaving China today' I began 'with a sense of amazement. The extraordinary thing for me is actually how much Marco Polo, and what he stood for, still means here in China.

'Marco Polo became the great bridge builder between East and West. The 700th anniversary of that remarkable man's death will be commemorated next year, 2024. I'd like to think our own Marco Polo project will also be seen as part of that commemoration.

'Back in 1961, I set out with two colleagues, sadly missed, to try and follow Marco Polo all the way to Beijing and didn't succeed. But today, 62 years later, my son Max and I finally got here. We finally made it.

'We managed to visit places people don't so often visit. We have met people other people don't often meet. We have been entertained in so many ways. We have learned so much. We have had experiences which we are never going to forget.'

Pete, the Camera, lifted his eyebrow while filming as though to say, 'keep looking at the lens.'

I kept looking at the lens. There was a bit of noise in the hall, the noise of a nation on the move. So I gave it some welly anyway:

'This has been our journey' I boomed 'IN THE FOOTSTEPS OF MARCO POLO'

POSTSCRIPT

OneTribeTV/CDIMC's 90-minute film "In the Footsteps of Marco Polo" was premiered in London's Curzon Cinema on July 3, 2024. The following report by Xing Yi appeared the next day in the China Daily.

Marco Polo's route across China retraced for documentary
Stanley Johnson, an author, environmentalist, and former member of the European Parliament, is the father of the United Kingdom's former prime minister Boris Johnson, who also attended the event.

Following the ancient trade route taken by the Italian merchant and explorer Marco Polo more than 700 years ago, presenters Stanley and Max recreated the ancient journey from China's western border to Beijing, crossing more than 5,000 kilometers in seven weeks.

The documentary showcased the country's astonishing landscapes while featuring engaging interviews with diverse locals and capturing the hilarious banter between the 84-year-old father and his 39-year-old son.

At Wednesday's premiere, Stanley recounted the story of his first failed attempt to retrace the ancient route six decades ago, when he was a student at the University of Oxford, and how that dream was finally realized last year with the collaboration of Chinese and United Kingdom teams.

"Sixty-two years ago, I first set out to try to follow Macro Polo's way to Beijing and didn't succeed. Sixty-two years later, we got there, we made it!" Stanley said. "We've met people, and we've been entertained by people, and we've had experiences which I will never forget.

"Macro Polo became the great bridge-builder between the East and the West, and he is still very much appreciated in China. To me, I hope this film will also help in a symbolic bridge-building."

Zheng Zeguang, China's ambassador to the UK, told the audience at the premiere: "This is a story about pursuing dreams … It's also a story about China-UK collaboration … This is also a story about cultural exchanges and mutual learning.

"I hope all of you, and people in the UK, will be following the footsteps of Marco Polo and also the footsteps of Stanley Johnson. Travel to China, see the culture, and meet the people. As the ambassador, I will do whatever I can to facilitate. So, please take up the invitation and travel to my country."

Sherard Cowper-Coles, chair of the China-Britain Business Council, said after watching the premiere: "Stanley's film was just wonderful. (It is) a powerful evocation of Chinese civilization, ancient and modern, delivered with taste, humanity, humor and brilliant cinematography."

INDEX

Afghanistan
  attempted abduction of Johnson in, 28–9
  Buddhist statues, Bamiyan, 25–7
  chai-khanehs, 31
  entry and exit from, 22, 23, 32
  festival of Jeshyn, 24
  Johnson family ties with, 27–8
  Kandahar, 23–4
  Khyber Pass, 32
  return route through, 31–2
  Wakhan Corridor, 25, 27, 45, 74, 91, 102
  World Fair, Kabul, 24–5
Ai Tao, 101–2
Aleo, Nadia, 114–15, 119, 123, 191
Anderson, Sir Donald, 31
Anglo-Chinese Friendship Society, 7
Art of Uyghur Muqam, 126–7
Ayton, Sue, 67

BBC (British Broadcasting Corporation), 29
Beijing
  Bell Tower, 87
  EEC delegation visit to (1975), 225–6
  Forbidden City, 226–31
  Marco Polo Bridge, 222–4
  Marco Polo in, 225, 228, 230–1
  road to Xanadu, 215
  Tian'anmen Square, 224, 226
  as the Yuan capital Dadu, 208, 212, 215, 223, 225, 229
Berlin Film Festival, 54–5
Billington, Rachel, 51
Biodiversity Conference, Montreal (CBD COP 15), 110
Bryan-Brown, Mr, 39, 41
Bryant and May, 27
BSA motorcycles, 4–5, 67, 194
Buddhism
  Buddhist statues, Bamiyan, 25–7
  Mogao Caves, Dunhuang, 143–7
  nirvana, 162
  Sleeping Buddha Temple, Zhangye, 160–2
  temple murals, Miran, 141

Cable, Mildred, 150
camels, 148–9, 150
carpets, 130–2, 233–4
Chaplin, Charlie, 40
Charles III, 86
Chen Dandan, 86, 88, 89, 110, 112, 119, 153, 159, 174–5, 178, 196, 204, 215–16, 233
Chiang Kai-shek, Madame (Mayling Soong), 59
China
  Anglo-Chinese Friendship Society, 7
  Chinese New Year, 63–4
  Chungking trip, 1986, 58–60
  civil service exams, 167–8

Covid provisions, 74–8, 79
demographic policies, 44, 45
desertification reversal strategies, 136–7
and the *Dragon River* plot, 58, 59, 61
Ecological Conservation Redlines (ERLs), 109–10
ecological goals, 109–10
EEC delegation visit to (1975), 45, 46–50, 98, 123, 157, 225–6
entertainment and propaganda, 48–9
environmental conferences, 108–9
Four Modernizations, 58, 59
Han dynasty, 141, 142, 169
the Internationale, 49–50
Lop Nur (nuclear test site), 8, 139
Ming dynasty, 156, 158–9, 184, 212, 219
national anthem, 158
Nixon-Kissinger US-China relations, 44, 157
Qianhai province, 109
respect for elders, 87–8
Song dynasty, 102, 103
Tang dynasty, 150
Three Gorges Dam, 59
UN's Convention on Biological Diversity (CBD), 64
visas for the Marco Polo Route Project, 6–10
Wakhan Corridor, 25, 27, 45, 74, 91, 102
wetlands, Shanghai, 63–4
women's football national programme, 120–2
see also Yuan dynasty (Mongols)
China Central Television (CCTV), 87–8, 89, 233
China International Television Corporation, 233
Chinese Embassy, Portland Place, London, 6, 10, 63–6
Clarke, Mike, 64–5

Coleridge, Samuel Taylor, 'Kubla Khan,' 170, 203–6, 207
Commissioner, The, 53–5, 58
Confucius, 129
Conservative Environment Network (CEN), 70
COP 26, Glasgow, 64, 71
Czech Embassy, 80

Daniels, Paul, 186
Deng Xiaoping, 59, 98
desertification, 136–7
Dong Chunjuan, 180
Doomsday Deposit, The, 51, 52–3, 56
Dragon River, 58, 59, 168
Dubai
  Global Banking School (GBS) campus, 71–2
  wild oryx reserve, 72–3
Dunhuang
  Crescent Moon Lake, 148, 150–1
  Marco Polo in, 67, 143, 148
  Mogao Caves, 142, 143–7
  Singing Sand Dunes, 148–50

Ecological Conservation Redlines, 109–10
Egypt, 36
English Path Language Schools, 73, 114, 221
environmental issues
  desertification, 136–7
  glaciers of the Hindu Kush-Himalaya region, 107–8
  Johnson's environmental work, 55–6, 64, 70, 82, 108–9
  pollution reduction measures, 170
Evening Standard, 11

Fang Liu, 88
Feng Fing, 141–2
Feng Wenli, 109
Fleming, Peter, 29–30

Flying Horse of Wuwei, 169
Forbidden City, Beijing, 226–31
French, Francesca, 150

Gansu province, 143, 152–4, 158, 160, 163, 167, 188; *see also* Lanzhou; Zhangye
Gansu Provincial Museum, 168–9
Gay, Owen, 200, 230, 233
Genghis Khan, 124, 187, 225; *see also* Yuan dynasty (Mongols)
Genghis Khan mausoleum, 187–92
Glass, Professor David, 43
Global Banking School (GBS), Dubai, 71–2
goat skin rafts, 175–6
Gobi Desert, 6, 8, 138–9, 141, 150, 152
Grass Skyline Drive, 216–17
Graves, Robert, 38
Great Wall of China, 49, 155–9, 217–20
Guo Hongwei, 105
Guozeng Tang, 160–1
Guterres, António, 136

Han dynasty, 141, 142, 169
Hanbury-Tenison, Louella, 157
Hanbury-Tenison, Robin, 157
Haschiluu, 187–9
Hayns, Peter, 76, 90–2, 112–13, 149, 165, 190, 191, 194, 199, 220, 221, 235
Helan Shan mountains
　Marco Polo in, 181–2
　Ningxia vineyards, 177–80
　rock paintings, 181–3
Heruo Desert Railway, 133–6, 137
Hexi Corridor, 155, 160, 166, 171
Highway 66, 216
Hindu Kush-Himalaya region, 107–8
Hinshelwood, Sir Cyril, 6
Hotan (Khotan)
　carpets, 131–2, 233–4

Jade Market, 128–30
Hua Mei, 70
Huang Wenbo, 153–4

Id Kah mosque, 117–18
'In the Footsteps of Marco Polo'
　China Daily report on, 237–8
　China International Television Corporation, 233
　China's backing of, 69–70
　Chinese visas, 70
　Covid quarantine requirements, 74–6
　English Path's sponsorship, 73
　'entry' into China, 89–90
　evening meals, 88–9
　false start in Chengdu, 74–8
　father-son relationship, 68–9
　filming programme, 74, 89
　financial backing, 70, 80, 83, 221
　in-car chats, 94, 200, 201
　Max Johnson brought on board, 67, 68
　motorcycles, 67, 69, 232, 233
　One-Tribe TV promotional brochure, 67–9
　OneTribe-CCTV team for, 73, 87–8, 89, 233
　pieces to camera (PTC) by Johnson, 90–2, 112–14, 135, 141, 145, 154, 171–2, 187, 189, 190–1, 194, 203–4, 228–9, 230–1, 235, 236–7
　Prado Land-Cruisers, 90, 92, 94, 133, 166, 186
　premier, 237
　return journey, 234–5
　route, 61–2, 67, 91–2, 111
　transport options, 67, 69, 74
India, 31, 33–4
Inner Mongolia
　animal herding, 193–4
　archery, 198–200

Index

Darkhads, 188–90
Genghis Khan mausoleum, 187–92
invention of the stirrup, 191–2
Sheep Offering Ceremony, 189–90
wild horses, 195
wrestling, 195–7
see also Yuan dynasty (Mongols)
Institute of Traditional Chinese Medicine, Anchang, 47–8
International Centre for Integrated Mountain Development (ICIMOD), 108
Iran
  the Magi (Three Wise Men), 18–20, 73, 110
  Marco Polo Route Project, 17–22
  Valley of the Assassins, 18, 110

jade, 128–30
Japan
  Johnson's visit to Tom Mori, 56–8
  Sino-Japanese conflicts, 46, 47, 60, 168, 222
Jenkins, Roy, 54
Jiayugan Fort, 155–6
Jiayuguan Pass, 155, 159
Johnson, Alexander (Boris), 52, 83
Johnson, Ayla, 92
Johnson, Gabriela, 92
Johnson, Irene, 4, 51–3
Johnson, Jenny, 54–5, 61, 70, 83, 118
Johnson, Jo, 55
Johnson, Julia, 54–5, 61, 83
Johnson, Leo, 27–8, 52, 55, 82
Johnson, Max
  acting experience, 184–5
  at the Berlin Film Festival, 54–5
  as co-presenter, 67, 68
  false start in Chengdu, 74–5, 78
  fluency in Mandarin, 63, 68, 92
  Mongolian wrestling, 196–7
  at Tsinghua University, 63, 153, 157, 224, 234
  see also 'In the Footsteps of Marco Polo'
Johnson, Rachel, 52
Johnson, Stanley
  attempted abduction of in Afghanistan, 28–9
  as Chairman of the GEDU Advisory Board, 71
  Chinese respect for elders, 87–8
  chopsticks, challenges of, 88–9, 173
  copy of Marco Polo's *Travels*, 15, 90, 91, 110, 113, 117, 201, 205, 209–10, 228, 230
  demographics studies, 43–5
  EEC delegation visit to China (1975), 45, 46–50, 98, 123, 157, 225–6
  environmental work, 55–6, 64, 70, 82, 108–9
  family farm on Exmoor, 3–4, 51, 92, 119, 194, 205, 216
  friendship with Ambassador Zheng Zeguang, 70
  'Grandpa's bookcase,' 27–8
  Harkness Fellowship, 38, 41–2
  Jakub Vlcek's bust of, 80–3
  Jan Mazaryk Medal, 80
  lack of correct revolutionary attitude, 49
  'Life Without Birth…', 43–4, 45
  at the LSE, 43
  as an MEP, 53
  National Policy Panel, United Nations Association, 43
  Newdigate prize for English Verse, 38–41
  novels, 51–5, 56, 58, 59, 168
  at Oxford, 2, 6, 12, 38
  parents, 3–4, 51–3
  at Ravenswood school, 7, 197, 199, 203
  at Sherborne school, 38–9, 49, 190
  at the State University of Iowa, 41–2

241

Sunbeam Talbot, 7, 8–10, 66
working for the European Commission, Brussels, 52–5, 98
Johnson, Taies, 28
Johnson, Wilfred, 3–5, 51–2, 53, 55
Johnson Wahl, Charlotte, 52
Juyong Pass, Great Wall of China, 217–20

Kandahar, Afghanistan, 23–4
Kashgar
  Great Gate, 112–14, 118
  Id Kah mosque, 117–18
  livestock market, 119–20, 125
  Marco Polo in, 112, 113, 117, 123, 125
  Muslim population, 113, 117–18
  restoration programme, 123, 125
  site of the former British Consulate-General, 140
  statue of Mao Zedong, 123
  Uyghur pottery, 115–16, 125
  women's football national programme, 120–2
  see also Uyghurs
Kissinger, Henry, 45, 157
Knight Ayton Management, 67
Koziell, Izabella, 108
Kublai Khan
  Cane Palace, 210, 213, 230
  Dadu (Beijing), 215, 225
  Marco Polo's time with, 201–2, 209, 213–14, 230–1
  Summer Palace, Xanadu, 69, 91–2, 177, 201–3, 208–10
  see also Yuan dynasty (Mongols)
Kuneralp, Zeki, 14
Kyrgyzs, 111

Lake Baisha, 111
Lanzhou
  Flying Horse of Wuwei, 169
  Gansu Provincial Museum, 168–9
  Noodle School, 170, 171–3
  pizza parlour encounter, 167–8
  Zhongshan Bridge, 168
Larrabeiti, Michael de, 11–12, 73, 110; *see also* Marco Polo Route Project
Lei Xingyi, 165
Li Cong, 174–5
Liang Fenfen, 133–4
Liu, Ambassador, 63–5
Liu Bingzhong, 208
Long Jihua, 129–30
Lop Nur (nuclear test site), 8, 139

Maimaiti, Zakar, 125–6
Mao, Frances, 79
Mao Zedong, 45, 46, 123, 157, 158, 220, 225, 226
Marco Polo Bridge, 222–4
Marco Polo Route Project
  Afghanistan, 22, 23–8, 31–2
  Bryant and May's sponsorship of, 27
  BSA motorcycles, 4–5, 67, 194
  cameraman, 11–12
  carpets, 130–1
  Chinese visas, 6–10, 65–6
  Dunhuang's Mogao Caves, 143
  expedition uniforms, 12, 35–6
  financial backing, 70
  Gobi Desert, 8, 138–9
  initial planning, 2–3
  Iran, 17–22, 110
  journey through Europe, 13–14
  Kashgar, 112
  the Magi (Three Wise Men), 18–20, 73, 110
  Mount Ararat, 17
  Pakistan, 22–3, 32–3
  press coverage, 6, 11, 19–20, 29
  return journey, 31–7
  road safety/rules of the road, 13–14, 16–17, 18, 20, 22, 25–6, 33

route, 6, 124–5
send-off party, 12–13
Turkey, 15–17
Venice, 15
Wakhan Corridor, 25, 27, 45
Ming dynasty, 156, 158–9, 184, 212, 219
Miran, 140
Miran Fort, 140–2
Mogao Caves, Dunhuang, 142, 143–7
Mongolia *see* Inner Mongolia
Mongols *see* Yuan dynasty (Mongols)
Mori, Tom, 56–8, 59
motorcycles
    BSA, 4–5, 67, 194
    for 'In the Footsteps of Marco Polo,' 67, 69, 194, 232, 233
    fuel for, 8
    in the Johnson family, 4–5, 14
    for the Marco Polo Route Project, 4–5
    road safety/rules of the road, 13–14, 16–17, 18, 20, 22, 25–6, 33
Muhetaer, Maiwulan, 131
Muqam music, 126–7
Muztagh Ata, 107, 111

Needham, Professor Joseph, 6–8, 10, 65–6, 151
Ningxia vineyards, 177–80
Nixon, Richard, 44, 45, 56, 157, 226
Norrington, Professor A. P., 40

One-Tribe TV
    and the CCTV team, 89
    promotional brochure for the Marco Polo Project, 67–9
Ordos, 186, 187
Oxford University
    Encaenia, 39–41
    Johnson's time at, 2, 6, 12, 38
    Newdigate prize for English Verse, 38–41

P & O, 31, 34
Pakistan, 22–3, 32–3
Pamir Mountains, 86–7, 91
Panlong Ancient Road, 104–6
Polo, Marco
    accusations of exaggeration, 110, 160
    in Beijing (Dadu), 225, 228, 230–1
    camels, 138
    challenges of cooking at altitude, 105
    Desert of Lop, 6, 138
    Ganzhou (Zhangye), 160, 162
    Helan Shan mountains, 181–2
    Hexi Corridor, 155
    house in Venice, 14
    Kashgar, 112, 113, 117, 123, 125
    Khotan (Hotan), 128
    at Kublai Khan's court, 201–2, 209, 213–14, 230–1
    Lake Baisha, 111
    the Magi (Three Wise Men), 18–19, 73, 110
    Marco Polo Bridge, 222–3
    Ningxia vineyards, 177–80
    noodles and pasta myth, 172
    Old Man of the Mountains, 18
    in Persia, 21
    return to Venice, 234–5
    route, 91–2, 124–5, 133, 215, 217
    Shazhou (Dunhuang), 67, 143, 148
    Silk Road, 3, 61–2
    statue of, 166
    the Tartars, 187
    Tashkurgan, 102–3, 104
The Travels of Marco Polo, 15, 90, 91, 110, 113, 117, 201, 205, 209–10, 228, 230
Wuwei, 169
Xanadu, 201–3, 209–11, 212–14
Yellow River (Qara-Muren), 167–8, 174

Al Qasimi, Sheikh Saqer Bin Mohammed, 72

Qiao Yajun, 223–4
Qinghai-Xizang Plateau, 155

Rana, Dr Vishwajeet, 71, 72–3, 80, 220–1, 233
Rana, Tatiana, 72–3, 221
Ravenswood school, Devon, 7, 197, 199, 203
Royal Society for the Protection of Birds (RSPB), 64
Rusk, Dean, 40

Salas, Rafael, 44
Samuels, Tony, 63
Sečka, Libor, 80–1
Severin, Tim, 2–3, 18, 24–5, 70, 110, 124–5, 143; *see also* Marco Polo Route Project
Shamanism, 188
Shangdu/Xanadu
  arrival at, 201
  Cane Palace, 210, 213–14, 230
  history of, 207–9
  'Kubla Khan' (Coleridge), 203–6, 207
  Marco Polo in, 201–3, 209–11, 212–14
  Summer Palace of Kublai Khan, 69, 91–2, 177, 201–3, 208–10, 213–14, 215
Shelley, Percy Bysshe, 140
Sherborne school, Dorset, 38–9, 49, 190
Shouhang Power Plant, Gansu, 152–4
Silk Road
  cultural transmission along, 145, 146
  Kashgar, 112
  Khotan (Hotan), 128
  Marco Polo's footsteps, 2–3, 61–2
  Miran, 141
  under the Mongols and the Yuan dynasty, 3, 103, 124, 188–9, 219
  Northern Silk Road, 155, 169
  route of, 45, 124, 133

Tashkurgan, 101, 102
Silver City Airways, 13
Sleeping Buddha Temple, Zhangye, 160–2
Song dynasty, 102, 103
State University of Iowa, 41–2
Stein, Aurel, 140, 141, 142, 144, 146, 147
Sunday Telegraph, 6, 19–20

Tajiks
  buzkashi match, 95–7, 99
  Eagle Flute and Eagle Dance, 97–8, 100
  hotpot restaurant, 98–9
  see also Tashkurgan
Taklamakan desert, 124, 133, 134–5, 143
Tang dynasty, 150
Tang Shiding, 233
Tashkurgan
  Marco Polo in, 102–3, 104
  modern-day, 100
  Stone Fortress, 101–2
Telensky, Alenka, 80, 83
Telensky, Dr Jan
  Jakub Vlcek's bust of Johnson, 80–2, 83
  as a Sinophile, 83
Templar, Dale, 67, 73, 74, 83
Templar-Gay, Mimi (Hermione), 150, 154, 184, 185, 186, 202, 203
Thiaw, Ibrahim, 136–7
Toghun Temur, 'Lament,' 210, 212–13
Turkey, 15–17, 130

United Nations
  Conferences of the Parties (COPs), 136
  Convention on Biological Diversity (CBD), 64
  Convention to Combat Desertification (UNCCD), 136

Framework Convention on Climate Change (COP 26), 64, 71
Fund for Population Activities (UNFPA), 43, 44
GeoParks, 163
United States of America, 44, 56, 157
Uyghurs
  carpet making, 131–2, 233–4
  in Kashgar, 114
  Muqam music, 126–7
  musical instruments, 123
  pottery, 115–16, 125
  see also Kashgar

Vlcek, Jakub, 80–2
Wakhan Corridor, 25, 27, 45, 74, 91, 102
Wang Guangyao, 229
Wang Jiangjiang, 127
Wang Jie, 164
Wang Wei, 45
Wang Yuan-Lu, 144
Wei Jian, 207–11, 213
Williams, Sir George, 35
Wills, Helena, 40
Woolf, Leonard, 201
World Population Conference, Mexico City, 44–5
Wuwei, 169

Xanadu *see* Shangdu/Xanadu
Xi Jinping, 93
Xiang Hua, Ambassador, 8, 65–6
Xige Wine estate, 178–80
Xing Yi, 237–8
Xinjiang province, 25, 88, 91, 101, 120, 127, 137; *see also* Kashgar; Tashkurgan
Xu Ellen, 88, 95, 119, 200, 209–10, 211

Yang Baorong, 135
Yang Gang ('Cino'), 88

Yarkant, 124, 125
Yellow River (Qara-Muren), 167–8, 174–6, 186, 187
Yimlakut bridge, 135
Yuan dynasty (Mongols)
  archaeological excavations of the former palace (the Forbidden City), 229–30
  Cloud Platform, 219
  Dadu (Beijing), 208, 212, 215, 223, 225, 229
  era, 103
  Ming wars against, 158–9, 212, 219
  Pax Mongolica, 103, 143
  Shangdu, 201, 208
  the Silk Road under, 3, 103, 124, 188–9, 219
  territories, 207, 208
  see also Genghis Khan; Kublai Khan

Zhang Fan, 218–20
Zhang Jianguo, 181, 182–3
Zhang Xianliang, 184
Zhang Xiao Dong, 159
Zhang Yanzhi, 178–9, 180
Zhang Yuanlin, 145–6, 147
Zhangye
  hot-air balloons, 165–6
  Marco Polo in, 160, 162
  Rainbow Mountains (Danxia), 163–6
  Sleeping Buddha Temple, 160–2
  statue of Marco Polo, 166
Zhenbeibu China West Film Studio, 184–6
Zheng Zeguang, Ambassador, 70, 79
Zhongshan Bridge, 168
Zhou Xing-guo, 172

Other books by Stanley Johnson

FICTION
Gold Drain
Panther Jones for President
The Urbane Guerilla
The Doomsday Deposit
The Marburg Virus (republished as The Virus)
The Commissioner
Dragon River
Tunnel
Icecap (republished as The Warming)
Kompromat
From Antique Land

NON-FICTION
Life without Birth: A Journey Through the Third World in Search of the Population Explosion
The Green Revolution
The Population Problem
The Politics of Environment
Antarctica: The Last Great Wilderness
World Population and the United Nations
The Earth Summit: The United Nations Conference on Environment and Development
World Population – Turning the Tide
The Environmental Policy of the European Communities [with Guy Corcelle]
The Politics of Population: Cairo, 1994
Survival: Saving Endangered Migratory Species [with Robert Vagg]
Where the Wild Things Were: Travels of a Conservationist
UNEP: The First 40 Years of the United Nations Environment Programme.

MEMOIR
Stanley I Presume
Stanley I Resume